ICI PERSPECTIVES IN CURATING NO. 2

Talking Contemporary Curating

Terry Smith

INDEPENDENT CURATORS INTERNATIONAL

Talking Contemporary Curating is the second publication of the series PERSPECTIVES IN CURATING developed by Independent Curators International (ICI). It offers timely reflections by curators, artists, critics, and art historians on emergent debates in curatorial practice around the world.

Published by Independent Curators International, New York

Independent Curators International
401 Broadway, Suite 1620
New York, NY 10013
Tel: 212-254-8200
Fax: 212-477-4781
www.curatorsintl.org

First Edition

Series Editor
Kate Fowle

Editor
Leigh Markopoulos

Copy Editor
Clare Fentress

Publication Coordinator
María del Carmen Carrión

Designer
Scott Ponik

Printer
SHAPCO, Minneapolis

Library of Congress Control Number:
2015949208

ISBN 9780916365905

Table of Contents

Preface

Kate Fowle

The seeds for this book were already germinating when Independent Curators International published *Thinking Contemporary Curating*, the first volume in the series PERSPECTIVES IN CURATING. Written by art historian Terry Smith in 2012, *Thinking Contemporary Curating* was a unique contribution to the emerging discourse on the profession, in that it objectively charted a range of curatorial methods that have evolved over the last twenty years, while postulating what is distinctive about contemporary curatorial—as opposed to art critical, or art historical—thought.

The book immediately generated discussions between curators, some of whom agreed, and others of whom who did not, with Smith's art historical delineations and his perspective as an "engaged onlooker." Realizing that critical responses could further expand how we both articulate and record the machinations of contemporary curating, Independent Curators International conceived of a series of conversations between Smith and leading curators, historians, philosophers, and directors who are currently setting the bar in the curatorial world.

From 2012 through 2014 dialogues were staged as both public events and closed-door sessions in Ljubljana, Munich, Venice, New York, San Francisco, Sydney, and Tokyo. Some involved people whom Smith has been talking with for years; others were the results of first-time meetings. All were then transcribed and used as the foundations for further discussion between Smith and each respective interlocutor, ultimately generating the texts you will read in this volume.

The question "how do we talk about contemporary curating?" elicits responses that are very personal, and often contradictory, or subjective, because they draw from a particular set of experiences and contingencies. In spite of this, certain common threads emerged when the question was posed to the intergenerational participants in this book, whether in the form of foundational exhibitions, shared urgencies, or speculations about the development of contemporary institutions that are responsive to art, culture, and publics today.

Just as the "thinking" in the title of Smith's first book does not represent the author's own thoughts per se, so the "talking" in *Talking Contemporary Curating* does not position Smith as the cajoling "host." It indicates instead an ongoing dialogue between people who are responding to each other's viewpoints, knowledge, and experience. As Smith writes in his introduction: "Curators now talk more often, and more publicly… less guardedly, and in more depth… building the sense that, for all of its competitiveness, conflicting orientations, and inner diversity, their enterprise is a shared one." In short, what unravels in the following pages is discourse in the making, emerging from talking, spurred by the "doings" of twelve practitioners who are immersed in the potential of curating now.

This book relies on the generosity of its contributors for its existence: the group of individuals who contributed not only their time and thoughts, but also their attention to the edited transcriptions of their conversations. We are grateful to each of them for their willing and engaged participation: Zdenka Badovinac, Claire Bishop, Zoe Butt, Germano Celant, Carolyn Christov-Bakargiev, Okwui Enwezor, Boris Groys, Jens Hoffmann, Mami Kataoka, Maria Lind, Hans Ulrich Obrist, and Mari Carmen Ramírez.

Once the talking was done, the work of putting the book together began and in this we were lucky to have an experienced team of collaborators on which to rely. On the home team,

María del Carmen Carrión, director of public programs, ably managed the project's many aspects. Particular mention is also due to former staffer Misa Jeffereis, who, as coordinator of public programs, was responsible for arranging the conversations in the first instance, and then to Kimberly Kitada, who took over her role to see the project through.

Talking Contemporary Curating would not exist in its final form without Leigh Markopoulos, who, as the editor, spent countless hours working with Terry Smith to ensure tight, terse dialogues were fashioned from extensive raw material, which was painstakingly transcribed by Carolyn Bergonzo. Then, after the i's were dotted and the t's crossed by our eagle-eyed copy editor, Clare Fentress, ICI's designer Scott Ponik set to work on the design of the book with his usual flair and fortitude, delivering a handsome companion to the first volume. Finally, Elisa Leshowitz at D.A.P. has been tireless in ensuring that the final results reach the widest possible audience. This book is testament to all our conspirators' significant abilities and it has been a pleasure to work with everyone over the last two years.

Of course none of this would be possible without ICI's dedicated and talented staff, led by Renaud Proch, executive director, who is a wise and willing collaborator; just as significantly, this publication, as with any of ICI's programs, would not come to fruition without the support of our funders and supporters. Special mention goes to the Robert Sterling Clark Foundation and the Hartfield Foundation, who have been central to the development of ICI's international reach and publishing endeavors for a number of years now.

Talking of a global perspective, ICI's International Forum was a gleam in our eyes in 2012, when the first volume in this series was published, but today its members are a firmly established part of our support network, inflecting what we do with greater richness through their passion for art and ideas around the world.

Thanks go to the late, and much missed, Melva Bucksbaum, Terry Fassburg, Michael Jacobs, Ingela Lorentzen, and Kathleen O'Grady. Our thanks also go to the visionary members of the Leadership Council, who continue to take ICI to new heights: Josh Brooks and Jung Lee, Füsun and Faruk Eczacibaşi, Agnes Gund, Alexei Kuzmichev and Svetlana Kuzmicheva-Uspenskaya, Toby Lewis, Dorothy Lichtenstein, Julie Mehretu and Jessica Rankin, Patricia Phelps de Cisneros, Mercedes Vilardell, and Helen Warwick.

As ICI celebrates its fortieth anniversary in 2015, it is important to recognize the long-term vision and generosity of our Board of Trustees, who have tirelessly believed in the organization through its various incarnations, willingly participating in its evolution while offering steadfast support and advice each step of the way. Thank you for making this book—and many others—possible over the years.

Finally, my heartfelt gratitude goes to Terry Smith, from whom I have learned so much since we first met in 2010, and without whom the possibility to find new language and clear perspectives around the myriad nuances of the universe of curating would be sorely lacking. His insight, patience, and continuous inquisitive spirit have enriched my life, and will enrich the lives of others who have the fortune to read this book and the previous in the coming years. It has been an inspiration and privilege to have this opportunity to work with someone who is as dedicated as Terry.

Acknowledgments

I thank first of all the twelve interlocutors who consented to engage in conversation, and then worked so carefully to bring the initial discussions into a readable dialogue worthy of our shared time and, we hope, the time of any reader.

In the course of preparing this book, I learnt much from public and private discussions about curatorship with Mary Jane Jacob, Julian Myers, Sofía Hernández Chong Cuy, Paul O'Neill, Johanna Burton, Liam Gillick, Qiu Zhijie, Manray Hsu, Hongjohn Lin, Zanny Begg, RoseLee Goldberg, Dan Byers, Daniel Baumann, Tara McDowell, Rebecca Coates, Chiara Costa, and Max Shackleton were also most helpful.

Thanks to my colleagues at the National Institute for Experimental Art, UNSW Art & Design, University of New South Wales, especially Jill Bennett, Ross Harley, Dennis Del Favero, and Lizzie Muller, and to those who offered comments on work in progress at my seminars there. My colleagues at the University of Pittsburgh, especially Barbara McCloskey and Isabelle Chartier, continue to provide a stimulating and supportive context for my work on curating, as do students in my graduate seminars on contemporary art and curating, and those in my undergraduate museum studies seminar.

At Independent Curators International, I am grateful to María del Carmen Carrión for her coordinating role, to Renaud Proch, and to all those who helped prepare the public events where many of the conversations in this book began.

Leigh Markopoulos has been a truly remarkable editor. Her grasp of the book's project, her sensitivity to the nuances in play within curating and in these conversations, as well as her attention to detail, have been pivotal to its quality.

Most of all, I thank Kate Fowle for her continuing support, her critical acumen, and her commitment to the cause of reflexive curating.

To Kate

The Discourse
Terry Smith

Perhaps the most significant development in curatorial practice in the last decade is that the field has become markedly more discursive in character. "Discourse" is an interesting word. Its general meaning is obvious enough: any written or spoken communication, or, as a verb, to talk at length about something. Its roots lie in the Latin *discursus*, or running to and fro, which made it perfect as a shorthand descriptor of what it was to argue in medieval times. In Late Middle English it denoted the process of reasoning in general, while in French, when a verb, it connoted the sense of running away (*discourir*). In the early 1970s, philosopher Michel Foucault used it to evoke the codes, conventions, representations, and habitual uses of language that he believed generated historically and culturally specific fields of meaning. He understood professions to be disciplinary practices, and social institutions to be disciplinary formations. He was concerned with highlighting the ways in which power operated in every kind of relationship, but was at the same time entirely contingent, thus open to challenge, and subject to change through individual and collective action.[1] These ideas have been influential on the interpretive and scholarly use of the concept of discourse today: it routinely designates the thinking practices and vocabularies of institutions, cultural domains, and practices; the language of particular social groups or cultures; the specialized fields of academic study; and even certain modes of intellection, or styles in the history of thought, such as psychoanalysis, structuralism, postmodernism, and deconstruction.

1. Michel Foucault, *The Order of Discourse* [1971] (New York: Vintage, 1994); *The Archaeology of Knowledge* (New York: Pantheon Books, 1972).

Curators will recognize themselves in every one of these senses of the term, if not in each subcategory. Discursivity is everywhere today. Curators now talk more often, and more publicly, about what they do and how they do it. They also talk less guardedly, and in more depth than ever before, about *why* they do it. They speak more searchingly about curating as a practice that is as grounded in processes of conceptualization, and as committed to the production of new knowledge, as it is in its more traditional pursuits: the pragmatics of caring for collections, planning programs, working with artists, mounting exhibitions, attracting viewers and educating them. Of course, curators tend to discuss such continuities and changes primarily with other curators, but they also regularly link their projects to the thinking of philosophers and historians, scientists and sociologists, while maintaining their long-running connections with the ideas in circulation within more closely related professions and pursuits, such as art history, art criticism, art dealing, and the cultural industries. Through these exchanges with each other and with others, curators are building the sense that, for all of its competitiveness, conflicting orientations, and inner diversity, their enterprise is a shared one. *Talking Contemporary Curating* is, first of all, a testament to the fact that discourse, in all of its various senses, is now upfront and at the center of curatorship.

These changes are not an accidental side effect of the "linguistic turn" that occurred within every academic discipline during the 1960s and 1970s, and which manifested itself in Conceptual art. They are, more exactly, a direct historical outcome of the intense exchanges between artists and curators during these decades, an interaction that has profoundly shaped both practices ever since.[2] While descriptions of the impact of artists on curating have focused on the loosening of museological

2. See Paul O'Neill, *The Culture of Curating and the Curating of Culture(s)* (Cambridge, Mass.: MIT Press, 2012), and Terry Smith, *Thinking Contemporary Curating* (New York: Independent Curators International, 2012), chapter 3.

constraints, and on the heightening of curatorial subjectivity, the cognitive and discursive aspects of artistic Conceptualism should not be forgotten. They, too, have left an increasingly resonant legacy, even if it has been somewhat slow in unfolding. Conceptual artists were also active in the internal politics of artworlds. They consciously took over the critical publication of their own work, displaced theoretical accounting for it, and intervened strongly in the ways it was exhibited. They were responding to the fact that all but a few curators, critics, and theorists—to say nothing of art historians—were able to accept the transformatory potential of art. In parallel ways during the 1980s and 1990s, a number of curators reacted to the art world they saw around them: to its obsession with money and markets, its recursion to anachronistic mediums and reactionary myths of the artist, its Old Master "blockbuster" exhibitions and creeping corporatism, its fear of far-reaching innovation, and its blindness to the art being produced in most of the world. Like the Conceptual artists they admired, they expanded the purview of curatorship to try out remedies to these maladies. The various kinds of curating that are identified in the practice of the curators who appear in this volume, and which I will describe shortly, are a direct outcome of this situation.[3]

What about the "contemporary" in the title of this book? It arises from another new, or at least recent, fact about curating: that it has come to be widely recognized as a significant profession, one caught up in the central impulses of contemporary life, yet also able to offer strikingly original and acute interpretations of the complexities and contradictions of our contemporaneity. The idea that everybody "curates" everything these days is a fiction, and a phantom of relative

3. For an expanded account of these kinds of curating since the 1960s, see Terry Smith, "Artists as Curators/Curators as Artists: Exhibitionary Form since 1969," in Germano Celant, ed., *When Attitudes Become Form: Bern 1969/Venice 2013* (Venice: Fondazione Prada, 2013), pp. 519–30 (for the Italian, see pp. 711–17).

privilege. To be contemporary today means more than simply being up-to-date with the latest news, ideas and attitudes, in tune with the times; it means more than increased, instant, global connectedness, the ability to travel in time and across space, immersion in a saturated image environment, and a quantitative increase in shared knowledge of the world. To be alive today also means being alert to the wild experimentalism of most systems of government, the implosion of globalizing economic frameworks, the yawning gaps between the haves, the have-lesses, and the have-nots, the incommensurability of purportedly universal belief systems, the contemporaneousness of disjunctive temporalities, the intense proximity of cultural otherness, and the evident fact that the modern contract with the planet has run out of options and that a new one is an existential necessity.

Artists everywhere are responding to this situation, and curators are being called upon to help, to join a worldwide effort to create a commons that will outlast the shocks of globalized capitalism, the resurgence of fundamentalism, and the impacts of climate change. Some time ago I attempted to articulate what these circumstances meant for contemporary art critics, theorists, and art historians. As it is a succinct formulation, I see no reason to modify it, so let me repeat it here:

> Place making, world picturing, and connectivity are the most common concerns of artists these days because they are the substance of contemporary being. Increasingly, they override residual distinctions based on style, mode, medium, and ideology. They are present in all art that is truly contemporary. Distinguishing, precisely, this presence in each artwork is the most important challenge to an art criticism that would be adequate to the demands of contemporaneity. Tracing the currency of each artwork within the larger forces that are shaping this present is the task of contemporary art history.[4]

4. Terry Smith, "The State of Art History: Contemporary Art," *Art Bulletin*, vol. 112, no. 4 (December 2010), p. 380

In *Thinking Contemporary Curating* I wondered whether it was possible to be as exact about what the current conditions (our "contemporaneity") require from art curatorship, and proposed that the purpose of curating today might be said to be this:

> To exhibit (in the broad sense of show, offer, enable the experience of) contemporary presence and the currency that is contemporaneity as these are manifest in art—present, past, and multitemporal, even atemporal.[5]

Elaborating this idea filled the rest of that book. It is the main topic of this one as well. The advantage now is that there are twelve other voices offering their understandings of how to approach this fundamental challenge. In these pages, they do so in direct discussion with me. But it is also obvious that contemporary curators, and those interested in the field, spend a lot of time in discourse with each other. Not only privately, or on panels, and in the growing number of journals devoted to curating, but also, and most thoroughly, through their main mediums: their exhibitions, their programming, and, if they are directing a museum, their policies.

Stepping up to the contemporary challenge requires not only pragmatic competences and managerial smarts; it also demands an acute analysis of one's resources, a clear picture of the field of operation, and a conceptual command of how, when, and where to act. Many curators are seizing this chance to more profoundly understand their profession, its histories and its possibilities, its capacities and its limits—in a word, to grasp it as a discourse. In so doing, they may, as a side effect, elevate their profession such that it becomes an art. But the main task is to shape a worldly practice, one that will deliver on the expectation that it exhibit the real relations that constitute our contemporary condition.

To those who think of curating as primarily a matter of managing practical problems, this might seem a strange starting

5. Smith, *Thinking Contemporary Curating*, p. 29.

place. Not so, if you accept the reality of the discursive shift that I have begun to sketch. A few years ago, when I noticed that this shift was occurring, I was puzzled by a contrary phenomenon. Why did such a prominent profession, one so deeply devoted to making art public, seem somewhat reluctant to articulate its premises in the written, discursive terms favored by the other professions dedicated to the distribution and interpretation of art, such as art criticism and art history? The obvious reason, I soon realized, is that curators articulate their thoughts, first and foremost, by staging an exhibition. They may augment this process by making statements in the accompanying catalogue, in educational handouts, or in publicity interviews. Museum-based curators articulate their thinking in the ways they arrange the display of a portion of a collection in a room in the museum, and by contributing to any didactics that accompany such displays. Less obviously, they do so by acquiring works for the collection, and explaining why to the museum's acquisitions committees. Yet I sensed a gap between the language that curators regularly use in their written statements and the kind of thinking that goes into shaping the exhibition or hanging the collection room. Up until recent years, their public language often read like a mixture of cited artists' statements, art-critic-like responses to individual artworks, art historical evidence-building about the development and direction of art, and the "human interest" stories favored by art journalists. Was curatorial thought nothing more than whatever came to mind when negotiating this jumble of interests?

If that were so, there was no good explanation of the origins of the empirical discoveries, the subtle connections, the striking juxtapositions, the resonant nuances, and the precise judgments that I was experiencing in so many fine and challenging exhibitions—and, of course, their absence from other not so good ones. Not all exhibitions are arguments, but they all generate meanings for their viewers that are different in kind from those we learn from reading the texts and looking at the illustrations in an art critic's article or in an art historical tome. In every exhibition, a conceptual framework is in operation, and curators have developed degrees of competence, often amounting to the highest skills, in deploying it, and in innovating within it. Further, in recent years, a number of curators—among them, and notably, those in this book—have sensed that articulating these competencies, reflecting on them, and searching out their histories could no longer be left to the generalizations of the museologists or the chance comments of critics, or wait upon the tardiness of art historians. Curators themselves, they believe, should take up these tasks, not as ancillary to their practice but as an essential part of it.

CURATING AS DISCURSIVE PRACTICE

In this book, curators of art, artistic directors of biennials, art museum directors, art historians, critics, and theorists reflect upon the challenges of curating art in contemporary conditions worldwide and in a variety of different contexts. They offer carefully thought-through answers to a number of questions that are central to debates within the field, and that often puzzle outside observers. What kinds of curating are most responsive to the world as it is, in all of its complexity, its intimacies, proximities and distances? What are the most responsible kinds of curatorial acts within such a world? What is so special about curating art when "curationism" appears everywhere in today's networked, spectacle cultures?[6] How much have professional curators learnt from the curatorial activity of artists, and vice versa? Is there really a fundamental divide between the modern museum-based, scholarly curator and the contemporary independent curator of temporary exhibitions, biennials, events, and processes?[7] More broadly, what are the similarities and differences between the modern, the postmodern, and the

6. David Balzer's *Curationism: How Curating Took Over the Art World and Everything Else* (Toronto: Coach House Books, 2014; London: Pluto, 2015) is an engaging profile of this phenomenon.

7. Hal Foster, "Exhibitionists," *London Review of Books*, June 4, 2015, pp. 13–14.

contemporary art museum, and how does curating operate within each of these paradigms? How does one negotiate an environment in which all three types of museum co-exist, often in the same city, and sometimes in the same building? In the larger, global cities, a vast array of exhibitionary venues continues to grow, and to refine its formats, whereas in many places around the world it is a daily struggle to simply build basic infrastructure for art to be seen and interpreted. These, then, are some of the challenges facing those for whom art remains the main avenue through which to understand our contemporaneity. They are taken up, boldly and with subtlety, in practice and in these conversations, by all of the interlocutors in *Talking Contemporary Curating*.

Like much to do with curating, this book took shape in somewhat adventitious ways, in response to necessities that became apparent, mostly, due to available opportunities and accidental conjunctions. It also exhibits, I hope, something of the projective planning, cooperative spirit, internal discipline, and plain persistence required to fully ground any curatorial project, and to bring it to fruition. The precipitating factor was the publication of *Thinking Contemporary Curating* in 2012. Its exploration of the question "what is contemporary curatorial thought?" led to widespread discussion among those interested in curating, in thinking about thinking, and in what it is to be contemporary. As I traveled in response to invitations to speak about the book, I participated in many such events. It soon became obvious that some of the most innovative curators and museum directors practicing today were reading it, and had strong responses that they wished to share. Here was a chance to learn more about contemporary curating from those most directly engaged in its practice, from among those who have given it the most thought. As well, questions concerning curatorship were engaging many art historians, theorists, and philosophers. In today's world, each of these professions seems to need something from the others in order to keep doing what it does, and to do it better. Talks turned quickly into debates, dialogues became conversations. Some are based on acquaintances, or friendships, that stretch across decades; others are the outcomes of first meeting.

Not everybody who might, ideally, be expected to appear in such a volume is included. Some were unavailable during the months of my journeying. Some conversations that did occur did not take a publishable shape. Thus these exchanges are partial in every sense of that word. Nevertheless, they provide, I believe, a vivid sense of contemporary curatorial thought at work: they show curators deeply immersed in thinking about the exigencies of practice, the contexts of exhibition making, the platforms on which art may be made public, the distinctive nature of curatorial discourse, and, above all, how curating might contribute to a better understanding of what it is to be alive today.

THE INTERLOCUTORS

Philosopher Boris Groys is well known for his astute and provocative comments on modern and contemporary art, and for his writings and exhibitions about Moscow Conceptualism, a Russian art movement that spanned the 1970s and 1980s, in which he was an active participant. In this book Groys argues that there is a fundamental distinction to be drawn between the curating of exhibitions that show an aspect of the traditional narrative of the history of art and those that manifest subjective selection by the curator—the latter often tend toward being *Gesamtkunstwerke*, or total works of art precipitating mind-blowing experiences for all the senses. The first kind of exhibition, he suggests, is the outcome of the revolutionary overthrow of the European monarchies, in France and Russia most influentially, which led to the spoils being presented to the new democratic publics, re-interpreted as art. The second has become prominent since the 1960s. That some curators seem to curate both kinds of exhibition comes up in our discussion of New Museum curator Massimiliano Gioni's central exhibition *The Encyclopedic Palace* at the 2013 Venice Biennale.

Carolyn Christov-Bakargiev, director of dOCUMENTA (13), among other major biennials, including Istanbul 2015, explores the arguments in *Thinking Contemporary Curating* in close, sympathetic, but skeptical detail. In response, I advance an interpretation of dOCUMENTA (13) as offering the visitor an experience of the often violent and tortuous impact of world differences, especially wars, on artists and artworks, and extend Christov-Bakargiev's metaphor of "the brain" to propose that the exhibition was designed across its venues as a brain inside a dispersed body. Throughout the discussion, Christov-Bakargiev paints a striking picture of her own, highly personal approach to exhibition making—as distinct from curating, a role that, she insists, should focus on the hands-on care of the material objects in collections. That she celebrates what might seem the more traditional side of this ledger might surprise many who see her as a prime example of the individualistic exhibition-maker. Indeed, the essays, statements, poems, and reflections that she issues as indicative of her curatorial intentions—always cast in the first-person voice, always intensely evocative of experiential intuition—would seem to reinforce this perception. In fact, as becomes clear, her practice oscillates between the two poles.

The curator of the 2015 Venice Biennale, Okwui Enwezor, revisits the passions motivating his series of exhibitions from the mid-1990s onward about historical transition on the African continent, and the ideas of provincializing Europe and the post-colonial constellation, which underlay his direction of Documenta 11 in 2002. His career might be seen as an outstanding instance of a third kind of curating, that which prioritizes a program of necessary change not only in art historical and art critical perceptions, but also in historical, social, and political worldviews. We might call it "programmatic curating." Enwezor argues that, despite the impact of the art market, art fairs, collectors, and neoliberal capitalism more generally, international contemporary art is, in fact, provincialized in its deepest senses, and has become what he calls "off-center." This transition occurred in the 1990s, and it is, he believes, a permanent one. It follows that the curator's job is to tell the micro-stories of what amounts to a critical regionalism in art practice, and to do so from a global perspective. This applies not only to the artistic direction of large-scale exhibitions such as the Venice Biennale, where worldwide flows of ideas and imaginings should be highlighted (Enwezor's edition is entitled *All the World's Futures*), but also to the mission of museums of all kinds. As director of the Haus der Kunst, Munich, he aims to program this Kunsthalle as if it were a collection-based museum, with multiple rooms permitting unexpected conjunctions, and also like a campus, with many kinds of platforms working together to precipitate new knowledge.

Best known among high-profile curators today is Hans Ulrich Obrist, whose ubiquity as an international art world figure is unmatched within the profession. Our discussion explores the conceptual underpinnings of his practice, especially the inspiration he has drawn from artists, his understandings of contemporary life, and his commitment to developing exhibitionary forms—from DIY enactments to interview marathons—that seek to enable the present to make itself manifest. As well as having curated over 250 exhibitions since 1991, he has conducted over 2,400 hours of interviews. More than any other curator, he has embraced discourse as a medium that can itself be curated, and, through the marathons staged at galleries, worked out a way of exhibiting it as it happens. Does his practice suggest a fourth kind of paradigm, in which curating becomes a medium in itself, a vehicle for exhibiting the processes of exhibiting as they are playing themselves out, in increasingly diverse forms, in the larger culture?

Many of the curators and museum directors who participated in these conversations established themselves outside the museum sector, as independent curators or workers within alternative art spaces. They came of age during the heyday of contemporary art that, along with biennials and temporary exhibitions, initially found its natural home in such spaces, before the growth of museums dedicated to today's art, and its dominance within the auction houses and the new private collection museums. How have these curators made the transition to the now quite elaborate cultural complex that supports art of all kinds?[8] Have their energies been absorbed by museums (where many of them now work), by the industrialization of culture, and by the private collector market, or have they been able to change these institutions and settings in significant ways? The next four conversations explore this possibility, and do so with a full awareness of the challenges posed by the commercial values pervading the system yet also with an optimism not shared by many of its critics.

Art historian and critic Claire Bishop, in discussing her book *Radical Museology, or, What's 'Contemporary' in Museums of Contemporary Art?* (London: Koenig Books, 2013), asserts that certain museums have again become loci of radical change, despite decades of institutional critique, capitalist incorporation, and conservative pushback. She highlights innovative changes in the recent re-installations of four European collecting institutions: the Van Abbemuseum, Eindhoven; the Museo Nacional Centro de Arte Reina Sofía, Madrid; and the Moderna galerija and the Museum of Contemporary Art Metelkova, both in Ljubljana, Slovenia. The differing models of spectatorship presumed by the modern, postmodern, and contemporary museum and exemplified in these case studies are explored. Other topics include the popularity of artist-curated exhibitions in museums; the contemporary museum as an "archive of the commons"; the failure of contemporary art historical scholarship to match the innovative work of radical museums; and versions of post-Marxism in contemporary critical theory.

These topics shape the daily work of Zdenka Badovinac, director of the Moderna galerija and the Museum of

8. For the concept of a culture complex, see Tony Bennett, *Making Culture, Changing Society* (London: Routledge, 2013), pp. 24–30.

Contemporary Art Metelkova, Ljubljana. Responding to the need to develop a new national museum of art after the breakup of Yugoslavia in 1992, while at the same time wishing to keep alive the spirit of internationalism that had inspired "self-managed socialism," she devised the concept of "the museum of parallel narratives," which allowed for two linked institutions and two different forms of collection display. She likens her museological innovations to the artistic practice of the avant-garde artist collective Neue Slowenische Kunst, with whom she has worked for many decades. Accordingly, at the Moderna galerija, the modern art rooms are shown as lines of continuity, one artistic movement leading to another, while the work of the early twentieth-century avant-gardists, the Partisan artists during the Second World War, and the art of the retro-garde art groups during the 1980s are shown as ruptures within this trajectory. Meanwhile, at Metelkova, the rooms are structured around the responses of artists to the variety of temporalities that co-exist today, of which no less than eleven distinct kinds are identified! In the conversation, the concept of post-war avant-gardes, important in Central and Eastern Europe in advancing art practice and discourse after 1945, is contrasted with the idea of the neo-avant-garde that prevails in European and North American criticism today. Contemporary art in the region continues this tradition of engaged artistic activism, to which Metelkova remains devoted, despite the recent rise of neoliberalism and conservative nationalism.

Curators working in Asia face challenges that parallel those in Eastern and Central Europe, but are quite distinct in other ways. During a conversation at the Mori Art Museum, Tokyo, chief curator Mami Kataoka discusses how Japanese art became contemporary during the 1950s, and outlines the development of the country's art institutions since then. The direct links between the country's socio-political conditions and its art history are exemplified in her analysis of the impact on current Japanese art of 3/11, the Fukushima nuclear disaster, which was showcased in her exhibition *Roppongi Crossing 2013: Out of Doubt*. Kataoka also details the vicissitudes of curating in the context of Asian, Western, and local perceptions of what it is to be Asian. These often contradictory viewpoints form the subject of some of her group exhibitions, such as *Phantoms of Asia: Contemporary Awakens the Past* (2012). They also surface in her exhibitions devoted to individual artists, such as Lee Bul and Ai Weiwei. Against culture-bound perspectives, Kataoka argues that the purpose of contemporary curatorial thought and practice should be to embody, and share, an expanded view of what it is to be human.

Wortham Curator of Latin American Art at the Museum of Fine Arts, Houston, and founding director of its International Center for the Arts of the Americas, Mari Carmen Ramírez has dedicated her career to countering essentialist perceptions of Latin America and reductive readings of art from this region—which, after all, consists of twenty nation states and many more ethnicities. Our conversation follows her pathways from her education in Puerto Rico and the United States to her curating of exhibitions in those countries, and throughout South America and in Spain. It reveals the contested nature of identity formation within this multitude of art centers, and the constant trafficking between them. More thoroughly and more boldly than any other curator, her exhibitions have addressed the question of Latin American vis-à-vis European avant-gardism, and the intersections between modernisms on both continents and in the United States.

Badovinac, Kataoka, and Ramírez are examples of museum-based curators who have broken the stereotypical view that art historical scholarship in curating is relatively passive and retiring. They bring reflexive museology out into the light, literally putting it on exhibition, and radically transform museums in the process. Similar innovations are being tested by a small but growing number of their colleagues: among them, Charles Esche at the Van Abbemuseum, Eindhoven; Manuel Borja-Villel at the Reina Sofía, Madrid; and Jarosław Suchan at the Muzeum Sztuki, Lodz.

Reflexive curating, that which takes the nature and history of curating as its subject, parallels theoretical reflection and art historical research in its modes of thought. But it works, often, by using the medium most natural to curators, the exhibition itself. The subjectivist, *Gesamtkunstwerk* mode of exhibition making that is now so prominent burst into visibility in 1969, when Harald Szeemann curated *Live in Your Head: When Attitudes Become Form: Works–Concepts–Processes–Situations–Information* at the Kunsthalle Bern. This event, which is a matter of vivid memory and of intensive photographic evocation, has become legendary, both within curatorial discourse and in the histories of curating now being written. Could it be revisited, directly, in actuality, as a re-curated exhibition? A very contemporary question, which was answered in the affirmative when a near simulacrum of the 1969 exhibition was displayed at the Fondazione Prada, Venice, in June 2013. *When Attitudes Become Form: Bern 1969/ Venice 2013* quickly became the most talked about exhibition of that year, and comes up in nearly all of the conversations in this book. In the conversation with Germano Celant, director of the Fondazione Prada, who gave the opening address at Bern in 1969 and was the curator of the 2013 restaging, both exhibitions are examined in detail. Celant has been closely allied with artists throughout his career: in the mid- and late 1960s, he gave the Arte Povera artists their name, and worked intensely to promote their work. Since then, he has exhibited and written monographs on a large number of artists, particularly those of his generation. He has also made a career of ambitious undertakings, mounting survey shows on broad themes, which often entail major interventions into the architecture of exhibition spaces.

When Attitudes Become Form is also a landmark inspiration for Jens Hoffmann, who, in 2012, while director at the Wattis Institute for Contemporary Arts, San Francisco, mounted an exhibition of works by contemporary artists who were inspired by the artists included in Szeemann's exhibition, and by its legacy. A miniature model of the Bern installation in the first room, together with historical documentation, set up the scenario. Throughout his career, and in his current position as deputy director of the Jewish Museum, New York, Hoffmann has continued to present exhibitions in relation to novels, plays, texts of various kinds, and other exhibitions. As a leading exponent of this style, Hoffmann has been influential in establishing the overtly staged, or dramaturgical, exhibition as a distinctive mode of curating. We can identify here—as in the museological innovations of Esche, Badovinac, and Borja-Villel, and in Celant's displaced replication of *When Attitudes Become Form*—a fifth paradigm within contemporary curating: re-curating past exhibitions, not with archaeological or antiquarian exactitude, but by restaging elements of them to articulate a relevance to contemporary art, life, or thought.

Beyond the museum sector, and outside the well-funded precincts of the private foundation, the mid-size and smaller, not-for-profit, often artist-run, collective "art spaces" that emerged in the 1960s and 1970s and then sustained themselves and expanded in many places are now undergoing a war of attrition due to cutbacks in public funding and competition from private foundations. Yet they were, and in many cases remain, the sites most conducive to experimental art and reflexive curating.

Infrastructural activism has become, in effect, a sixth mode of curating; it is especially urgent in situations where contemporary art is a rarity, and has a fragile existence in complex cultural, legal, and political settings. Zoe Butt is executive director and curator of Sàn Art, a small space in Ho Chi Minh City that has become a vital center of experimental activity since it was established in 2007. She is inspired by groups of local artists as they build platforms on which artistic ideas can be proposed and discussed. Only some of them are actually realized, usually against the grain of intense, uninformed, and inconsistent official interference. Connections overseas, and partnerships with institutions elsewhere, become crucial in such a context. Provisional platforms such as these are appearing in many places: they hold out hope for the future of art, and for engaged curating, in an increasingly troubled world.

Almost all of the themes that occur throughout these conversations come up in the discussion with curator, art center director, and theorist Maria Lind. We explore in depth her controversial concept of the curatorial; the artist-curator interface; activist curating; organizing visual arts infrastructure at the "relative peripheries" within the European Union during the neoliberal turn; and her policies as director of the Tensta Konsthall, an alternative art space in a Stockholm suburb heavily populated by immigrants. Lind initially described her distinction between curating and the curatorial as analogous to Chantal Mouffe's differentiating the political from politics, that is, an agonistic, experimental practice of political negotiation toward genuine democracy in contrast to acting within a supposedly consensual but in reality fundamentally conflicted domain dedicated to the impossible task of imposing hegemony through the institutionalization of its processes.[9] In her 2009 *Artforum* article, Lind stated that "the curatorial should be beyond the expanded field, a multidimensional role that includes critique, editing, education, and fundraising."[10] In our conversation in this book she refines this claim by adding that:

> "Curating" encompasses the technical side of things, and can take different shapes and forms: making an exhibition, commissioning an individual artwork, organizing a screening or seminar series, a workshop, et cetera. But "working curatorially" implies doing these things with a sensibility and urgency as to why they are being done *precisely* this way, *precisely* right now in relation to *this* art and the questions that it raises or proposes. And it is based on an ambition to go beyond the status quo.[11]

9. Chantal Mouffe, *On the Political: Thinking in Action* (London: Routledge, 2005).

10. Maria Lind, "The Curatorial," *Artforum*, vol. 68, no. 2 (October 2009), p. 103.

11. Maria Lind, this volume, p.321.

We are just beginning to grasp the dynamic at play here. It is a relatively recent phenomenon, still finding its shape. For some, it will, or should, always remain in this nascent state. For others, it is already being absorbed back into the institutional apparatus, and being saturated with the values of spectacle culture, leaving a small remainder of critical content for those able to discern it. My view is that the most advanced and interesting curatorial practice today frequently generates the curatorial as it responds to the challenge to exhibit our contemporaneity, and that, in doing so, it regularly innovates within the technical competencies of exhibition making. Each is necessary to the successful realization of the other; and both are essential to the sufficiency of the exhibitionary outcome. Critical content remains exceptional, but there is more and more of it on show, and, one hopes, more to come.

THE DISCOURSE OF CURATORSHIP

What have I, as an art historian, learnt from my involvement in these conversations? Let me get to that via a brief explanation of how I usually go about trying to learn. When exploring any subject, I usually start by focusing on a highly visible concentration of instances, looking for patterns of connection between them, watching them change through time in similar and different ways, meanwhile searching out the less visible aspects, and the outliers. I listen closely to how this practice explains itself to itself, to the many voices that compete to do so, aiming to build up a picture of its discourse, of its layers of invitation and enclosure, self-questioning and self-protection. I then move out, back to the worlds to which it is contingent, all the while comparing and contrasting its self-portrait with those of the worlds around it. This is when the most interesting questions arise, and answers begin to suggest themselves. I then test these against what others have said about these matters, and, most importantly, against what I know about the world, and what it is asking of the practice. Induction and deduction are the names of these methods for pinpointing truth. Using one to check the other is to subject them to a deconstructive dialectic.

Applying this approach, I soon saw that curators activated a whole constellation of ideas about art that don't configure in quite the same way as they do for critics or theorists or historians. The question immediately arises: what is shared and what is different in each approach to what is, after all, the same object—art? Evidently, each of the interpretive professions exhibits its own style of thought. There is a superficial, misleading level on which this is the case. For instance, many curators claim that, like artists, they are driven by pragmatism, intuition, and instinct, rather than by the kinds of applied reason that, they say, historians and theorists employ. This bland generalization did not fit my experience of curators of the kind you will meet in this book. So, in developing *Thinking Contemporary Curating*, I figured it would be interesting to go against the grain of such stereotypes and ask, what is contemporary curatorial thought? Conducting the conversations in this book led me to expand and deepen the answers I gave in 2012. Let me revisit those answers, and share them with you in a developed form.[12]

To me, answering the question "what is contemporary curatorial thought?" required due acknowledgement of what curators share with other art world actors, but primarily it meant trying to distinguish what was distinctive about how curators think and what they actually do when they present art to audiences. Generally speaking, art critics strive to articulate in writing an immediate response to the works in exhibitions, taking them one by one or comparing them to others. By an act of projective imagination, they strive to show how, in *this* work of art, *this* artist has worked to transform form and formlessness into figure in meaningful or, perhaps, not so meaningful ways. Critics also compare the exhibition they are looking at to other exhibitions on the same subject, or similar ones, and often provide relevant contextual commentary. Importantly, they add evaluations to their descriptions, thus indicating how much

12. The following paragraphs develop passages in Smith, *Thinking Contemporary Curating*, chapter 1.

attention should be paid to this artist, these artworks, and this exhibition. In sum, critics write monologues in the present tense, spoken words that evoke what a reader might experience when he or she comes to look at the same works, in the same exhibition, quite soon.

When art historians visit museum installations and exhibitions they do so, mostly, to confirm art historical facts, that is, to explain the historical formation and development of a school of art, or the evolution of the work of an artist, hopefully in some illuminating relationship to the society in which she works or worked. Usually, they are trying to add something to a story that is larger than that which any given museum, even all of the world's museums together, could ever show. It is the story of art's presence within the history of humanity, its salience within human life, in all of its many dimensions. (It needs, now, to become a planetary discipline, but that is another story.) Thus, for an art historian, the real excitement arises when scrutiny of the artworks and the documents pertaining to them provokes an unexpected meaning, a resonant relationship that illuminates the artwork, art around it, and the larger story of art's valiance in the world. Art historians, then, write narratives for the ages, accounts of the event after the event, accounts that evoke the eventual moment of the artwork, of exhibitions, and of art itself, but also that trace the resonance of each through time and across space.

But *before* any of this can occur, a curator has already examined these works for their exhibitionary potential and selected them, usually in relation to others, thereby unlocking meanings inherent in each work, and in their relation to others. These meanings are pre–art critical, but are immanently so. And they may be pre–art historical, but potentially so. They are the meanings that art has in and for itself, as produced by an artist, or, if the work has been circulating through time, the meanings that have accrued to it due to its passage through the world, including its presence in previous exhibitions. Analogous to the art critic's affective insights and the art historian's historical hypotheses, these inherent meanings are the curator's raw material, embodied in the actual and figurative stuff with which she works to make an exhibition.

What kind of thinking goes into discerning this exhibitionary potential, and into prefiguring such meaning? If we can say that a historian, critic, or theorist searches for a conceptualization (usually a mental image) that encapsulates the apparently disparate elements of his or her analysis into a definable "shape," a discursive figure that holds up when explicated (thought through, written out, contested in dialogue, measured against the works) in detail, then the equivalent kind of curatorial thinking might be a process that gathers all of the elements under consideration (artworks, objects, documents, texts, their histories, their implications as to meaning, along with facts about the physical setting, and information about its location within its city and within the exhibitionary complex) into a pre-visualized exhibition, or, more explicitly, into a projective imagining of the viewer's journey through such an exhibition. If it is an event that is being curated, the curator will try to imagine, to the degree possible, the likely immediate or accumulative experience of the participants. While many curators still envisage one (ideal?) viewer's pathway, others prioritize a number of possible routes for that viewer, or the passaging of numbers of viewers, moving in parallel or in concert. The exhibition—in this expanded, extended sense—works, above all, to shape its spectator's experience, taking her on a journey of understanding that unfolds as a guided yet open-weave pattern of affective insights, each triggered by looking, a passaging through particular spaces that takes its own time—in fact, it creates its own particular temporality. These sequenced, structured responses accumulate until the curator has fully realized (and, for the first time, completely understood) her initial intuition, the curatorial hypothesis that the exhibition was shaped to test.

The curator of an exhibition is, thus, its pre-viewer, and its first actual viewer. For the visitor, these same, first-time-like experiences also accumulate until she has understood the curator's statement and, hopefully, arrived at feelings and meanings previously unfelt and unknown. At this moment, the artworks begin their careers as public objects. At the same time, the exhibition begins its career as a curatorial act, a fresh statement about the art that constitutes it, as an original intervention in art critical and art historical discourse about the art involved, and as exemplary in some way within the discourse of curating. In time, as it echoes within public realms, it might remain in the memory of those who saw it as a turning point in their lives, and, if exceptional enough, accumulate significance as definitive of a moment in the history of human world-perception.

Curators are, then, the first people to *make art public* in the true sense. They bring it out from the studio or off the drawing board or laptop, *before* a critic sees the work (usually at an exhibition), before an art historian writes about it, and before a philosopher theorizes it. If a critic writes a monologue to be read usually in private, and an art historian a narrative to be read by every future reader interested in the past's shaping effect on possible futures, then a curator organizes a public dialogue between actual, material objects in a specific, real space, an encounter among unequals, and an exchange of silent voices that visitors come to hear, one which enables viewers to become members of that exhibition's audience.

EXHIBIT, EXPLICATE: THE TALKING CURE

According to the *Oxford English Dictionary*, the word "exhibition" acquired its current meaning in the early to mid-eighteenth century, the moment of modernization in Europe, of the Industrial Revolution, the invention of the stockholding company, the creation of the middle class, and the expansion of the British Empire. "Exhibit" derives from the Latin *habare*, "to hold," and from *ex*, "out." Thus the meaning: to "hold out or submit (a document) for inspection, especially as evidence in a court of law," or, more relevant to us, "show (an item) publicly for entertainment, instruction, or in a competition; have (an item) on show in an exhibition." Curatorship of all kinds fulfills these definitions, as do all kinds of exhibitions, from a booth in a trade fair to an international biennial.[13] Definitions are not absolute pronouncements; they are fallible, changeable descriptions of everyday language use, which is, in itself, descriptive and fungible. It is the persistence of usage that suggests qualities that have stuck, and that may be fundamental to the ongoing formation of a discourse.

Let us, then, revisit the word "exhibition," imagine "inhibition" as its implicated opposite, and so re-read curating as the process of removing the inhibitions from works of art, of freeing them into the space of the exhibition—that is, "ex-inhibiting" them. Further, because an exhibition is a framework larger than any individual work of art, it is at the same time able to display art's inhibitions, as after-effects of its having given each artwork its freedom—or, at least, the qualified freedom of the companionship of the other works in the exhibition. We find here, perhaps, a nuance of curating as a kind of caring for art, an idea that echoes the Latin meaning of the word *curare*. We also find a confirmation of Boris Groys's observation that curating is necessary to "cure the powerlessness of the image, its inability to show itself by itself," and his qualifier that the public exhibiting of works of art in museums, insofar as those works aspire to absolute freedom, also infects them with an unfreedom, with the illness of institutionalization. It also implicates them within the historical, political, class struggles that have been fought in museums, albeit silently and symbolically, yet just as definitively as they have been on the streets and in the squares.[14]

13. See Terry Smith, "The Logic of Biennials," in Kwangsu Oh, ed., *The Symposium 2013 Busan Biennale: Biennale Ecology in Contemporary Art* (Busan: Busan Biennale, 2014), pp. 11–21 (for the Korean, see pp. 22–30).

14. Boris Groys, "The Politics of Installation," *e-flux journal*, no. 2 (January 2009). http://www.e-flux.com/journal/politics-of-installation/.

In the context of my emphasis on the discursive character of contemporary curating, its adoptions of many kinds of speaking out after careful reflection, let me add to the mix the concept of explication. The dictionaries tell us that the term comes from the Latin *explicat*, to fold (*plicare*) out (*ex*), or unfold, and has, since the mid-sixteenth century in England, meant "to analyze and develop [an idea or principle] in detail," and to talk at length about it in public. Discourse is, in this sense, a talking cure. Its potential to heal curating is what I have been arguing for throughout this introduction. The contemporary curatorial process, at its best, is as thought-filled, as cognitively driven, as the processes of the best critics, historians, and theorists of art who are currently practicing. The conversations in this book are their own demonstration of this fact. I hope that your reading of it will convince you that the discourse itself—in the person of these curators and their colleagues, as they operate through and between the modes of contemporary curating that we have identified—is also contributing significantly to the ongoing articulation of what it is to curate our contemporaneity, and to do so critically. Whether the discursive cure will have unforeseen side effects remains to be seen.

Carolyn Christov-Bakargiev

On not Having an Idea: dOCUMENTA (13)

Director of the 14th Istanbul Biennial (2015), Carolyn Christov-Bakargiev is an organizer of events and exhibitions; a researcher into artistic practices, the histories of art, and the politics of aesthetics; and a writer. She was recently appointed director of Castello di Rivoli Museo d'Arte Contemporanea and Galleria Civica d'Arte Moderna e Contemporanea, Turin. From 2009 to 2012, she was the artistic director of dOCUMENTA (13), which took place in 2012 in Kassel, Germany, as well as in Kabul, Afghanistan; Alexandria and Cairo, Egypt; and Banff, Canada. Previously, Christov-Bakargiev was the artistic director of the 16th Biennale of Sydney (*Revolutions—Forms That Turn*, 2008) and chief curator at the Castello di Rivoli (2002–8; interim director in 2009). She was senior curator at P.S.1 Contemporary Art Center, New York, from 1999 to 2001. Other group exhibitions she has organized include *Faces in the Crowd*, London and Turin (2004), *The Moderns*, Turin (2003), and *Citta' Natura* (1997). Her books include *William Kentridge* (Brussels: Société des Expositions du Palais des Beaux-Arts de Bruxelles, 1998), *Arte Povera* (London: Phaidon, 1999), and, for dOCUMENTA (13), the *100 Notes – 100 Thoughts* series as well as *The Logbook* (Ostfildern: Hatje Cantz, 2012) and *The Book of Books* (Ostfildern: Hatje Cantz, 2012). She has recently held academic positions, including the Edith Kreeger Wolf Distinguished Visiting Professorship in Art Theory and Practice at Northwestern University (2013–15).

We spoke at the New Museum, New York, on October 14, 2012.

Terry Smith: I am fascinated by the fact that so many curators claim that they operate, like artists, mostly through a mixture of pragmatism and intuition, and by reactive, instinctive response, rather than by applying reason in the way of, they say, historians and theorists. I reject this stereotype, for curators as much as for artists. I find it interesting instead to ask, what is contemporary curatorial thought? How can it be expressed in an exhibition? How do you show the frictions of world difference, and of world proximity, or of world sameness? How do you show the way we live in the "conditions of contemporaneity," as I call them? How do these conditions actually impact exhibitions? I think that in many ways, curators around the world are very interested in answering these questions, one way or another. I believe that you did through dOCUMENTA (13), and so I hope we can talk about that.

Carolyn Christov-Bakargiev: I have an allergy toward curatorial discourse in general, and thus to any sort of discourse that would attempt to define the field of contemporary art. Furthermore, I warn you that I always speak with skepticism and, fundamentally, with Adornian suspicion: whenever one says anything, it's false the minute it is said. So, it is difficult to hold a conversation about curatorial practice generally, let alone my own.

I also believe in projects and utterances that resist summary, the easy idea of the list as exhibition, or a Wikipedia-like abbreviation of everything. What I like the most about an artistic project is the resistance of the text to the subject matter it's trying to imbricate. Everything needs to be apprehended at the time that it is said or done, and not outside of its historical and cultural context.

But you include people like me in your book—the so-called reticent curator who says, it's all in the exhibition, don't talk about it, don't do congresses or conferences about curatorial practice, because you can only *do* it, you can't speak about it. Theodor Adorno rightly identified the speechlessness of art in Europe in the period just after the Second World War.[1] Then, in later decades, once criticality, also in the name of Adorno, became a pre-requisite for meaningfulness in art, some Conceptualists accused the Art Informel artists and the Art Brut generation—the artists who understood and embraced this speechlessness—as constituting a reactionary, conservative impulse. They were wrong. Certainly, in 1967, to say "I cannot speak about art, I can only paint" would have been idiotic. But to say, as Adorno did in 1949, faced with the horrors, the unspeakability of the Second

1. Theodor Adorno, "Cultural Criticism and Society" [1951], in *Prisms*, trans. Samuel Weber and Sherry Weber (Cambridge, Mass.: MIT Press, 1988).

World War, "To write poetry after Auschwitz is barbaric," that was the *only* thing to say. (Yet, maybe, one could also say: *only* lyric poetry was possible at that time…)

The advanced, digital age of cognitive and financial capitalism in which we live today is based on the verbal, which is why images are much less important than they were ten, or twenty, years ago, at the tail end of the age of spectacle.

TS: These counter-intuitive observations are very important for us now, if we are to maintain a critical, historical perspective on the present, which is so adept at misleading us.

"THE CURATORIAL AGE"

CC-B: So, let's discuss your book, *Thinking Contemporary Curating*, which came out last year. I love it. What I'm going to do is give you some comments, things that came to my mind, not in a rational way, because reading it was like being in therapy. I constantly kept seeing myself, in earlier versions, mostly.

In the introduction, Kate Fowle speaks about the 1990s as the curatorial coming of age, the period of professionalization. I would agree with that, but I think that is part of the problem today. During the modern period the curator cared for collections, and the role was more service-oriented. There is something in the modesty of the research-based, service-oriented, old-fashioned curator of a collection that appeals to me more than the narcissism of the curatorial protagonist involved in the co-production of recent art. Which is why, in a way, the whole of dOCUMENTA (13) is an anthology of different kinds of curatorial practice. It is a sort of meta-exhibition, with many possible curatorial models at play, and many also denied.

From this perspective, we can read *Thinking Contemporary Curating* as a large-scale artwork that has enabled you to exhibit curatorial practice. Two hundred years from now, when someone like you looks back at our age, he or she will write a chapter called "The Curatorial Age," recognizing a time when no one could speak about art without acknowledging the curatorial presence. So, most probably, with hindsight, we might see that you, Terry Smith, are actually making art with "curatorial practice." It is the most topical material that you could be using. This places your work as an intellectual and researcher in relation to those artists—you mention them at certain points in the book: Goshka Macuga, Liam Gillick, and so on—who are using the curatorial as material for their work. One can go back also to Marcel Broodthaers, whom you mention in another capacity: the artist as curator.

Being a Conceptual artist, a member of the Art & Language group, one of the founders of Conceptual art, you've come full circle and are doing the same thing that was done in the late 1960s, but within a different context. (I'm superficially analyzing you right now!) That was a very important turn, because it was the moment when the artist found a kind of emancipation from the art critic, from the Greenbergian position that imposed its taste on everyone. It is as if there was a voice inside the artist saying: I must be able to use these words myself. I don't need to have this art critic interpreting and deciding what I'm trying to say.

This was a power relationship, a slave/master axis that developed because, as we said before, ten years earlier the artist had said, I cannot speak because the conditions are unspeakable. So, ten years after the art critic seized power, Conceptual artists took back the voice and the conceptualization of their own practice. In a way, I feel that what you're doing with curators is the same. It's another turn in this spiral of love, which is, each time around, a different one, but is also the same. So, that is kind of cool.

TS: Your analysis is acute. Actually, my first rejection of Clement Greenberg came when he visited Australia in 1968 to deliver a lecture, "Avant-Garde Attitudes," arguing that the core driver of avant-garde art throughout the late nineteenth and twentieth centuries was the efforts of a few artists to match the Old Masters in terms of quality.[2] To those of us who dreamt of making avant-garde breakthroughs, especially from within such distant places, this was too reactionary to be borne. I was the youngest member of the staff of the institute that brought him out, the Power Institute at the University of Sydney. My first article as an art critic was an attack on that lecture, and all of Greenberg's principles. Of course, the key people in Art & Language—Terry Atkinson, Michael Baldwin, Joseph Kosuth, Ian Burn, and Mel Ramsden—had already gone through this spurning of the formalist father. And it is true that that spurning spurred us on, for a number of years.

Coming right up to the present, one of the blurbs on the book is by Boris Groys, who describes the book as an "act of global meta-curating."

CC-B: I think you are turning it back into art, which is a more interesting thing, and exactly what Art & Language did with verbal commentary.

TS: Yes, but we did it in a particular way, with what came to be called "institutional critique" as the goal. There was an interesting moment in 1972 when Daniel Buren, Robert Smithson, and others refused to participate in Harald Szeemann's Documenta 5. This struck us at the time, and ever since, as strangely anachronistic. Even though, at that point, these artists were denying the romantic view of the artist as author, they retained the view that they should remain in total control

2. Clement Greenberg, *Avant-Garde Attitudes: New Art in the Sixties* (Sydney: Power Institute of Fine Arts, 1969), in Clement Greenberg, *The Collected Essays and Criticism, Volume 4: Modernism with a Vengeance, 1957–1969*, ed. John O'Brian (Chicago: University of Chicago Press, 1995), pp. 292–303.

of their work, at every stage from conception right through to presentation and publication. Like the early Conceptualist approach to photography, they thought that exhibiting was a relatively neutral means to an end. There was simply no anticipation that curators would be creative. It was like they were saying, you will show my work in the way I want it shown; you will not use it in accord with any other logic or any other approach; you cannot have an idea that is as provocative, or critical about exhibiting, as mine; if you try that, I won't allow you to show it. When Art & Language was included in Documenta 5, in the section "Idea/Light," curated by Kasper König, the members involved simply took over their allotted space and did their thing, exhibiting *Index 01*. Szeemann was fine with that, they told me.

Like many artists from that time, we put a lot of thought into connecting with audiences and, I believe for the most part, we actually did it better than the curators. We showed work—not only ours, but also that of others—in a more interesting, critical, and analytical way than most of the curators around at the time, just like we thought about it, and wrote about it, better than the critics and others. Whether I'm still doing that, I'm not sure.

CC-B: We're always doing the same thing, all our lives.

TS: If you say so, but it wasn't conscious in the book.

CC-B: No, of course not. But the only interesting things are non-conscious; they come from the other side of the brain.

TS: I was just trying to learn something.

CC-B: And you did! You brought together an incredible archive of possibilities for positioning oneself in relation to art. One of the first things you introduce is a picture of a blackboard. You are Australian, and I know something about Australia because I directed the Biennale of Sydney—

TS: Curated the Biennale of Sydney, in 2008.

CC-B: Yes, but I don't use that word. I would never use the word "curator" to define myself, and I didn't call anybody who worked on dOCUMENTA (13) a curator. Chus Martinez was head of a department, but we never gave the department a name. I actually tried to liquidate this word, "curator." I always say "directed." More like a traffic controller. I actually find it a more humble, more modest term.

Anyway, one of the people I met in Sydney was Nick Waterlow, who is not known in New York City particularly, but who happens to have been a fantastic, as you would say, "curator."

TS: That's what he called himself, by the way.

CC-B: Yes, he did use that word. He directed the Biennale of Sydney at various times, and was the first person to bring traditional Aboriginal art into a contemporary art venue, something I also did in dOCUMENTA (13)—as a secret homage to Nick, actually—through the works of Doreen Reid Nakamarra and Warlimpirrnga Tjapaltjarri.[3] I wanted to break with one of the big snobbisms of the contemporary art world outside of Australia, which is to exclude art that is, in fact, contemporary, but is not made with a critical consciousness of participating in the same story as the rest of modern or contemporary art. This is an exclusionary boundary that allows us to say, ah, now, in 1979, art has arrived in Hanoi. Ah, now it's arrived in Singapore, with the founding of the artists' village. It's a colonial viewpoint that looks around the world through a telescope based on an Enlightenment idea of what art is, an idea that may have no relevance in the twenty-first century. Nick Waterlow did this really revolutionary thing, so I went to see him. He became my secret advisor for the Biennale of Sydney.

3. Nick Waterlow, *Australian Biennale 1988: From the Southern Cross: A View of World Art c. 1940–1988* (Sydney: Biennale of Sydney, 1988).

READING A CURATOR'S TESTAMENT

CC-B: Shortly before being killed by his son, Waterlow wrote a text he called "A Curator's Last Will and Testament." It takes the form of seven statements, written as if on a blackboard, and I was so happy to see them reproduced on the first page of your book. Number 1: "Passion." That's the left side of the brain. Number 2: "An eye of discernment." Number 3: "An empty vessel." Number 4: "An ability to be uncertain," which is one of my main principles: uncertainty. I'm deeply skeptical and that's why we only offered "maybe-education," not education, in dOCUMENTA (13). I don't even know if dOCUMENTA (13) was an exhibition. You tell me. Number 5: "Belief in the necessity of art and artists." I would agree with that, although I don't necessarily believe that the *field* of art will exist as a field in fifty or one hundred years, which doesn't mean that the people who make it, and their specific, situated knowledges, will not exist. They have existed since time immemorial, but they have not always been called "artists." They have been called all sorts of things—"alchemists," for example. Number 6. "A medium: bringing a passionate and informed understanding of works of art to an audience in ways that will stimulate, inspire, question." And 7: "Making possible the altering of perception."

There's only one word that is repeated—"passion"—in statements number 1 and number 6. So I went to look for that word in your book. And the word—or something very similar to it—comes up on page 255.

TS: That is a very thorough reading.

CC-B: You use the word "love," which is quite connected to passion. And the word "caring" is connected to love, which is connected to Nick Waterlow. But, when you look at them, "caring" and "curating" are actually formed using the same letters, except that you have to take out the "u" and the "t" in order to make the first from the second. So I thought about this "ut," and of course it is the reverse of "tu." But in Latin, *ut* means "for," or "in order to," as in *ut, eum amaret*, "so that he or she would love him." Curating in order to care. "Passion" used to mean the suffering of Christ on the cross. It comes from *passio* in Latin, which means "to suffer" or "to endure pain." It came to mean "a strong desire" in the thirteenth century, but in the 1600s, when John Donne was writing his incredibly sexual, yet also very religious, poems, the term began to imply what it does today.

On page 255, you wrote, "I would love to see curators keeping detailed records of every stage of their thinking and planning." I did it! I kept hundreds of notebooks in connection with dOCUMENTA (13), documenting, like you say, "... every stage of [the] thinking and planning." We published a lot of these notebooks. I also published "statements of how they pre-visualized exhibitions, including how these ideas changed during the hang," in volume 2 of the catalogue, called *The Logbook*, so I hope you're happy with that.[4] "I would love"—this is a repetition of the word in your text—"to follow their version of learning by walking through the exhibition and their sense of what various audiences made of it. Of course, it would be great to have records of visitor responses, of the spectator's emancipation." I love the word "emancipation" and I hate the word "freedom" because of its misuse in politics (by the Bush administration, in particular). "But it would be a major step forward to see more writing by curators about other exhibitions that have inspired their own, or were curated in response to theirs, or simply were devoted to the same artists or about a similar issue." In fact, the narcissistic disorder of many so-called curators like myself has meant that I have never really written that much about other exhibitions that have inspired me.

4. dOCUMENTA (13), *The Logbook: Catalog 2/3* (Ostfildern: Hatje Cantz, 2012).

TS: Why is that?

CC-B: Well, I don't know, it's like some disease…

So, we go to page 227, where the word "passion" appears, in this passage: "For most curators, wherever (and whenever) they are situated across the infrastructural spectrum, the ideal is to strive to work from an independent, relatively autonomous professional perspective based on a passion for art itself, an approach that balances respect for the vision of particular artists against commitment to developing audiences for art and that brings these two together in exhibitions that enable shared insight into the contemporary world—its dark, its dazzling, and even its dull, ways of being." That's a beautiful sentence. I love it also because, strangely enough, as I was searching for "passion" I found the other word that I really like right next to it, which is "commitment." This to me comes from Judith Butler, who might say dOCUMENTA (13) was a "committed" exhibition, if one were to ask her. I think a lot about commitment—*cum mittere*, "to put together," "to put with." It has an unfortunate relation to "communion," but we can leave that religious aspect aside. But, I really haven't given you any theory at all…

THE EXHIBITION AS A BODY

TS: Let me now put before you my thoughts about dOCUMENTA (13) because this is a really unique chance to spend some time with someone who has, I think almost for the first time, made an exhibition that exhibits curatorial thinking as part of its core content. Which is to say, the exhibition shows the results of thinking about what it is to be in the world today, and how art is in the world today; how art is in fact impinged on, and acts on, and transforms the world today. So, it's not just an exhibition that is *about* something, in the sense that many exhibitions are about this or that topic.

CC-B: It actually resists being about something in that sense.

TS: Particularly in the section called "The Brain." For those who haven't seen it, let me conjure the main exhibition building, the Fridericianum. The ground floor rooms are virtually empty except for a couple of key quasi-footnotes. In the main space is a work by Ryan Gander, some breezes induced via air-conditioning, which serve to clear your mind and open you to the exhibition itself. Apart from a few small (and, in my view, unnecessary) nuances on this experience, the next thing you come upon is a transparent window wall bearing the text of a work by Lawrence Weiner, entitled *The Middle of the Middle of the Middle.*

The wall demarcates the entry to the rotunda space, which is called "The Brain," and which is full of a variety of, maybe thirty-five or forty, objects: works of art, photographs, and artifacts... some in vitrines, some on walls. Featured on one wall are some beautiful paintings by Giorgio Morandi, made during the fascist period. In the area behind that wall are works by Lee Miller and Man Ray, plus objects that were crushed in bombings or destroyed in some way or another. To the side, in vitrines, are some absolutely stunning, fragile, yet intact Bactrian princess statuettes. It is an extraordinary collection of items and images, all of which were produced in situations of violence or confrontation, evasion or disappearance. The world created them and they all bear the marks of that world-ing. So, I felt that I had entered the mind of the curator, your mind, as you were conceiving the exhibition, but also actually the mind of the exhibition itself.

Then I thought, if "The Brain" is the exhibition's mind, you might think of the other buildings in Kassel as its body, not necessarily a human body, but some kind of animate body *in extenso* connected with other bodies: other buildings, in the parks, through the city. We, the spectators, become the circulatory system.

CC-B: The veins, the blood, yes.

TS: But what are the works of art? In this metaphor, what are all the things you show? Are they in fact what *was* in the unconscious: your unconscious, or, really, that of the world itself? To me, the works of art have come from the unconscious of this exhibition and, as it were, surfaced. True, you could move from one room to another and pick up certain narratives that you obviously intended. But, often, that doesn't happen. It is a little like what Freud says: the detritus of the unconscious constantly fills our conscious minds.[5] He did not mean simply bits and pieces of random stuff. He meant *breccia*, an aggregate made up of various kinds of crushed materials that are held together in some kind of binding medium. One of his metaphors for the conscious mind was the Roman forum as we see it, all of those beautiful ruins. The unconscious, however, is all the rocks and stones and sculptures and buildings that have, over the centuries, been crushed and re-used as the core materials for successive layers of architectural structures—like foundations, platforms, columns, whatever. Much of it is lying around in plain sight but we never consciously look at it. So, that's how I read your show, as exhibiting what has been, and is being, crushed and repressed. Does that make sense to you?

CC-B: Yes, it does. But I never thought of the artworks as the unconscious becoming manifest.

TS: Items from the unconscious. That's what Freud talks about. Not the unconscious itself, which always remains invisible, but eruptions from within it.

5. Sigmund Freud, "The Dream-Work," Lecture II, *Introductory Lectures on Psychoanalysis*, in *The Standard Edition of the Complete Psychological Works of Sigmund Freud*, vol. 15 (London: Hogarth, 1955–74), p. 181–82; also in *The Interpretation of Dreams* [1899] (Harmondsworth: Penguin Classics, 2006).

CC-B: I think that's very interesting. I have to think about it. I mean, you catch me off-guard, I've never thought about it that way. I always think in other terms. Such as temporality, spatiality, and partiality. I think dOCUMENTA (13) is basically about transforming temporalities into spaces. I really resist the idea of compressed time. There are other moments that are more about reflection, such as the seminar. Which is why we did three years of seminars in Kabul as part of dOCUMENTA.

When you try to construct something that has no concept, no "idea," you have to find a system so that it is not always collapsing. I used "The Brain" in an open polemic with neuroscience, because I find its fundamental premises anti-philosophical and unable to address the complexities of what's in the brain. Neuroscientists eliminate from the field of research that which is complicated: the palimpsests, the associations with memory, the psychoanalytic, and so on. To them, philosophy died during the twentieth century. Then there is a political danger in neuroscience, a potential return to phrenology, to the idea that the mechanics, the hardware, are the important part. So I use "The Brain" intentionally, polemically, against that perspective. The word "mind" is not an adequate option, because it suggests that there is something produced by the body but somehow disembodied. I side with the Imagists, the poets, who would say, with William Carlos Williams, "No ideas but in things." Therefore, there is a language, which is more like a hieroglyphics, in "The Brain."

TS: But it's not grammatically grounded in the same systematic way.

CC-B: Well, hieroglyphs are not as grammatically grounded as we think. They operate on three simultaneous levels: the image, or the thing that you are writing about; the pronunciation of that word in ancient Egyptian; and then there's a purely syllabic level.

I agree with you that dOCUMENTA (13) is also a project about curatorial practice; as I actually mentioned earlier, it's an anthology of all the modes currently in use, ranging from the most classical modernist display, like in "The Brain," to the idea of activist public art. AND AND AND did projects all over the world, for years, as part of dOCUMENTA. And then in Kassel, they have done projects that were absolutely not controlled or programmed by me, projects dealing with different political problems within the city or in the world at large. These are activist art projects, none of them foregrounded through documentation or publications. They just happened and were what they were. Art outside art venues is another mode: Theaster Gates's work in the Huguenot House, or Sam Durant's work in the park, where passersby rub up against the destination audience. As well, there is the sculpture park model stretching to the outer park. And the so-called educational turn—the "maybe-education" program as an example of a curatorial project—the art-as-education model. Altogether, this is more or less an anthology of every exhibitionary mode you can think of.

META-CURATING

TS: *Thinking Contemporary Curating* ends on the question, why don't curators articulate curatorial thinking? It's a creative act, as you say, and in a certain sense it's an artistic act. So, why not be explicit about it in statements, texts, even in exhibitions, which, after all, are your main medium? I call that "meta-curating," and called for it in the book, hoping that it would happen in your show.

CC-B: Yes, you did. You predicted it in the last chapter, which you wrote before the exhibition opened. It's such an honor that the last words are about dOCUMENTA (13), based on that one text that I circulated when you were finishing your book.

TS: And then you did it.

CC-B: I did it. I always do what I say. Everything in the exhibition is suggested in "Letter to a Friend," which was sent out to 17,000 people in October 2010 as an attachment to a press release, but intentionally hidden in a pdf so that most people wouldn't even open it because they're afraid of computer viruses. Really, only artists read it. It speaks about my journeys to Afghanistan, and everything we did subsequently. It's in the form of an intimate dairy—like an epistolary novel, in a way. It's a 5,000-word text, now available as one of the notebooks, and I got many reactions after it was published in this form.[6]

Let us go back to your question: what are the artworks? Well, most of them didn't exist before dOCUMENTA (13). I'm allergic to the practice by which existing artworks are brought together by curators to demonstrate their connoisseurship, to show off their visual intelligence by juxtaposing works. Of course, if the artworks already exist, and you pick them, you're going to get an exhibition full of really good art. If you have any taste or ability to discern, it's easy. I believe instead in the journey that you go on with artists to create the works, fresh works, for your exhibition. The last thing I talk about with artists is art. We talk about food. We talk about love. We talk about death. We talk about trauma. We talk about politics. We talk about the world. And, then, while I write something for the catalogue, he or she makes the work. Then we walk "together with" the work, and then we welcome the visitors…

If "The Brain" somehow exhibits the detritus emerging from the unconscious, I can think of some examples: the ceramics by the Paraguayan potters Julia Isidrez and Juana Marta Rodas; the puppet used for Wael Shawky's film, the second of his *Cabaret Crusades* series, which was projected in the Neue Galerie; Etel Adnan's palette knife, with which she has from 1957 through today painted all her paintings, a selection of which were shown

6. Carolyn Christov-Bakargiev, *Letter to a Friend: 100 Notes – 100 Thoughts; Documenta Series 040* (Ostfildern: Hatje Cantz, 2011).

in the Documenta-Halle. I put the knife in "The Brain," right next to two ancient Roman sculptures that had been burnt during the Lebanese civil wars and so were fused together into this horrendous, incredible, abstract sculpture that looked like something from post–Second World War Art Informel. So in that sense, yes, there is that kind of relationship within the exhibition.

But I would only agree with the analysis if the unconscious were understood as simultaneously producing itself and, at the same moment, throwing up the detritus, which is revealed, perceived, and articulated. I would reject the idea that the detritus is being caught at a second moment, if you think about it temporally, by me as a curator operating consciously to do exactly that. So, does that answer your question?

TS: Yes, that distinction is what I had in mind when using the extended metaphor of Kassel as the body in relation to "The Brain" in the Fridericianum.

CC-B: I have to read, from page 22, the sentence I like most in your book. I didn't quite get it, and I'm not sure that you did when you wrote it, which is why it's beautiful. I think you're making a logical jump, but not explicitly, which is really nice: "Think of the terms of my title"—the title of the book—"that flash independently, in bold isolation, but then combine into a number of almost sentences"—I love "almost sentences," it's like the "maybe-education" of our project—"seemingly located at levels below and more basic than those allowed by the surfaces of spoken and written language, through which they often, these days with accelerating insistence, break." So maybe the relationship between what's outside and inside "The Brain" has something to do with these "almost sentences"?

TS: That's, actually, exactly right. It's a very good parallel to the way I'm reading your exhibition. It's not that you, yourself, have the ability to predict what's going to come up from the unconscious of either artists or the world, but you set up a range of conditions so that this is somehow elicited by the framework of the show.

CC-B: Yes. That's why most of the projects are new. But they aren't new and fetishized as being new, they were just a journey "with," you know. Like in a marriage, or in a life. It's a journey with someone…

THE CONTEMPORANEITY QUESTION

CC-B: I have a question about the difference between "contemporary" and "contemporaneity." Why do you use these terms in that way? And why am I allergic to "contemporary"?

TS: Well, for people who haven't read my recent material, let me explain that I start from the idea of opening out the word "contemporary" in terms such as "contemporary art," and in a phrase we often hear, "the contemporary." I object to the sense that these terms can describe a singularity, for example, immediacy, or being of the present, or being up to date, or being more contemporary than someone else. In effect, this reduces the multiplicity, the differentiation that shapes what it is to be in the world today, and turns it into one kind of world being. That's not just inaccurate, it's oppressive. I became very concerned with the question of contemporaneity after 9/11, particularly when the post–Cold War idea of the United States as the country that, due to the forces of history, had come inevitably to dominate the world's agenda became the official policy of the Bush administration, a policy it then sought to impose by force. The whole idea of a "War on Terror"—a warring on things that will go on forever—was an effort to make a declared state of emergency into a kind of constant contemporaneity.

CC-B: To make it permanent.

TS: Yes. That's the kind of "contemporary" that I am utterly against. We have versions of it in the art world, and various other worlds. So, what I've tried to do is go back to the core concept, to see how "contemporary" points us to the many different ways in which all of us—individually and, necessarily, together—exist in time, always at the same time as others. And always with the sense that others, even when they're sitting right next to us, are actually, or have the potential to be, in a different time. That's immediate and personal. On world-picturing levels, all of us can have a sense of belonging to our own time, but also feeling out of joint with it, or being disposed against it, being what Nietzsche calls "untimely," to which I would add: in a way that's different from everyone else. But we can also, at the same time, share some, perhaps many, things with others; we can become each other's contemporary. In short, there is a multiplicity of ways of being in time in the present. To be contemporary in this sense is a very rich, very layered experience. It is the exact opposite of what is promoted as "contemporary" at the great auction houses of the world, and by the highest-priced artists—whose time, perhaps, has come.

I think that exhibitions like dOCUMENTA (13), whether consciously or not, are in fact impacted by the layering of the world—by the different temporalities that exist for people throughout the world. It's possible for curators to exhibit this contemporaneity, it's important for people to write about it, for artist to grapple with it in the work that they make. I cannot make it a rule, but to me, it's a very deeply important thing to be doing. So, that's what I mean by "contemporaneity." Do you have a different understanding?

CC-B: No, no. I would agree with that definition of the word "contemporaneity." I would agree that that is what I was trying to do with dOCUMENTA (13), what we were all trying to do—to live with this sense. I think you are suggesting a very interesting breakaway from the word "contemporary," while you keep using the root of it. You know, *cum tempore*, "with the times." I know you trace it back through the centuries, but for me the important moment is after the Second World War—after the atomic bomb, basically. Since the 1960s, especially since the late 1960s, the word "modern," or "modern art," was increasingly substituted with "contemporary." So it is a twentieth-century word defining the culture of the second half of the twentieth century, which for me, as a culture, is not really relevant right now. Because it has to do with this celebration of the *hic et nunc*. The obsession with the "here and now" is really about trying to understand what the hell dropping this atomic bomb means. What is the meaning of that cloud, that instant during and just after the bomb falls?

TS: The world could end. Time has shrunk to that kind of moment.

CC-B: Yes, it is the instant. So it's very different from the notion of time, or untimeliness, or anachronism… I mean, "contemporariness" is a modern idea. It's somewhat synonymous with the late nineteenth-century notion of *il faut être absolument moderne*. But it's articulated differently because it takes away the Bergsonian idea of duration and wants to expand this instantaneity as if one could look at the time one is in with a historical gaze. As if one could be, at once, outside and inside of time. So, to understand that "contemporary" means to be outside understanding the now is a presumptuous idea of the twentieth century, an extraordinarily destructive belief.

It is similar to the more recent usage, more or less also starting in the 1960s, of "global"—a word that is now extremely popular. It appeared when we began to see images of the Earth taken by satellites in the late 1960s, and it expresses the hubris of thinking that you can both be in the world and see it from a detached, outside perspective, a perspective of power. I don't wish to use either of these two terms, "contemporary" or "global." I prefer to use the word "worldly."[7] So, I love the way that you make

7. Carolyn Christov-Bakargiev, "Worldy Worlding: The Imaginal Fields of Science/Art and Making Patterns Together," *Mousse*, no. 43 (March 2014). http://moussemagazine.it/articolo.mm?id=1095.

"contemporaneity" into almost the opposite of "contemporary." You make it mean something like the palimpsest of different times...

TS: ... all at the same time, exactly.

CC-B: Yes, but I'm not so interested in the "at the same time" part. The rest I'm very interested in. If we think about it in terms of space, it has something to do with the partialities that I discussed earlier. dOCUMENTA (13) was not just exhibited in Kassel. Yet its existence there created a kind of partiality that allowed for the Kabul seminars to have meaningfulness. And vice versa. This sense comes from Judith Butler, because I'm thinking about the notion of grievability and precarious lives: only if you know that something can be lost, or that there is something that you cannot have, can you fully appreciate what you have. So, it's through the possible negative that any positive is perceived. That's one kind of partiality.

TS: And you required every artist who was invited to dOCUMENTA to visit Breitenau, a former monastery, prison, work camp, concentration camp, girls' reformatory, and psychiatric clinic, not far from Kassel.

CC-B: Exactly. Documenta itself emerged out of trauma, after the rise and fall of fascism in Germany, through the impulse to reassess positively what had been the exhibition *Entartete Kunst* [*Degenerate Art*] in Munich in 1937 organized by the Nazis. It also emerged historically as a wish to reconstruct civil society after the horrors of the Holocaust, the breakdown of international relations during the fascist period, during the Second World War, and more. In this context, art became a vehicle for a form of transnational alliance that could be built more easily through artists and cultural practitioners than through other fields. Unlike other international exhibitions, such as the Venice Biennale, Documenta doesn't come out of the history of the commercial world fairs of the nineteenth century. It comes out of a wound. This gives it a different premise.[8]

The layering of the works that artists have made in the past creates a context for the artists invited to participate in Documenta. They might be thinking about Walter De Maria's *The Vertical Earth Kilometer* [1977], or Joseph Beuys's *7000 Oaks* [1982]. As director, you are preceded by Catherine David, who brought incredible things to the project, and Okwui Enwezor, among others. In Venice, when so many things are going on in parallel exhibitions, and there is also Giorgione's *Tempesta* nearby, the path of precedents is less clear. It all becomes a blur, not a context. After the war, Kassel was a blank slate, a neutral platform that permitted a clear perception of the history of artworks that were made in that palimpsest. None of my predecessors wanted to question that neutral platform—out of fear, because naturally they wanted to protect it. It's like the United Nations building. If we all start speaking about it as being in New York City because the U.S. is the dominant country in the world, delegates from some countries might not come anymore, or certainly might not come as the representatives of their countries. So everyone politely ignores the obvious, which is that the UN building is not a neutral space. This also happened with Kassel until this edition of the exhibition. To question a neutral platform is a very risky thing, especially when you want a platform on which to speak together with others. But I did it anyway. I did it because I believe in reality and in these forms of commitment.

But just as I say this, I also say the opposite: it could have been anywhere. I would have done it anywhere. There's a certain history of pain in Kassel, and there's a certain history of pain in Kab ul. They actually share something. Documenta emerges in Kassel with the need to rebuild Germany after the trauma of a war.

8. Carolyn Christov-Bakargiev, Dario Gamboni, and Michael Petzet, *On the Destruction of Art—Or Art and Conflict, or the Art of Healing: 100 Notes – 100 Thoughts; Documenta Series 040* (Ostfildern: Hatje Cantz, 2011).

To rebuild it as a *nation*, knowing that *nationalism* can bring the most horrendous consequences. Today, Afghanistan is an Islamic country that is rebuilding itself after the Taliban regime, or that needs to do so, knowing—the same way that nationalism in Europe lead to Nazi fascism—the consequences of an extremist religious state. It is a country that can only be Islamic, because it has extreme ethnic diversity, but it understands the paradox of this. There are 150 languages; there are the Uzbeks, the Pashtuns, and Tajiks. This strange contradictory condition somehow resonates with Germany during the 1950s.

This thing you say about co-temporalities... I don't believe that time is linear. I know that's a postmodern idea, but actually time is layered, and different historical periods exist simultaneously. That's why there's one page, only one, I don't agree with in your book.

TS: Let's look at that, then, as a kind of wrap-up.

ALWAYS CRITICAL, EVERYWHERE

CC-B: On page 257 you say something like, "Of course, all that I've written about before is valuable for a place that is advanced, which already has all the infrastructure, a deep history of work around art, so we can question ourselves and discuss how we do this questioning. Of course, I don't mean to say that in places that don't have art, or that don't have an art system, or that don't have artists, it's invalid. For them, it's valid just to be able to make art. And therefore I don't want to criticize their lack of critical consciousness about the curatorial." I disagree with that.

TS: So do I. Did I say that?

CC-B: You say it in a positive way, yet I find it somewhat paternalistic—not from the point of view of Western culture as a whole, but as a curator. I believe that you can start from a blank slate anywhere. And you can learn things that you don't know everywhere. For example, there are things in traditional Australian Aboriginal painting that would be important lessons for people in places that have the burden, unfortunately, of knowing the history of Mondrian and Brice Marden. It would be so great to forget all of that—to undergo some kind of lobotomy and start all over in a different way. That's not neo-exoticism or primitivism at all; it's just rejecting the idea that there is one linear history of art and civilization.

TS: At some points in the book, when I'm writing about some very subtle efforts by curators and artists to activate overwhelming infrastructure, too much institutionalization, lots of money concentrated perhaps in the wrong places, I zone out to the larger world picture, and zone in elsewhere. I think of Brazil, or Argentina, much of China, through to Oceania and much of Africa, places where there is infrastructure, but it's fragile and could collapse at any minute. When the political regime changes, everyone is sacked and the other "team" comes in, dismantling everything. Or the buildings are destroyed. Artistic and curatorial activity has been pivotal in bringing about positive social change in these parts of the world, and in many others. I am saying: commit to the infrastructures, build them, but never for their own sake, or in the vague hope that interesting art will appear. It won't. You can never let up on critical practice, not anywhere, it doesn't matter what the circumstances are.

Boris Groys

Exhibitions, Installations, And Nostalgia

Born in East Berlin, Boris Groys studied philosophy, mathematics, and logic at the University of Leningrad during the 1970s. He wrote about Russian artists in underground journals, and continued to do so after 1981, when he emigrated to the Federal Republic of Germany. From 1994 to 2009, Groys taught the history of avant-garde art, as well as philosophy, at the Staatliche Hochschule *für* Gestaltung Karlsruhe (Karlsruhe University of Arts and Design). Since then he has been Global Distinguished Professor of Russian and Slavic Studies at New York University and a senior research fellow at Karlsruhe University of Art and Design and the International Center for Cultural Studies and Media Theory at Bauhaus University in Weimar, Germany. He is the author of a number of books, among them *The Total Art of Stalinism* (Princeton, N. J.: Princeton University Press, 1992), *Ilya Kabakov: The Man Who Flew into Space from His Apartment* (Cambridge, Mass.: MIT Press, 2006), *Art Power* (Cambridge, Mass.: MIT Press, 2008), *History Becomes Form: Moscow Conceptualism* (Cambridge, Mass.: MIT Press, 2010), *The Communist Postscript* (London: Verso, 2010), *Introduction to Antiphilosophy* (London: Verso, 2012), and *On the New* (London: Verso, 2014). Among the exhibitions he has curated are *Specters of Communism: Contemporary Russian Art* (2015), at the James Gallery, CUNY Graduate Center, and e-flux, New York; *After History: Alexandre Kojève as a Photographer* (2012), at BAK, Utrecht, and traveling; *Total Enlightenment: Conceptual Art in Moscow 1960–1990* (2008) and *Dream Factory Communism* (2003–4), both at the Schirn Kunsthalle, Frankfurt; and *Fluchtpunkt Moskau* (1994), Ludwig Forum, Aachen.

We spoke at Independent Curators International, New York, on October 22, 2013.

Terry Smith: As well as curating a number of exhibitions in recent years—exhibitions of quite different types—you have made what are, to me, some of the most insightful comments on curating in modern and contemporary contexts. Concentrated versions of your ideas can be found in essays such as "On the New," written in 2000, and my favorite incidentally, where you highlight particularly how essential the museum, as a spatial entity that sets itself apart from lived time, is to the very possibility of novelty, itself temporal. This is an unfashionable, but essential, idea. Your 2007 essay "On the Curatorship" explores the role swapping between artists and curators that has been going on since Duchamp's (in)famous display of a urinal in 1917.[1] You relate this issue to current art and curatorial installations in your 2010 essay "Politics of Installation," to my mind the indispensible theorization of this quintessentially contemporary art form. In "Comrades of Time" you offer a reading of contemporaneity not too dissimilar to mine.[2] There are ongoing themes here, which are carefully, philosophically considered, but which are also propelled by provocations that come from angles that often seem unfamiliar, not to say strange.

TWO TYPES OF EXHIBITIONS

Boris Groys: Can we start from a very general point about the nature of art exhibitions? I think that there are basically two types, each asking to be seen in a very different way. One shows us a fragment of a traditional narrative about the history of art, while the other reveals a subjective act of selection on the part of the organizer. Everything we might want to say about curating works of art into exhibitions flows from this distinction.

TS: Can you elaborate on those differences?

BG: Well, as I see it, traditional exhibitions have two specific characteristics. First of all, they illustrate already established narratives, like, for example, the Latin American art of a certain period, or the life and work of, say, Paul Cézanne. In this case, the narrative is already known, broadly speaking, and what's important is that the exhibition is created to afford access to the individual works. You go from one work to another, like you turn the pages of a book. You can say, I like this particular work, but I don't like that particular work. The questions that arise are mostly about why something is included, or excluded.

TS: The inclusion or exclusion of this or that work reinforces or changes the established narrative?

1. Both essays in Boris Groys, *Art Power* (Cambridge, Mass.: MIT Press, 2008).

2. Both essays in Boris Groys, *Going Public* (Berlin: Sternberg Press, 2010).

BG: Yes, but now we must ask: what is the ontological status of this type of exhibition? The answer is that the exhibition itself, unlike an artistic installation, does not exist as a total space. So, the second characteristic of this type of exhibition is that its space is neutral. It is only a medium of access to individual artworks. How they relate to the announced subject of the exhibition is dependent on the visitor's focus, and not inscribed into the exhibition itself. If interrogated by the public, the curator has a hard time explaining why s/he ignored this work or narrative, but included another. The situation becomes political very quickly.

TS: So compared to the individual artworks in it, this type of exhibition appears to be almost invisible, a kind of "natural" surround. Bringing the curator to the foreground changes that equation, and presumably leads us to the second type of exhibition. How is it different, in your view?

THE INSTALLATION AS *GESAMTKUNSTWERK*

BG: To highlight the distinction, let's use the term "installation" instead of "exhibition." Immediately, the question of inclusion and exclusion disappears. If you look at, for example, Harald Szeemann's projects, it makes no sense to ask why something is included and why something is excluded. It is included because it fits into his individual project and excluded if it doesn't. There is no claim to neutrality, or of normative narrative, or of representation. The claim is a semi-artistic, or quasi-artistic, one: "I did something that expresses my personality." That's the end of it.

I think this kind of curatorial installation is best understood as a *Gesamtkunstwerk*. As we know from Wagner, who developed the idea in relation to his operas, the *Gesamtkunstwerk* is an artwork that includes every possible art form. Indeed, contemporary curatorial projects often present objects traditionally understood as artworks alongside artifacts, texts, soundtracks, or videos.

Individually, these objects, processes, documents, or texts might or might not make sense. In the framework of the curatorial *Gesamtkunstwerk*, however, they are instrumentalized, and entirely subject to the will of the curator. They cannot be seen independently. They have no meaning outside of the project. They are completely integrated into the whole. Captured. They are not representative in a social, political, or other way. They do not stand for anything but what they are, a part of the *Gesamtkunstwerk*. The placement, lighting, position, whatever is only an expression of the curator's general idea. Everything is subject to it. After the exhibition is over, the artworks remain, while other elements, such as the exhibition architecture, are discarded.

Like an artistic installation, the curatorial installation is a temporary artwork. It has a beginning and it has an end. For its duration, however, the curator is like a dictator, or a theater director, and the exhibition space is a stage. It's not a traditional art space; it has no autonomy. It is a stage where the *Gesamtkunstwerk*, or the installation, is performed. It's no accident that Harald Szeemann introduced this kind of subjective, performative installation. He was an admirer of Bayreuth, where the Wagnerian festivals are held.

TS: He began his professional life as an actor, I believe, after studying art history, archaeology, and journalism.

BG: To explain his particular attitude, he made the exhibition *Der Hang zum Gesamtkunstwerk* [The Tendency toward the Total Work of Art] in 1983.

TS: Hans Ulrich Obrist recalls that it was the first show he ever saw. He visited it forty-one times.[3] Taking up your idea that the

3. Paul Holdengräber, "Hans Ulrich Obrist Interview," *Surface*, issue 104 (December 2013/ January 2014), pp. 126–33, and Hans Ulrich Obrist, *Ways of Curating* (London: Allen Lane, 2014), pp. 30–32.

first type of exhibition is a neutral medium for art, you could read Obrist as a medium for curating, although this foregrounds him as a curatorial figure, a cipher in a not-so-neutral way. After that conversion experience at *Der Hang zum Gesamtkunstwerk* he seems to have wanted to become a living, human rhizome, or *the* medium connecting that exhibition, or any exhibition, to all of its possible viewers. Perhaps with all of its possible curators, and all of the artists whose work might have been in it? Also, maybe, with all of the philosophers or scientists and so on, whose ideas might be relevant to it.

BG: The strange thing about Bayreuth as a precedent is that Wagner and his people drew the line between audience and stage in a more radical way than ever before. They introduced a major change in the auditorium lighting, putting the public into darkness, and they lowered the orchestra into a pit, hiding it from view. Sitting in the auditorium now feels more like being in a film theater. The fusing of drama and music happens at a distance, up on the stage, as if on a screen. It's no accident that the artist Christoph Schlingensief, in his 2004 production of *Parsifal*, used the stage of Bayreuth as a large screen for the projection of his videos—the set up is very, very cinematic.

Actually, Szeemann, as some other curators and artists have done since, did something that Wagner aspired to, but never achieved. They really, physically, corporeally included the visitors *inside* the exhibitionary space. In traditional theater, the fundamental division between the public and the stage remains. But in a curatorial project, the visitors are inside the art space. They come to the venue, they step on the stage, and they enter the scene. Every visitor automatically becomes an artwork, or part of the *Gesamtkunstwerk*.

TS: An artwork? What do you mean?

BG: When I go to traditional museums, to the narrative kind of exhibition I mentioned before, I look at the paintings, the sculptures, whatever artworks are on display. But when I go to curated exhibitions, I almost never look at the objects. I look at the other visitors. You know, it is essential to understand their behavior. How much time do they spend looking at a video? Do they go back to a work or not? Do they read the texts? I am particularly interested in how visitors react to the curator's and/or the artist's implicit or explicit commandments. Installations—such as those by Mike Kelley, for example, or by Gregor Schneider, which you have to crawl inside to experience—ask us to take literally the idea that the viewer "completes" the artwork. So, this is the sense in which I say that what I really find most entertaining, interesting, fascinating, even, are the visitors as artworks.

TS: Let's try to unpack some of these ideas a little bit more. In terms of historical trajectories, when do you think the split occurred between these two kinds of exhibitions? Or has it always been there?

BG: Well, I think it started with the idea of introducing temporality into individual artworks, and also into the presentation of art. During the Russian Revolution, to take one instance, the new government feared that the museums would be looted, or that they would have to close due to the economic collapse. Kazimir Malevich, on the contrary, advocated that they should be burned down and their ashes exhibited.[4] He believed that a new kind of life was being born at that time, and the old institutions were blocking its conception. Their ashes, however, might contain the DNA of that new life. The idea of showing those ashes was one of the first curatorial projects of the kind I am talking about.

4. Kazimir Malevich, "On the Museum" (1919). See Boris Groys, "Becoming Revolutionary: On Kazimir Malevich," *e-flux journal*, no. 47 (September 2013). http://www.e-flux.com/journal/becoming-revolutionary-on-kazimir-malevich/.

TS: A massive *Gesamtkunstwerk* in reverse.

BG: Precisely what I mean. When you exhibit things, you transform them. Malevich's idea was to thematize temporality, yes? To exhibit the temporal mode of existence. Around that time, there were many attempts to do this. From a contemporary point of view I would say that the two most interesting are El Lissitzky's projects and those of Marcel Duchamp. El Lissitzky's exhibitions represent the Constructivist, let's say, or really the Suprematist, side of the avant-garde, and Duchamp's installations attempted to present the Surrealist side. Neither was understood in their time. But by the 1960s, when ideas of temporality, performance, context, interaction, and so on became very central, these projects came into their own. In turn, the 1960s conception of exhibitions as performative acts gave birth to contemporary installation practice.

I have a student here at New York University who is interested in the Russian exhibitions of 1918–19, organized by Nikolay Punin, notably the *Avalanche Exhibition*, for which he invited artists to fill a particular space with artworks, whatever they wanted to show. And after the whole space was filled, it was closed. So, you know, what was exhibited was this concept of an avalanche of art, thus demonstrating that the time of artworks is infinite but space is finite. It is always particular and limited. And exhibitionary form is not something infinitely indefinite, or potentially immortal. Rather, exhibitions have moments of coming into existence and maybe even of development, of becoming—and then of ending. Temporality is, I think, central to the idea of the exhibition.

EXHIBITION ARCHITECTURE

TS: How does your trajectory as a curator relate to these questions? From where I sit, it looks as if your exhibitionary work has mostly been an extension of your engagement, as an art critic, in Moscow Conceptualism.

BG: Well, I must say that my own curatorship has developed mostly in response to offers to do something. When I came to the West at the beginning of the 1980s, there was zero interest in Russian art, or in Eastern European art more generally. This changed a bit with perestroika and the end of the Cold War. I was asked to be an advisor, then to write for catalogues, and soon to make exhibitions.

If you are asking why I curate, I think the driving force has been a desire to show something that was previously not visible. On the other hand, I have wanted to make very subjective shows. To emphasize this, I have always designed my own exhibition architecture. I even had the spaces rebuilt in established institutions, such as the Schirn Kunsthalle, so they were totally unlike what they were before.

TS: How does this logic work in the case of particular exhibitions?

BG: Well, as mentioned, in Frankfurt I organized two major surveys, one about Socialist Realism and the other about Moscow Conceptualism. During my early years in the Soviet Union, Socialist Realist images were never shown in the kind of modernist, neutral, white cube settings that were standard in the West, but always in a palace environment, or as part of huge thematic exhibitions dedicated to different aspects of Soviet life, while sculptures were placed in very public places. So, for the exhibition *Dream Factory Communism* [2003–4], the architect Wilfried Kuehn and I created a progression of palace interiors. For *Total Enlightenment: Conceptual Art in Moscow 1960–1990*, the idea was the opposite: I wanted to show something like an experimental laboratory, or office space, in action.

TS: I saw that show. The upper rooms were like studios in the artists' apartments, housing big projects by Ilya Kabakov, for example, or they were like mini-exhibitions, of, for example, Dmitry Prigov's concrete poetry, or like an outdoor, amateur art show, in the case of some early photographs by Boris Mikhailov. The lower floor was laid out like an open-plan office.

BG: Yes, it was modeled on the office spaces of the Centre Pompidou, half open, half closed, so that individuals can concentrate but also communicate. For the exhibition at the Venice Biennale in 2011, the large, domed, central space of the Russian Pavilion was transformed—by very abstract, minimalist means—into a space evoking a Soviet labor camp. And then, in the lower gallery, I re-created the Andrey Monastyrsky and Collective Actions section from *Total Enlightenment*, that half-intimate, half-official space.

TS: Yes, going through those spaces was a disjunctive experience. You were following, obviously, the *Gesamtkunstwerk* model rather than the narrativizing, art historical one.

BG: I didn't want it to look like Russian art is easy to inscribe into Western art history, because it is not. There are breaks and gaps; it has a different temporality, no? When I speak with Western art curators, from different museums, most of them honestly believe that Russian art became contemporary after perestroika, which is the first time they saw it. They don't get that it had been conceptual, process-oriented, experimental since the late 1950s. To disturb that perception, I tried to create this feeling of discontinuity, the sense that Russian art occurred in different kinds of spaces with different relationships among participants and artworks.

THE REVOLUTION INVENTS ART

TS: It is now conventional to locate the first type of exhibition you distinguish within the history of museums and the history of exhibitionary spaces, particularly from the fifteenth century to the present, starting with the displays of the art collections of the princes, cardinals, and popes, and continuing to the industrial design expositions, such as the Great Exhibition in

London, in 1851. These expositions were huge, sprawling affairs, lasting for a few months. Similar versions were staged all over the world, especially during the later nineteenth century, so there was a sense of the world's manufacturers being permanently on show somewhere. It's argued that there's a parallel activity in fine art museums throughout the nineteenth and twentieth centuries. Put the two together, as Tony Bennett argues, and you get the exhibitionary complex. Caroline Jones is writing a book about this development as being pivotal to the exhibitionary structure of contemporary art, especially biennials.[5]

BG: I don't think there's any relationship whatsoever between industrial exhibitions and art exhibitions.

Industrial exhibitions show things that are used in life, whereas art is for the most part the exhibition of what is already dead. Our attitude toward its possible use is ultimately negative, while our relationship to the use of technology is positive. That is the basic difference between how art functions in our culture compared to industry. It is an absolute divide, one you can't cross.

There is a bigger story informing that period. If one asks, what is art? one must answer that art is an effect of the French Revolution, that is, the outcome of the question having faced the bourgeoisie at that time: how do we deal with the heritage of the aristocracy? The logical thing for the French revolutionaries to do with the riches that they inherited from the old regime would have been to destroy them. Instead, the French made art out of them. They defunctionalized items of wealth, and of religion, and kept them as objects of pure contemplation. One can hate a political system, and feel alienated from the palace (the Louvre) that embodies it, yet at the same time one can find this palace beautiful.

5. Tony Bennett, *The Birth of the Museum: History, Theory, Politics* (London: Routledge, 1995), especially chapter 6, and Caroline Jones, *Desires for the World Picture: The Global Work of Art* (Chicago: University of Chicago Press, forthcoming).

So, intrinsic to the bourgeois conception of art is the iconoclastic moment of its birth. Art embodies the modern way of destroying things—by defunctionalization, aestheticization. If you go into European art museums you see icons that have been desacralized, signs of power that are disempowered, Egyptian mummies that cannot be resuscitated, and Inca gold that we no longer accept as currency. This is a collection of things we no longer accept on their own terms. We don't like the religions that commissioned these items, we don't accept the social relationships that produced them, nor do we accept the politics of their times.

TS: Yet these items are also displays of various processes of selection and classification. They are the results of campaigns of conquest, or the outcomes of archaeological expeditions, or scientific efforts to classify natural phenomena, to trace human tool making, or the history of the world's art...

BG: I agree, of course, that there's always selection, in both situations. But if you read the commentaries on exhibitions written in the eighteenth and nineteenth centuries you will find they are critical of the organizers for being too subjective in their choices. It was believed that curators should attempt to overcome their prejudices, their personal attitudes, their individual tastes, and present something objective and socially, politically, and historically relevant.

Today, in contrast, curators are required to be subjective, to formulate their own position as clearly as possible. They are expected to follow their individual tastes, preferences, and even political convictions. Indeed, if they do something that conforms to the norms of public taste, their exhibitions are dismissed as banal. What was once uncorrupted curatorial strategy, exercised according to "objective" criteria, now looks like banality. And what was, say, an honest attitude toward art's actual history appears, now, one hundred percent ideological. So we have this radical reversal, but we should not think that things always remain similar, or that the traditional and the individual exhibition are the same kind of thing simply because both are exhibitions.

THE ENCYCLOPEDIC PALACE

TS: How would the 2013 edition of the Venice Biennale, curated by Massimiliano Gioni, fit into your distinction? Clearly it's an exhibition that tries to offer a certain history of modern art, emphasizing two trajectories and their interaction—actual, trained, professional artists who happen to be very interested in human obsessions, on the one hand, and, on the other, amateur, outsider artists, some of whom are certified as mentally ill, who unabashedly draw or collect or accumulate their obsessions. Isn't it, in a sense, halfway between your two models?

BG: No, I wouldn't say so. Gioni exercised a very individual principle of selection, and he selected artists who were also very subjective in their approaches. So, for him, it seems to me, it was irrelevant if they were recognized, not recognized, or recognized as outsider or insider artists by art history. His project was very consistent precisely because it disregarded all these traditional boundaries, separations, and evaluations.

TS: But the show was structured as a historical narrative. You entered the Central Pavilion via illustrations by the psychologist Carl Jung; storyboards by mystic teacher Rudolf Steiner lined the main room, where you also encountered a Tino Sehgal performance of two people making "primitive" sounds at each other. Then, as you progressed through the side halls, you moved through an implied narrative that unfolded from the 1910s up to the present. It wasn't a strict chronology, true, but there was historical movement. There was a sort of subtext, asking us to go back and revise the history of modern twentieth-century art, to expand it to include these artists. So, the question of inclusion and exclusion was there, recalling that contentious space between your two kinds of exhibition.

BG: Yes, it does tell this history, but tells it in a different way. I think that the exhibition had a certain polemical edge. To me, Gioni is trying to outline an alternative history of art rather than revise the orthodox modernist account. Instead of beginning from the idea that art comes from previous art, he is asking us to imagine a kind of art—really, an outpouring of imagery, call it "art" or not—created by people who are driven by unconscious or subconscious energies, some religious, some having to do with sexuality, or psycho-social disturbances.

Let me put it another way. I see a huge misunderstanding in art history, and in art historical writing, about modernism and the avant-garde. Not so much in professional scholarship, but in popular writing about modern art, which is in love with the idea that avant-garde art is all about breaking the rules of art, of social convention, of culture, of everything. But the avant-garde was never about rule breaking—it was committed to rule making, to introducing rules, and usually these new rules were much more restrictive than the previous ones. The whole history of the avant-garde, De Stijl obviously, but even Surrealism, is about narrowing the freedom of artists. Greenberg understood this better than most, as you can see from his early essay "Avant-Garde and Kitsch" and the late one "Avant-Garde Attitudes."[6] The artistic avant-garde is like the radical ascetic movements that erupt from time to time within established religions. They practice self-purification; they are always more restrictive than the current regime, right? In a similar way, the avant-garde is about self-restriction, and self-submission to the rules; it's a kind of self-torture.

TS: This does not sound like the Miesian, Frankfurt School line about negative capability, which advocates that the point of

6. "Avant-Garde and Kitsch" [1939], in Clement Greenberg, *The Collected Essays and Criticism, Volume 1: Perceptions and Judgments, 1939–1944*, ed. John O'Brian (Chicago: University of Chicago Press, 1986); "Avant-Garde Attitudes" [1968], in Clement Greenberg, *The Collected Essays and Criticism, Volume 4: Modernism with a Vengeance, 1957–1969*, ed. John O'Brian (Chicago: University of Chicago Press, 1995).

greater narrowing is to enable more to be done, more profoundly, with less.

BG: No, because it's simply restrictive, restrictive, restrictive, restrictive. Every step is further restricted by the next step. Not only fewer subjects, but also fewer and fewer genres. Successively, you can no longer paint Rubens's "fat ass of Venus"—as Malevich put it—and then you can't paint portraits. Finally, you can only paint white on white. Then, even painting white is too much. The whole tendency is devoted to generating restrictions, restrictions, only restrictions, one after another.

In total contrast to this, Gioni's heroes care nothing about aesthetic restrictions: Jung just painted what he dreamed. Gioni's biennale is a presentation of the non-restrictive, non-monkish art being made during the past century.

TS: For me, this idea of the unrestricted dangles in some unspecified psychic space, whereas all the artists included in the official parts of the biennale were, in fact, into repetition of one kind or another. Even Jung spent time developing generalized theories about the conscious and the unconscious: the drawings show him trying to illustrate the archetypes that dominate it, in his view. The "heroes" who introduce the exhibition, like Steiner, were in fact people who devised these massively generalized systematic theories, all of which have, at the same time, this strange quality of being over-particularized.

BG: Yes, true, but we can't say their theories were unscientific, because they were of another kind altogether, neither scientific nor unscientific. They were full of rules but not systematic. Remember that Jung broke with Freud because Freud rejected his return to mythology. Jung was not alone at the time in creating unsystematic systems that don't follow their own rules: don't forget, this is the moment of quantum physics, too.

In Moscow in the 1970s, I met artists who followed this kind of approach, such as Mikhail Schwarzman and Eduard Steinberg. They are now almost completely forgotten, maybe unjustly so. They disregarded all the rules of what Minimalism is, what Conceptual art should be, in order to do something mythical, or mystical, something coming from another place that does not fit into the art system. I don't like that myself, and I couldn't quite follow what they were doing, but at the same time, I understand what it is and how it can work. So, I appreciate Gioni's position.

SEMIOTIC SURREALISM

TS: It is curious that there are very few Surrealists included in Gioni's exhibition, and yet latter-day surrealists, of various sorts, were featured in many of the national pavilions. I am thinking of Mark Manders in the Dutch Pavilion, Berlinde De Bruyckere in the Belgian, and Sarah Sze and her entrancingly obsessive worlds in the United States Pavilion. To me, these artists, together with others scattered throughout the city, resolve the tension that Gioni set up in the main galleries. Maybe this was because the curators of those pavilions wanted to second-guess Gioni, or perhaps it is because this mood is so widespread among artists these days.

BG: If we look attentively at André Breton's writings and objects, if we really examine René Magritte, we discover that the Surrealists' work had nothing to do with any kind of unconscious. The whole movement was about logic. If you study Magritte's work, it's very obvious. He looks at certain kinds of logical relationships, and pictures them through certain kinds of spatial relationships. He distorts them in a very systematic way. It has nothing to do with reality, or the unconscious, or subconscious. It's a very systematic play with logical possibilities that follows certain kinds of logical rules. The paradox is that these rules exclude everything that looks banal, trivially logical, or familiar in some way. I think that Gioni tries to follow this rule, the rule of avoiding any rules whatsoever. You can accept this tactic, appreciate it, even like it—or not. Whatever the case, I find that it is a consistent position.

TS: Thinking about the Magritte exhibition currently at MoMA, I have to agree with what you're saying about his work not manifesting the unconscious, even though that is its overt topic, time and again, if you go by the titles of many of the paintings. *The Pleasure Principle* [1937], for example, which is a kind of anti-portrait of one of his patrons that could be seen as a pretty obvious illustration of Freud's idea of life or death. Overall, Magritte's procedure seems very controlled, careful, and conscious. Also on display are the brief statements and drawings that he made for an essay about his thinking process, which he contributed as a double-page spread to the magazine *La Révolution surréaliste* in 1929. Halfway through, he makes a statement along the lines that the nature of the word we use for something is not necessarily like the thing itself. Premise number one of semiotic theory. To illustrate this, he first draws a horse in space; then a painting of a horse in a meadow set on an easel; next, that horse actually in the meadow; and finally, he draws the figure of a person saying the word "horse." One and three horses. Very proto–Joseph Kosuth.

BG: We find the same ideas in the Renaissance humanists' writings, in Galileo's work, and then again in Mondrian and Malevich. The fundamental laws of this world are logical and geometrical at the same time: this is the basis of European science. Magritte, too, plays with the sense that geometrical and logical laws are to be understood as one law. Do we find this kind of tradition in other cultures? I don't know. Edmund Husserl, for instance, was absolutely sure that it could be found only in the West. Perhaps it is a specific, Greek way of thinking.

DISBELIEVING DUCHAMP

TS: Let's test your idea about what underlies these two types of exhibitions against the case of Marcel Duchamp. Let's take his famous act of submitting, in 1917, to an exhibition of current art—an alternative, independent exhibition—a toilet bowl that he found in a plumbing shop, which he signed with an invented or appropriated name. This urinal, or *Fountain*, as he titled it, was, he claimed, a gesture of "aesthetic indifference." If we take him at his word, this establishes a counterpoint to what you say is the willful and subjective nature of the *Gesamtkunstwerk* approach to the artistic and curatorial installation, does it not?

BG: In this respect we should believe Duchamp not at all. His background is quite clear; he comes from a certain kind of Surrealism, from André Breton and Raymond Roussel. Like their imagery, *Fountain* is full of sexual symbolism, and has all kinds of connotations, including the very traditional idea of revealing something hidden, or showing something repressed. Roger Caillois and Georges Bataille, for example, wrote about *sacré* [the sacred] as being filthy, infectious—something that you cannot touch. In Latin, *sacer* means "what is in the domain of the gods," and then, afterward, "what is filthy." So, there is a certain kind of analogy between the divine, on the one hand, and, on the other, something forbidden because it's dirty.

TS: Divine excrement.

BG: Both of them are *sacré*. It's obvious that *Fountain* is about a specific type of sacrality, and a dirty joke about sexuality, like his inscription on the image of the *Mona Lisa*, and many of his other puns. The whole thing about aesthetic indifference is complete nonsense, a deliberate diversion. You know the small avant-garde magazine that Duchamp and others edited called *The Blind Man*? In the issue in which they defend themselves from critical attacks, there is an article entitled "The Buddha of the Bathroom," which highlights the erotic shapes of the urinal.[7] But the more interesting point is that while the Buddha himself might have been indifferent to aesthetics, the figure of Buddha is never aesthetically indifferent to any observer.

7. Lois Norton, "The Buddha of the Bathroom," *The Blind Man*, no. 2 (May 5, 1917), pp. 5–6. She comments on Alfred Stieglitz's images, "The photographs of *Fountain* make it look like anything from a Madonna to a Buddha."

If you work against established aesthetics, you do not disregard them, but rather you counter them with another aesthetic. Like many others in France at the time, Duchamp was interested in the *sacré*, in the metaphysical, the sexual, more than aesthetic problems proper, so his work was not aesthetically neutral.

TS: My sense is that Conceptual artists understood Duchamp's use of the urinal as a provocation, or a challenge to a prevailing cultural attitude. Some contemporary artists, however, draw from him the lesson that an installation can be made up of anything—any object or material—and that its components will accumulate without connotations, or with so many that whatever shape they take will be a random one. This is the "Duchamp effect" on steroids.

BG: If one is told that one can use any object, it doesn't mean that one will use *any* object. It simply means that one can use the object one needs to make a statement, to make a point. As I said, Duchamp did not choose a random object, he chose one that was relevant to his interests at the time: it was sexually charged, quasi-sacred, and manifested desire in the face of nothingness.

TS: But these days, lots of artists have taken that as permission to be relatively unselective aggregators. I am thinking of artists such as Jason Rhoades, or Ryan Trecartin, who gather everything they possibly can into a space and overload it, to make an environment of excess, of endless impacts.

BG: I don't see these installations in that way. To me, they replay American Pop art, a nationalist thematic: American flags, logos, junkyards, media, games, and so on. They are highly selective, there's nothing inconsistent, and no sense of historical contingency. I go through the spaces, I look at the things, the statement is clear to me.

WHEN ATTITUDES BECOME FORM REDUX

TS: *When Attitudes Become Form: Bern 1969/Venice 2013* has provoked a lot of discussion, not least between us. Out of all the exhibitions that could have been selected for repetition—

BG: —this is the one that demanded to be chosen. Yes. Actually, this extremely subjective choice—a personal choice that turns out to be the one that everyone in the art world feels that they have to make—begins with Szeemann himself. In fact, it begins precisely with this exhibition. This exhibition made a certain claim to present the art of its time. But it did not offer a representative overview. Szeemann did not fear that he might disregard something, or someone, he should have included. On the contrary, he excluded and disregarded almost everything and only focused on what he personally believed to be important.

The repetition of such a project raises the general problem of reproduction. A reproduction of a traditional artwork is usually congruent and, mostly, commensurate with the original. Walter Benjamin argues famously that it is only the absence of an aura of uniqueness that differentiates the two.[8] Nevertheless, potentially we can imagine a complete identity. But when art becomes involved with temporal processes, as contemporary art definitively does, this possibility is excluded. Today, we do not create reproductions of processual works or exhibitions, we produce documentation—of works, of exhibitions, of curatorial projects, of performances, and so on and so on. All these documentations are incongruent, incommensurate with the original. The break is absolute.

8. Walter Benjamin, "L'œuvre d'art à l'époque de sa reproduction méchanisée," in *Zeitschrift* für *Sozialforschung*, Jahrgang V (Paris: Félix Alcan, 1936), pp. 40–68; for an English translation, see Walter Benjamin, "The Work of Art in the Age of Mechanical Reproduction," in *Illuminations*, ed. Hannah Arendt, trans. Harry Zohn (London: Fontana, 1968), pp. 219–53. The current preferred translation is "The Work of Art in the Age of Its Technical Reproducibility."

TS: Is that because objects are subject to entropy, because you can see the traces of time pretty quickly? What about replication?

BG: You can't replicate them, even if you reproduce them exactly. This is because you can't replicate time—you can only document it. The gap between then and now is unbridgeable.

I think the project team of the Prada Foundation exhibition understood these limits, or at least they discovered them when they tried to make a reproduction of what was essentially an event. To attempt this is to challenge the basic temporality of any curatorial project. My sense is that they tried to repeat it in Benjaminian terms, as a reproduction that would, in a certain way, coincide with the original, minus its aura.

I understand that everybody today is frustrated with exhibitions that look like mere documentation, and I very much sympathize with this frustration—there are too many of them, they are everywhere. In my view, the Prada curatorial team made a heroic attempt to overcome the dichotomy between reproduction and documentation. But a pre-condition of any *Gesamtkunstwerk* is that the space where it takes place is an integral part of it. It's finite, temporary, and radically contingent. You cannot repeat it. No way. Even if you take the elements of the exhibition, and combine them in the same layout, within a reproduction of the original venue—all of which they did in Venice, and in the best possible way, in detail, with exactitude and care—you end up with wonderful, very seductive *documentation*, rather than a repetition, of the original exhibition.

TS: Restaging it at its original site in the Kunsthalle Bern would have even less chance of success, in your view?

BG: Even there, it would be impossible. Because, you know, there is a kind of irreversibility of time. What is the structure of the curatorial project? It's not a space—although, of course, space is an element—the medium is above all an event. Curatorial projects are inscribed in a certain moment in history, and are part of it. They are events, and you cannot reproduce them, because you cannot take an event out of its own time. It's like a human being, a human life, in that sense.

TS: I understand that during the opening period of the biennale the spaces at the Prada Foundation were so crowded that the visitors became the exhibits—like you said earlier—maybe you would have enjoyed that. The attendants, immaculately dressed in Prada clothes, directing people, showing them this work and that work, also became part of the performance. The "Prada" aspect of it, that palace, the cost of the venture, stood out as a kind of surplus, which offended many people and led to negative comments.

Whereas when I went a month or so later hardly anyone was there. I became intensely aware of the interaction between my imagined memory of the exhibition—the picture of being in Bern in 1969 that I had conjured up out of photographs—and the rooms of the Ca' Corner della Regina. This was a dichotomy that grated at every level, leaving me with a very disjunctive feeling, and a fragmented sense of what I had learnt. I believe that the curatorial team, especially Rem Koolhaas and Thomas Demand, deliberately set out to induce such a response. Perhaps this was their way of responding, concretely, to the challenge that you have identified.

By the time I finished my second visit, however, I'd actually forgotten I was in this building, and somehow I found myself in a space where the works, for me at least, were alive. They seemed to be really working as artworks, and in most of the rooms the interaction between them was absolutely fantastic. Everything was totally fresh. I am as embedded in the historical detail of the original exhibition as anybody, but there I felt as if I was actually present for the first showing of each of these works. In an extraordinary way, each work became totally contemporary, as did the exhibition itself. This occurred through a strange effect: by wiping out all subsequent art, by disappearing all contemporary art from then until now, by erasing it from my memory bank. I'm exaggerating my response, but it was something along those lines.

BG: Mostly, art is about destruction and nostalgia. Generally, when you go to an exhibition, you can choose between hating the times that it represents and loving the images as they are here and now, or hating your time and feeling nostalgia for the time depicted. I think that documentary exhibitions are, in this sense, even more likely to induce you to hate your own time than a traditional exhibition is. Because they tell you how wonderful it was then, and how everything around you now is not as good. The people who complained about the Prada Foundation's reenactment were actually so much under the spell of the exhibition that they began to hate everything that was not this exhibition. They hated the space, the building, the Venice Biennale, Venice, the contemporary art world, contemporary life, world politics, everything. They experienced a kind of disassociation from their own time, a distancing from it. I am not objecting to that, no, I think it's good. We are so much captured, imprisoned by contemporaneity, are we not? We cannot escape contemporaneity simply by introducing some fascinating images from the past here and there, because it is so easy to inscribe the past in the present.

By showing a certain past inside our present we demonstrate our betrayal of its promise. We see again its promise, the promise we have memorized, and held dear. We are reminded of this promise, but then we look around and see how radically we have betrayed it. I think that this makes us much more critical toward our own contemporaneity.

Benjamin, in his famous image of the Angel of History who sees the winds of progress piling up detritus and garbage before his feet, protested against the illusion that the past is inscribed within our present in a smooth way.[9] This exhibition is a reminder, a

9. Walter Benjamin, "Theses on the Philosophy of History" [1940], in *Illuminations*, ed. Hannah Arendt, trans. Harry Zohn (London: Fontana, 1968), pp. 254–69.

documentation, that shows us how we are living now, and does so in negative way. It's critical.

TS: Do you mean that the kind of art that's been made since 1969 fails the premises or the possibilities projected by the original *When Attitudes Become Form*? Or are you also saying that the, let us say, openness to possibility that enabled that show to happen is one that we can't find, or that is incredibly difficult to see right now?

BG: We believe that a certain kind of art born in the 1960s—the kind that is shown in this exhibition—established itself, was recognized, and began to influence, or even define, its time. But if one looks at the artworks in this exhibition, one immediately understands that this is no longer the case. In our mentality today, we are far away from this time. There is no continuation in terms of art history, or on any other level. When you see this exhibition within the context of Venice Biennale as a whole you see only the break. It is absolute.

MUSEUMS OF CONTEMPORARY ART

TS: Speaking of this break, it is also present in the way many museums deal with contemporary art. In effect, they ignore it. Or they use architecture to disguise it. The effect is to keep the universal art historical narrative going—moving us from late modern to contemporary art—simply by passing through a doorway into the next white cube.

BG: That is precisely where attitudes do not become forms. They become neglected and distorted. Even temporary exhibitions of contemporary art try to create the illusion that when you are confronted with the artwork it will speak to you. If it doesn't seem to, it's your fault. Especially in the contemporary world, when context and attitude are so different, one ends up with a huge mass of objects that make absolutely no impression.

TS: Do you mean to say that a museum of contemporary art is a contradiction in terms?

BG: Of course it's impossible if one understands the museum in the traditional way, as a place of permanent collection. It's only possible as a new Bayreuth—where the museum of contemporary art is a stage where *Gesamtkunstwerke*, that is, curatorial projects, are staged more or less successfully. Or where there is documentation that demonstrates the impossibility of overcoming time, for the reasons we discussed before. There, one has to take a position for or against one's own time.

TS: In general, it also follows from what you are saying that collections of contemporary art are an oxymoron.

BG: Yes, because contemporary artworks are not objects, they are events. Events cannot be collected. You can collect and exhibit documentation of the event, you can try to re-enact it, or you can create a new event using memories of the earlier ones. Re-enactments, re-readings, re-interpretations—all are possible. But you cannot collect an event as an object. Some people make collections of luxury objects by Jeff Koons, Damien Hirst, and Takashi Murakami, but this is like dressing in Gucci, Prada, or any of those brands. You can create a certain kind of luxury lifestyle, but this has nothing to do with contemporary art. Now we have a new financial aristocracy and art is a part of its luxury lifestyle, like a Chinese vase, or a Persian carpet. We are living at the end of the era of the middle class, a well-informed, stable, culturally educated, but at the same time not very rich middle class; a very specific social strata that has supported the arts for so long, but that is being evaporated in the gap between the one percent and the rest of us. In some countries, instead of the middle class the state was the supporter of museum collections, of theaters, operas, of all that public culture. Now, however, in many places, the state is collapsing, running out of money, shrinking…

The whole art system is a machine for the articulation of frustration with contemporaneity and for the production of nostalgia for the past. Nowadays, these are the only two things that everyone in the art system does.

TS: But artists everywhere project all kinds of possible futures, mostly small in scale. They imagine localized, but real, advances on the present implosion.

BG: I have no belief in futures. I think the only person who truly expressed the contemporary European mindset, which is also mine, is Lars von Trier, in his film *Melancholia* [2011]. I really believe that the asteroid is coming to destroy everything.

TS: Having an Antipodean mentality, I read that asteroid as Earth, and I saw the whole last scene as an appeal—obviously against the odds—to renegotiate our contract with it before the differences between us and the planet become fatal for us. You, however, seem to be echoing, on a planetary scale, Malevich's call to burn all museums in the hope that something might generate from their ashes.

BG: It seems to me that the only thing that we have, all of us, is the present. The only thing—there's no future, no past. But we don't like being in such a situation. So, we feel compelled to find the language to articulate this unhappiness. Contemporary art has nothing to do with criticality per se... it has to do with the articulation of dissatisfaction with the only reality that we have.

Okwui Enwezor

World Platforms, Exhibiting Adjacency, and the Surplus Value of Art

Okwui Enwezor is a leading curator and theorist of global contemporary art, with a special interest in African art. Born in Nigeria in 1963, he was based in New York from 1982 until 2011, when he became director of Haus der Kunst in Munich. Enwezor's wide-ranging practice spans international exhibitions, museums, academia, and publishing. He was artistic director of the 2nd Johannesburg Biennale, South Africa (1996–98); Documenta 11, Kassel, Germany (1998–2002); the 2nd International Biennial of Contemporary Art of Seville, Spain (2005–7); the 7th Gwangju Biennale, South Korea (2008); the Triennale d'Art Contemporain de Paris at the Palais de Tokyo (2012); and the 56th Venice Biennale (2015). From 2005 to 2009, he was dean of academic affairs and senior vice president at the San Francisco Art Institute, and he has held positions as visiting professor in art history at the University of Pittsburg; Columbia University, New York; University of Illinois at Urbana-Champaign; Umea University, Sweden; and the Institute of Fine Arts, New York University. In 1994, with Chika Okeke-Agulu and Salah Hassan, he founded *Nka: Journal of Contemporary African Art*, which is published by Duke University Press. He is the author or co-editor of numerous books, among them *Contemporary African Art Since 1980* (Bologna: Damiani, 2009), *Antinomies of Art and Culture: Modernity, Postmodernity, Contemporaneity* (Durham, N. Car.: Duke University Press, 2008), *Reading the Contemporary: African Art from Theory to the Marketplace* (Cambridge, Mass.: MIT Press; London: INIVA, 1999), *Mega Exhibitions: Antinomies of a Transnational Global Form* (Munich: Wilhelm Fink Verlag, 2002), *Archive Fever: Uses of the Document in Contemporary Art* (New York: International Center of Photography; Göttingen: Steidl, 2008), and *The Unhomely: Phantom Scenes in Global Society* (2nd International Biennial of Contemporary Art of Seville, 2006).

The following conversation took place at Haus der Kunst, Munich, on August 30 and 31, 2013.

Terry Smith: You are known for your passionate commitment to drawing the world's attention to the agency of Africa, especially to that of its artists, on the continent and throughout their global diaspora. I have valued that, but also see you as taking on a broader responsibility, one that I share, to the contemporary art of the world, to its multi-faceted grappling with the our current condition, wherever it is made, and wherever it circulates. Am I right about this as how you see as the curator's role in the current situation?

Okwui Enwezor: To me the fundamental challenges that a curator faces today are how to provoke an engaged confrontation with works of art, how to make that experience legible, and how to use it to open up forms of engagement with the world. Exhibitions, in this sense, stage the surplus value of art. They create value of many kinds, simply because each time artworks are exhibited they accrue new meaning, new force, and open out new possibilities, while not necessarily changing or shifting their shape. In turn, art changes the perceptions of those it engages—so, to make an exhibition is to theorize the place of art not only in institutions, but also in public spaces, and, if you will, in the world. This raises the issue of what we mean by "world" in such contexts. These are very big questions...

CONSTELLATING THE POST-COLONIAL

TS: Your concept of the post-colonial constellation, which you developed in the later 1990s, has been a very illuminating and influential approach to these issues. It certainly was crucial to my theorizing of what I call "transnational transitions," which I see as the broadest current in contemporary art. At a time when most people in international art worlds accepted that globalization, Western-style, was the most powerful set of forces defining the world, you argued that these forces were actually saturated with post-coloniality and continuing efforts at nation building. In such complex conditions, you claim, "the legacy of the Western historical avant-garde seems inadequate to the job of producing a unified theory of contemporary art," not least because "the structure of contemporary art's relationship to history is more transversal, asynchronous, and asystematic in nature" than modern art's relationship to modernity.[1]

1. Okwui Enwezor, "The Postcolonial Constellation," in Terry Smith, Okwui Enwezor, and Nancy Condee, eds., *Antinomies of Art and Culture: Modernity, Postmodernity, Contemporaneity* (Durham, N. Car.: Duke University Press, 2008), pp. 222, 223.

In your essay on this subject, you highlight five different "effects" of this change upon curators, artists, and art worlds everywhere. You have explored these elements in all of your exhibitions, from *The Short Century* [2001], one of a series of shows about historical transition in Africa, through to Documenta 11 [2002] and the 2012 Paris Triennale. Let me list them because I want to discuss their continuing relevance, and how they might have changed. The first one is the messy proliferation of exhibitionary forms and their constant mutation; second, the fraught and contradictory experiences of decolonization and of nation building that have obliged us to think about identity and tradition as operating in more layered, antinomic ways; third, the impact of heterogeneous art practices on the logic of the museum, which has managed to absorb many but not all of them; while, fourth, culture everywhere has been heavily mediated, indeed mediatized, which is to say turned into a provider of spectacular experiences. The fifth element, the strongest one, is the globalization of economies and cultures, and the digital revolution that has fused cultures with economies. The net outcome, you say, is a new historical circumstance for all of us, a state of *permanent transition*, in which the adjacency of difference, or "intense proximity," as you call it, prevails as the most definitive contemporary experience.[2] That's your main argument, as I understand it, and it clearly drives your practice as a curator. Do you think that it remains acute, in all of its elements? Does it still add up to a total explanation?

OE: These ideas have been percolating through my thinking and work for some time, but the concept of the post-colonial constellation really took shape—constellated, you might say—after the opening of Tate Modern in London in 2000. In the lead-up, I had been fascinated by the prospect of a museum of modern art

2. Okwui Enwezor, *The Short Century: Independence and Liberation Movements in Africa 1945–1994* (New York and London: Prestel, 2001), and Okwui Enwezor, ed., *Intense Proximity: An Anthology of the Near and the Far* (Paris: Centre national des arts plastiques, 2012).

being inaugurated *after* the liquidation of modernism, or, at least, after the compelling character of modernism as an idea had faded considerably. What could that possibly mean? What kinds of opportunities and challenges would such a museum face, and what sorts of insights could it provide? Would a subtle or polemical position would be taken? Perhaps the grounds of canonical modernism would be destabilized and traditional narrative streams opened up to include works previously excluded from accounts of modern art around the world?

Visiting Tate Modern, I was disappointed to find that it had not, as far as I could see, risen to the challenge.

TS: Do you mean the grounds of contemporary art today, or the historical grounds, those of the various kinds of modern, traditional, and indigenous art that have shaped the present?

OE: Well, both, of course. This failure crystallized, for me, in the section of the permanent displays entitled "Nude, Action, Body," which proceeded from a formalist understanding of how the figure was represented, produced, understood, and interpreted in earlier modern art, to a mid-century sense of a more abstract or surreal representation, and, finally, to the subjective experience of an embodied body—in art actions, happenings, performance, et cetera. What struck me was that at each step of this slow progression from inanimate, to animate, to subjective, it was the African figure that was used as the antithesis.[3]

My concern was not entirely with the *location* of Africa as the antithesis. This exclusion also applied to Asia, Central Europe, Latin America, and so on. But as these are societies that have actually re-emerged in the aftermath of colonialism, or what you call the "aftermath of modernity," how might we understand the argument of modern art in the shadow of this aftermath?[4] Why

3. Enwezor, "The Postcolonial Constellation," pp. 213–22.

4. Terry Smith, *The Architecture of Aftermath* (Chicago: University of Chicago Press, 2006).

would such a museum—in the capital of what was once a great empire, and what is still a hub within what Hardt and Negri call "Empire" in a more general way—set out to interrogate "Nude, Action, Body" without considering what the empire produced, the figures it generated, and the forms of disfiguration that have emerged after its demise?[5]

Actually, the challenge is more interesting even than that: it is to show history and the aftermath of history co-existing, to show how they have come to be together now, how they have come to be contemporaries.

THE CONTEMPORANEITY QUESTION

TS: In your essay, you say that the "post-colonial constellation" is the prism for understanding "late modernity," which, for you, is the term for our overall present situation. This puzzles me, not only because I prefer "contemporaneity" as the term for our current "condition," as David Harvey calls it (although he sticks with "postmodernity" as his name for the condition), but also because both of us highlight the particularly intense proximity of difference today.[6] As you know, I argue that the contemporaneity of these differences is leading to, or has in fact already established, a larger or different kind of condition.

OE: Let me take up what I think is one of your premises: that, historically, there were societies whose relationship to modernity emerged specifically from different kinds of contact with Western modernization. I would argue that there never was a pure modernity to which some other non-modernity suddenly became exposed. Because modernity was always double-sided, the "others" were always there. The "non-modern" had to be there *from the beginning* in order for modernity to define itself.

5. Michael Hardt and Antonio Negri, *Empire* (Cambridge, Mass.: Harvard University Press, 2000).

6. David Harvey, *The Conditions of Postmodernity: An Enquiry into Cultural Change* (Oxford: Wiley-Blackwell, 1991).

TS: This is the argument that European modernity defined itself as much by confining its non-European others to a contemporaneous pastness as it did by defining its own prehistory as "the past."

OE: Exactly. Contact was, and remains, the manifestation of the dark side of modernity. It is the attempt to dominate, to subjugate, to replace the life-world of the "non-modern" with the knowledge of the colonizer. This series of substitute experiences begins from the process of evacuation of—let's call them "native knowledges." Knowledges rendered as primitive, as underdeveloped, relegated to the past, with no proximity to the future or the present. The result is that the artist is not, never was, and can never be contemporary. This is really the key dilemma, right?

Modernity today is based precisely on this set of tangled relationships between the colonial and the post-colonial world. The difficulty lies in the fact that the old colonial system cannot recognize itself in the post-colonial experience even though it remains fundamentally co-extensive with it. The idea that the post-colonial is over there, is elsewhere, and therefore does not belong here is an attempt to distance present modernity from the darkness of its origins.

When you highlight a certain kind of contemporaneity as a problem—with-it-ness, presentism, "pure" contemporaneity—you are echoing a critique that came up in the 1980s and 1990s. What is the "post" in postmodernism and what is the "post" in post-colonialism? Transposing that question to the present, we might ask: is there a point at which the post-colonial terminates and contemporaneity continues, therefore putting us into a state of perpetual present-ness? I do not believe that the disentanglement of contemporaneity from modernity works quite so simply. There cannot be a radical break between the two, because the structures of the post-colonial transition mean that the consequences of modernity are still being lived through.

That is why I prefer the term "societies in transition" over "developing countries" or "developing societies," as a way of marking this constant engagement with change, with transformation, with transition. This is a process of what I call "permanent transition," a process that is very deeply embedded within the structures of modernity.

TS: My argument acknowledges that different kinds of modernity are still very powerful, and that they're contemporaneous with currents that are not modern, and have never been (such as indigeneity, the fundamentalisms, surviving feudalisms, et cetera). What I call the "transnational transition" is a worldwide effort to overcome the cultural priority of the West in the name of energizing—in fact, internationalizing—various national and regional cultures and networks. As well, there are currents emerging now that are taking different, more dispersed, and occasional shapes, reflecting a world that is changing beyond the dialectics that drove modernity.

OE: I'm saying precisely that the post-colonial constellation may be understood as one layer of contemporaneity. I think it's very hard to define temporal or even spatial boundaries. I believe there is a close relationship between modernity, post-coloniality, and contemporaneity. And this alone can enable us to come to the point where we can have a radical sense of contemporaneity, of real being in the world.

FOLLOWING THE PROVINCIALISMS

OE: In his analysis of the global art world, Hans Belting says that contemporary Western artists see themselves as being in a post-historical situation, whereas non-Western artists wish to be in a post-ethnic one. To be no longer identified by race, ethnicity, or tribe. Western artists are not concerned with identity, with ethnicity, because that value is clear to them, they're Europeans. Their self-recognition, self-knowledge, sense of self-hood are all there, given. Therefore, the main struggle of contemporary

Western artists is to come to terms with the logic of tradition, with the way in which history is both a resource and a negation of the now. In the rest of the world—India, China, Africa, wherever—the self-consciousness that follows from established historical identity has not been achieved. According to this model, those parts of the world are still obsessed with broader definitions of identity.[7]

TS: The logic of that analysis rests on a Western dialectical structure: Hegel's master vis-à-vis slave. Belting highlights the fact that artists from outside the West are always subservient. The only way they can actually become post-ethnic, or get beyond the ethnic, is to become post-historical.

OE: They have to become historical first, because they have to become historical subjects...

TS: ...in conditions within which the West has set the terms of what it is to be historical and to be a subject within history. To me, Dipesh Chakrabarty's *Provincializing Europe* is the best analysis of this conundrum.[8] Like you, he argues that European modernity manifests in its colonial exploitation as much as in its historical achievements, such as Enlightenment thought and critical theory. Today, however, understood as a set of economic, social, and political formations and models, Europe is reaching its limits. Decolonizing cultures are inheriting the world's future, at a time when they have yet to develop the capacity to take it on, not least because of what Europe took from them. Nevertheless, to succeed, decolonial thought needs not only to develop its own distinctive capacities, drawing on its "native knowledges," it has the additional task of contributing in a major way to the future of what is now Europe. This is a crude summary of his arguments, and I have cast them rather more in Walter Mignolo's terms,

7. Hans Belting, "Contemporary Art and the Museum in the Global Age," in Peter Weibel and Andrea Buddensieg, eds., *Contemporary Art and the Museum* (Ostfildern: Hatje Cantz, 2007), p. 34.

8. Dipesh Chakrabarty, *Provincializing Europe: Postcolonial Thought and Historical Difference*, 2nd ed. (Princeton: Princeton University Press, 2007).

but I think that they pinpoint acutely what is, in fact, happening in world thinking today.[9] Certainly, they underlie my ideas about contemporaneity, which is intended as a contribution to this enterprise of rethinking ways of world picturing.

OE: The other key component of Chakrabarty's notion of provincialism is his refusal of the idea that big history is Euro-American and small histories occur elsewhere. We must always approach history with a small "h"—not with a big one. This takes us back to the point I was trying to make that it is time to reconsider regionalism. Critical regionalism, I mean, not as a form of withdrawal, but in the provincial sense that Chakrabarty is arguing. His point is illustrated in the dissolution of the imperial architecture, if you will, of what used to be called "the art world." Now, there are so many different worlds. Of course, this does not mean that they all have equal power, equal influence, or equal epistemological force. Rather, it means that while the so-called centers are doing their thing, these other art worlds continue doing theirs. They do not close up shop and say, well, the real art world is over there, there is nothing for us to do here.

TS: Recently, for the first time, I read a lecture on this subject by Sir Kenneth Clark, which he gave in 1962 in London, when he was elected president of the English Association.[10] Looking back through the history of art, he proposed that art is at its greatest when it's produced at the centers, but as you head away from the centers, it becomes more and more provincial. He understood this to be a natural state of affairs. This is almost a parody of the view from the center, the imperialist gaze. My teacher Bernard Smith argued that, on the contrary, the initiating energies that transformed modern art at its breakthrough points came from the so-called provinces.[11] This was a minority view when I, and

9. Walter Mignolo, *The Darker Side of Western Modernity: Global Futures, Decolonial Options* (Durham, N. Car.: Duke University Press, 2011).

10. Kenneth Clark, *Provincialism* (London: The English Association, 1962).

11. Bernard Smith, *Modernism's History: A Study in Twentieth-Century Art and Ideas* (New Haven: Yale University Press, 1998).

others, advocated for it in the 1970s, but now—if you think of the international prominence of many Chinese and South American artists, or artists from Africa, India, and the Middle East—we're reaching a point where it is not unreasonable to say that their energies are driving art. Can one envision a future in which even the post-colonial will fade from view?

OE: Perhaps so, but for now, a certain kind of modesty in our attempt to remake the history of art is necessary. I can illustrate this in what seems an immodest way, by taking myself as an example. If I look at my relationship to contemporary art, and think about other curators of my generation, I see a distinctive difference. Throughout my career I have worked, in a committed way, within contemporary African art and, at the same time, within the so-called international contemporary art world. I've worked with artists in most parts of the world, in a continuous, consistent manner, for a number of years, so I can, with a certain sense of natural ease, without attempting to learn a new vocabulary, make connections between art in many different provincial places. I'm not seeking to impose some kind of all-inclusive universalism, but I am searching for specificities in order to see how they might excite new moments of insight.

Of course, many other curators know what's going on in Africa, in Europe, in the United States, in South America, or in Asia. But very few people have actually deployed such worldwide knowledge in a consistent, constant way, or made it their article of faith, the basis of their careers. You know, you can look at work of a certain merit made in Australia, or London, or Johannesburg, and find a value in that work by thinking seriously about it. You can also look at work from these same places, or others, and make an argument about why it's of lesser interest.

In this sense, my work has been about following provincialisms. That's what I mean by modesty; that's my own version of it.

THE LIMITS OF THE AVANT-GARDE

TS: Within Western modernism in general, and within the idea of the avant-garde in particular, there is a double directionality: toward autonomy, on the one hand, and, on the other, toward social purpose. The avant-garde artist wants to remove himself *from* society and yet have a critical relationship *to* society. (I am deliberately using the gender that almost entirely dominated twentieth-century avant-gardism.) It strikes me that, if you transpose that idea to the primitivist presumption, the individual Western artist remains a creative, innovative individual, but what he sees as the antithesis is not a parallel set of artists who, like him, work within and against their culture, but rather an array of objects that embody a generalized idea of African-ness, or otherness, or blackness—a massive, empty difference. I mean, the array has no people in it, no authors, actors, and no agency. The objects are magical, strangely compelling, and rippling with great artistic ideas, but they have issued from this big, dumb, passive, opposite other. In effect, this is the same kind of logic that you highlighted at Tate Modern during those opening years.

OE: That is precisely the problem with the specifically Western idea of the avant-garde. It can be a productive, or interesting, even valuable idea in specific circumstances, but as a way of understanding innovation in the arts, it cannot be universalized. Even if there were avant-gardes everywhere around the world, then each would respond to various local traditions and not to one, universal, homogenized tradition. To universalize it is to flatten the antithesis. The question one has to ask is this: *why* does the avant-garde idea always seem to emerge against the backdrop of tradition? For in many places, art does not emerge out of rupture, or out of an attempt to break away from tradition, but is something much more subtle, contemplative, gradual. If we were to suppose that there is no avant-garde in, say, Africa at the moment, or that the people producing the masks that so excited artists in Europe a hundred years ago were not avant-gardists with regard to their traditions, that hardly makes them deficient as artists, or demonstrates a lack of innovative thinking. Nor does it prove that they did not challenge the conventions that constitute their tradition. For me, the great mistake that we make when we want to identify the avant-garde of this place or of that time is that the concept has become so broad that it loses the specificity that it had as an image of the artistic innovations in Europe in the early twentieth century.

TS: Some distinctions need to be made, surely. I am thinking of settler colonies, such as Australia and Canada, that have been, until very recently, dependent cultures. If we think about how the idea of an avant-garde plays out in the history of art made in such places, we can see that, from those perspectives, it over-signifies as being definitive of art practices in the metropolitan centers, and seems impossible to achieve in the peripheries. The cultural logic of dependence is telescopic: it is always inverted, refracted, and exaggerated. From a sufficient distance, avant-gardism seems to drive art in cultural centers, when, in fact, breakthroughs are by definition exceptional, chancy, and often tentative. But, for modernist artists, avant-gardism is an irresistible idea, because its core promise is that a small number of artists, working together, can transform Art altogether. The extra load carried by artists in colonial settings is that they feel compelled to transform their national artistic tradition in the process—to, in effect, denationalize it, which is a huge task, as this local art has been produced inside a dependent culture, and its national character has been shaped by the provincialist bind for decades.

The good news is that, for some time now, this perverse logic has been losing its governing power. Rather than attributing this change to globalization in some nebulous, generalized sense, we might more accurately see it as another "effect" of post-coloniality, of the very idea of nationality going into transition—one hopes permanently.

In former settler colonies like Australia, for example, artists working in remote communities have continued to elaborate and pass on their achievement as painters primarily, while increasing numbers of city-based artists with indigenous backgrounds have since the 1990s developed more complex and more subtle ways of working through the issues of identity and belonging. Tracey Moffatt, Destiny Deacon, and Gordon Bennett led this push, and now we see it taken up by Brook Andrew, Yhonnie Scarce, and others, who understand indigeneity as an opening to broader issues, such as temporality, mourning, historical mystification, et cetera. You and Chika Okeke-Agulu explored parallel notions in your book *Contemporary African Art*.[12]

ART WORLD ECOLOGIES

OE: I would say that the 1990s were pivotal for a number of reasons. The main one was the implosion of the ideological conditions that supported the Cold War, a conclusion, if you will, of the project of late imperialism. The obvious signs were the fall of the Wall and the reunification of Germany, the breakup of the Soviet Union, and so on. But there were effects all over the globe. Many nations, previously obliged to ideologically affiliate in one way or another, or to play off the superpowers against each other, began to envisage different understandings of how world power could be configured. Curators prominent in the 1960s, 1970s, and 1980s were formed during the Cold War. Few of them were ready for the changed world picture that emerged in its aftermath.

During the 1990s we began to create new networks and dialogic systems, and it was out of these that new exhibitionary models emerged, and proliferated, most obviously the biennials: large-scale, temporary, recurring exhibitions that became grounds for staging the world differently. Mary Louise Pratt called them "contact zones," places where many different impulses in art, many kinds of artists, curators, and interested audiences could

12. Okwui Enwezor and Chika Okeke-Agulu, eds., *Contemporary African Art Since 1980* (Bologna: Damiani Editore, 2009).

meet.[13] During the 2000s, these developments became much more global, and took into account what became known about a decade ago as the educational turn, when pedagogical models became the medium through which certain kinds of intellectual projects could be elaborated.

Over the same period, of course, we saw the rise of the market, and its appropriation of the biennial's exhibitionary form. And conversely the proliferation of residencies, which proposed an informal economy, as a retreat through which artists who are not visible either in the biennial or the art fair complex could have access to resources to create and show new work. We could say that the art fair and residency models have led to the production of more commodities, more consumer goods, more collectible works and so on. If we recognize that mega-exhibitions have enabled a new scale of artwork—bigger, more impressive, with longer temporalities in the case of videos and cinematic installations—what sort of works are being produced within the residency context? Does the itinerant nature of these residencies generate work that is portable, modest, infinitely re-creatable, and mobile?

For me, these are very important questions. When I look at the responses by artists to new conditions of production, and these new options for presenting work, I ask myself, how does art's surplus value emerge in each of these specific contexts?

TS: Some people, such as Chris Dercon, the director of Tate Modern, argue that the increase in the number of these relationships for producing work is, in effect, splitting the art world internally into two art worlds. Perhaps this will lead to the concurrence of two kinds of art: art that really depends on a close relationship to a willing, informed, and conscientious audience,

13. Mary Louise Pratt, "The Arts of the Contact Zone," *Profession*, no. 91 (1991), pp. 33–40. http://learning.writing101.net/wp-content/readings/pratt_arts_of_the_contact_zone.pdf.

versus art that depends on very large but changing audiences for museums and biennials.

OE: I do not agree. Today, the art world should be understood as a complex ecology, with many micro-climates and some macro ones. The metabolism of the art world, in this sense, depends on the sort of practice each ecology rewards.

TS: You see them going on together? You don't see one replacing the other over time?

OE: No, no, together. Let's look at the spectacle of Art Basel, for example. Everything turns around one simple fact: selling the work. Museums might visit to find missing links within their collection, private individuals to begin collecting. Some curators might seek out work to present at exhibitions. Whatever your micro-interest, it is a meeting point for people wanting to keep up with the macro-picture of contemporary art. This is what I mean by metabolism.

Something much more important to me is the diminishing of absolute centers and the re-emergence of "off-centers." You can go even further and call them "regional events." The Joburg Art Fair, for example, is a regional art fair; so is Art Basel Hong Kong. None of them are international art fairs, but they want to behave as if they are. Even Art Basel, up until 2000, was not visited by many non-institutional curators. During the 1990s the place to go was ARCO, in Madrid, because it was hospitable toward younger curators, it staged conferences, meetings, discourses, publications—Basel wasn't doing that. But we have very short memories.

TS: I've been going to New York a lot over the last ten years, and the extraordinary persistence of the kind of Tate Modern model we've spoken about has become really obvious to me in the broader market for modern and contemporary art. If you imagine that all the galleries of Chelsea, or Midtown, plus SoHo and around the New Museum are a single venue for contemporary art, you realize straightaway that you are seeing lots of American art, some European, and very few shows by artists active elsewhere. Of course, this is a local art scene, primarily committed to local artists and collectors. It is huge in scale, but provincial. It serves an international market, but one that is extraordinarily narrow, with its greatest wealth concentrated more and more at the top end. We can't expect it to show the world's art. It never has, and probably never will. But surely we are entitled to expect this in New York's museums?

OE: Well, I've gone on record repeatedly to defend biennials. I'm not necessarily arguing that biennials represent the answer to the lack of complexity that you've described in Chelsea. Not all biennials can be weighed together, but because of their cyclical nature and their immediacy exhibition makers are able to react, respond, and address some of these questions. They can challenge some of the conventions that we find in museums, especially their function as canonical passageways through which everything has to pass. The extreme contingency of biennials is highly productive for enabling us to think about the various genealogies of contemporary art. This does not happen sufficiently in commercial galleries, or in museums.

TS: What about those galleries, such as Gagosian in New York and elsewhere, which regularly present museum-style shows?

OE: Actually, I want to contest that. It is a fantasy, a market fiction. Borrowing tons of first-rate works from major museums does not a museum make. What I don't like about the Gagosian model is their transposition into the primary market of the pretention to connoisseurship that prevails in the auction houses. We all know what the end game is: the inflation of sales prices through the sheer economic power of the gallery. Gagosian certainly does this very well. But it's quite a conventional gallery. It takes no risks. It doesn't support young artists. Unlike Leo Castelli, who started with artists who were making groundbreaking work and stayed with them for a very long time, no matter what they made. This is a gallery that trades in commodity objects at the top end of the market, so although they may trade on "museum quality," the idea is inappropriate.

In general, though, I admire the work, the serious work, that galleries do. I think, again, that they are part of that complex ecology that we talked about. I admire the investment they make in bringing art to public attention for free. You can walk in, look around, and nobody asks you if you want to buy anything. So, it's wrong to think that simply because there's money involved there's bad faith at the base of it all. That's not what I'm arguing.

RE-IMAGINING THE CIVIC

OE: Recently, I have become a little bit tired of the blanket use of terms such as "public sphere," "the public," "the commons," the whatever. Traveling constantly in Africa, in places with very "underdeveloped," or with no, infrastructure, I have become preoccupied with what I call "civic imagination." However much it might be considered a failure today, the Arab Spring was a real example of the upheaval of civic imagination on a massive scale. When you go to societies in transition, places where the rule of law is not yet deeply rooted, where individuals struggle for respect, you realize that it is only through the attempt to construct civic relationships that it becomes possible for imaginative action to occur. If you go to towns in Lebanon, Jordan, Nigeria, or Palestine, you find artists working at the intersection of their artistic practice and creative, quasi-institutional structures that enable civic exploration. These actions are nothing to do with public-ness. It's a question of civicness.

TS: Because there was no European-style public sphere for them to act within, they had to imagine a different kind of collective appearing to each other? In *Thinking Contemporary Curating* I ended up highlighting infrastructural activism as a major way of curating contemporaneity.[14] Is that what you mean?

OE: Yes. When look at the work that so many artists and curators are doing today… Lamia Joreige is an artist, but she's also the co-founder of Beirut Art Center. Also in Beirut, there is the Arab Image Foundation, whose work has been supported and undertaken by many artists, including Walid Raad, Akram Zaatari, Lara Baladi, and Yto Barrada. Christine Tohme, a curator, is the founder of Ashkal Alwan and its platform Home Works. Tarek Abou El Fetouh founded the Young Arab Theatre Fund in order to facilitate a range of projects. In Cairo, a group of young women created CIC, the Contemporary Image Collective; they are artists, but also use this collective to build civic bridges. In Tangiers, Yto Barrada and Bouchra Khalili created the Cinémathèque de Tangier. In Ramallah, the Riwaq Biennale is led by artist Khaled Hourani. In Lagos, there's Bisi Silva at the Centre for Contemporary Art; in Dakar, Koyo Kouoh at Raw Material Company; in Rabat, Abdellah Karroum at L'appartement 22, and so on. It's an amazing proliferation…

There were times in the West, during the 1970s especially, when artist-run spaces and alternative galleries played this kind of role. But that was in response to official circuits of culture, and was more specifically related to the struggle for space within the public imagination. These other places are trying to bring different constituencies within societies together, to meet each other, to speak to each other, to find a point where a shared experience of co-existence can be explored. This is very, very interesting, because they've done it through the domain of representation, of art, a domain in which things that cannot be spoken can be shown.

Their activism is not conventional; it is embedded in the very act of making things appear without protest. This is the

14. Terry Smith, *Thinking Contemporary Curating* (New York: Independent Curators International, 2012), pp. 249–58.

dimension of civic imagination that I am very invested in now, in view of all the things that are happening around the world. The evolution of what one could call "civic insurgency" is not a fight against dictatorship per se. It's not like the Minjung [People's] art movement in South Korea that was really clearly political. It is not the China avant-garde. It has a completely different character. I'm extremely interested in what this means, in how one can understand it within the conceptualization of contemporary art.

MUSEUM MISSIONS: EXHIBITING ADJACENCIES

TS: Returning to my point about the world picture of contemporary art offered by the art scenes of what used to be the metropolitan centers, I sense a kind of defensive lessening of attention to art coming from the rest of the world. There are exceptions, of course. From its home base in New York, the Guggenheim is making serious efforts to connect to Asian arts through special programs and key shows. Doubtless, this is part of building its international franchise, something that major museums everywhere are striving to do...

OE: Yes, I have also noticed a reduction recently. But this doesn't really bother me, precisely because of what I said before, i.e., that the art world is off-center, structurally, deeply, everywhere, and for the foreseeable future. If you go to Australia, you'll probably see something completely different. If you go to Beirut, you know, they have a completely different vibe. The same is true when you go to Istanbul, or Ramallah, or Brazil, and so on. Recognizing these specificities tells us that it's okay that what is going on in New York is going on in New York.

That is not to say that one cannot challenge the situation one finds in each of these provincial setups. I was recently in the Museum of Modern Art in New York, and I can't tell you how appalled I was by the permanent collection of contemporary art from 1980 to now. About sixty percent of the artists displayed lived in New York! It's okay if MoMA wants to be a conventional, local museum, but then they should articulate that as their mission, and not claim to offer a universal context for contemporary art. Sure, zillions of people come to New York specifically to see Picasso's *Les Demoiselles d'Avignon*. Who is MoMA to deny them that pleasure? However, there's a level at which these rooms begin to feel like propaganda for modernism. They are too settled, too hide-bound.

What I would really like to see in museums is a more highly conceptualized way of looking at adjacencies in contemporary art, and a way of exhibiting adjacencies that feels fresh, rather than didactic. I think that contemporary art institutions would benefit from mimicking the encyclopedic museum model, in which you have both horizontality and verticality. A wide geographic spread of contexts of production, of particular practices, and conditions of reception, all treated specifically. And a deep time frame in which the local production of art has occurred. When I go to the Metropolitan Museum of Art in New York, my favorite museum in the city, I enjoy stumbling from, you know, the Greek galleries into the Babylonian, the Egyptian, then into Oceania, Africa, and so on. Of course, the area reserved for Western art in the museum overall is massive, but nevertheless, these adjacencies really can be very, very productive when seen not as separations, but as apertures.

So, how can we do this in a modern art museum, given the very limited time span? We can use the horizontality, the geographic spread, to create apertures that show that modern art was, at the same time, quite different in each particular set of circumstances.

TS: Do you have successful examples of this?

OE: Mostly temporary exhibitions. MoMA's *"Primitivism" in 20th Century Art: Affinity of the Tribal and the Modern* is a classic example. I actually saw that show as a very young person in 1984.

I didn't know I was supposed to dislike it. I enjoyed it specifically because of the kinds of things that I am mentioning now. How can you provoke people into thinking about how a work of art from one time and place meets works of art from elsewhere, from other times? I believe that MoMA is a powerful enough institution to be able to undertake that challenge. Obviously, it received enormous criticism for how it did so with that exhibition. But the ambition was pointed in the right direction. As it was at Tate Modern in 2000…

TS: Actually, the Tate curators did impose chronology, you remember, in the sense that they introduced each theme by juxtaposing an early modernist masterpiece with a contemporary work, and then, in the next rooms, or soon after, took you back through time to the beginnings of modern art, after which you progressed from there back to the present. So, it was multi-chronic, you might say. I have argued that, like most modern art museums since around 2000—in fact, most art museums period—it "contemporized" its collection displays.[15]

I'm trying to think of examples of contemporary art museums that would meet your criteria. Mostly, they vote to downplay their collections and operate like Kunsthalles. However, Zdenka Badovinac has conceived a very interesting strategy for the two major museums in Ljubljana that she directs. As you enter the first, the Moderna galerija, you can choose, with minimal guidance, between a sequence of galleries that trace what she calls "the line of continuity" through modern Slovenian art, or another, shorter, more abrupt sequence following "the line of ruptures." The continuities within modern art—from Impressionism right up to the New Image painting of the 1980s—are sustained, substantial, but not radical. The ruptures—a room of prints and posters by Partisan artists from the Second World War period, the OHO group, et cetera—

15. Terry Smith, *What Is Contemporary Art?* (Chicago: University of Chicago Press, 2009), chapter 4.

erupt, but they don't add up to an ongoing, self-generating avant-garde. So, in this sense, she's utilized the footprint of the galleries to propose quite a complex historical picture of art in Slovenia during this period.

The second, the Museum of Contemporary Art Metelkova, is situated elsewhere in the city, in converted barracks (useless now that there is no longer a Yugoslav army) and shows contemporary art. It is not restricted to Slovenian artists, although their work predominates, along with the work of artists from Central and Eastern Europe. Here Zdenka has created repetitions of significant exhibitions that were previously shown at the Moderna galerija. But the really original curatorial move was installing a series of mini-exhibitions in the top floor galleries showing how artists have imagined, and are imagining, many distinct kinds of time: "lived time," "future time," "no future" time, "war time," ideological time," "retro time," "time of transition," and so on. The ground floor is used for larger, often archival, exhibitions that explore these times in more depth. This is the only museum of contemporary art that I know of that has understood that contemporaneity is a state of temporal multiplicity.

OE: You are describing exactly what I have been trying to emphasize. As the art world is no longer bound to centers we can begin to appreciate certain forms of critical regionalism. Our job is to tell these multiple stories, these micro-narratives that add to the great fund of knowledge that we need to build and develop and grow in relation to our understanding of the work of museums, and the practice of thinking about contemporary art, or about modern art after modernism.

CONTEMPORARY ART AND ITS AUDIENCES

TS: How have you been thinking about these challenges in your job as director of Haus der Kunst, here in Munich?

OE: Well, we are agreed that the main task of the contemporary art museum today is to put forward new ideas and concepts about the development of contemporary art. Few would disagree with this. But in general, the modern art museums of the world have not offered audiences experiences that have taught them to be fluid in their thinking. So, the main challenge that I face is audiences who have not been brought to the point of appreciating what it means, for example, to turn over our prime gallery to a comprehensive survey of the life work of Ivan Kožarić, a leading member of the OHO group, whose work you would have seen in Ljubljana.

We need to continue to find new ways to keep people interested in returning so that we can introduce these other more difficult, under-known, unknown, under-theorized, under-historicized practices. But how does one do that? How does one build a constituency for serious engagement with this kind of art? How do you teach the audience to unlearn their former experiences in order to be able to enjoy new experiences?

TS: Most audiences for modern and contemporary art have been taught a certain rather straightforward avant-gardist narrative following the work mainly of European and American artists and occasionally a few others. They have also learned to accept the spectacularly contemporary, overwhelming, and striking as somehow the natural extension of this modernist narrative. Partly because, for decades now, more and more people have been coming to the visual arts for the first time, the capacity of museum educators to tell stories that have more depth and critical character has been overwhelmed. Instead, museum directors with populist agendas are being rewarded. The pressure of increasing audience numbers, the dominance of market values, the sheer quantity of contemporary art makes it seem impossible to enable more than a few people to be questioning spectators, to form themselves into critical audiences.

OE: I want to question the conventional wisdom that there are more and more people seeing contemporary art. There were periods, here at Haus der Kunst, during the 1960s, 1970s, and 1980s, when exhibitions regularly attracted 500,000 visitors. Those were blockbuster-type shows, which won't be possible here in the immediate future.

Yes, it is true that more people go to museums, but this is simply because there are more museums and, of course, many more people in the world. But the question is: are these people going to museums that really grapple with contemporary art? It's quite clear that MoMA wouldn't attract the kind of audiences it attracts if it didn't have its historical collection. I do not want the number of visitors to Haus der Kunst to be the arbiter of the quality of our programs. The question is, how can we transmit ideas to our public so that they understand that it can also be rewarding for them to participate in contemporary art debates without always being constantly entertained? There's nothing wrong with being entertained, of course, if that is the way in which you start the conversation. But my challenge is to put forward the kind of exhibitions that we think should be in museums while protecting the fragility of the institution itself. Can I do a Kožarić exhibition and then after that do survey of the work of, say, Artur Barrio, or even of Cildo Meireles? Of course not.

But what I have said to my colleagues is that while many of these exhibitions might not enjoy a robust public, we must absolutely defend them. The historical merit for the institution lies in the seriousness of our commitment to its mission, which is to constantly reward the visiting public with a new set of propositions, to introduce them to the active state of our research, to show them how far afield we are taking that research, and how we are applying it to the present. So, I think it's important to figure out a way to protect those kinds of fragile, under-known, under-historicized, under-represented artists and exhibitions. We must become known for taking them on, when others—in this city, in the region, anywhere—will not do so.

PLATFORMS IN THE HOUSE OF ART

OE: Thinking about these questions is very challenging, simply because Haus der Kunst is essentially an exhibition venue. Yet, I want to insist on the idea that, even though it does not have a collection, it is, nonetheless, a museum. This is a place of transmission, not only of art but also of the ideas and the histories that come with that art. We bring, for example, a lot of value to the engagement with our public through the very generous and educational materials that we provide.

I see the building—this (in)famous structure, with its vast public spaces, its huge galleries—as an alimentary canal. Some parts of it metabolize more quickly than others, giving visitors an energy rush. This is where we introduce the things that the public thinks it knows and understands, that it believes to be part of its common experience of art. In other parts with a slower metabolism we introduce those nutrients that nourish the circulation system of the whole institution. Striking a balance between these two regimens is the challenge. Which is why I hope that it might, in due course, be possible to think of our building, and our exhibition program, in the same way one might conceive of an encyclopedic museum.

As I said before, we need to think in a chronological, synchronic—or, as you say, multi-chronic—dimension, but we also need to rethink the horizontality—let's simply say the adjacency—of spaces in order to create a certain kind of porosity across the usual boundaries, areas of overlap, meshing points through which we filter our rethought genealogies of modernity and contemporary art. Over the next period, we will always have at least one under-historicized, under-known, under-presented artist in our exhibition programs. The overall aim is not to invent a wholly new model but to learn something from the adjacency we find in the encyclopedic museum, to see if it will work in the context of a contemporary art museum.

TS: So, will you install your post-colonial constellation in the halls of the museum? In other words, will you have exhibitions that show the work of different kinds of artists, from different time periods, different parts of the world, and artists of different generations? Visitors will come to this building, enter these co-temporalities and adjacent spatialities, and traverse them as if traveling within the world's art domains. Is that your goal?

OE: Absolutely. Technically, we can achieve some of this by how we break things down. I think we also need to question the retrospective model, where you present everything in a straightforward chronological order. So, rather than presenting an entire retrospective of Kožarić, for example, we could present a room that provides an exquisite experience of a key aspect of Kožarić's work. We will only find fresh meshing points when we actively understand the exhibition as a theoretical construct, rather than simply as a format through which to present things. Yet we must also provide bridges for our audiences. But it's not possible to do all this in an instant. I've been here for two years, and have learned that you cannot simply put a museum into gear and go. One must proceed with deliberate speed.

TS: Let me pose this question in more overtly political terms. Germany is at the center of "old Europe," as the Americans say, or "*Kern-Europa*," as the Eastern Europeans say. It is clearly part of a huge political experiment in re-invention to situate itself in what it sees as a globalizing world. The obvious question that everyone wants to ask is, how and in what way do you introduce your post-colonial and contemporary vision here? Do you have something specific in mind—in parallel to, say, Charles Esche's *Be[coming] Dutch* program, which comprised a whole series of exhibitions, programs, plays, and events that challenged public conceptions of "Dutch-ness"?[16]

OE: I admire much of Charles's thinking and much of what he has done, but that's not the kind of axe I want to grind. I don't want to explore "German-ness." I think identity politics can only be fruitful if it proposes a framework of understanding that is not directly connected to place. I want to avoid using this museum as a place of commentary. I work in an institution that carries huge historical baggage. This baggage can be really quite relentless, and, indeed, can become a boring cliché that prevents people moving forward. Nevertheless, the history of the institution itself can also be used in order to think through the post-colonial constellation more productively.

Along with the Tate Modern and the Centre Georges Pompidou, we have begun a six-year project to explore the historical conditions under which art around the world has developed since 1945. Through a series of conferences that will lead into exhibitions, we will re-value the concepts "postwar," "post-colonialism," and "post-communism." Instead of focusing just on Europe and North America, we want to rethink them in an archipelagic way, from the Pacific and the Atlantic toward the continents. It is amazing how many art-producing centers come into view from this perspective, and how different art in the older centers begins to seem.[17]

TS: In the upcoming renovation of the building, you will be working with David Chipperfield to re-conceive the interior spaces and, I presume, aspects of the external presentation. What are some of the principles you have been discussing with him?

OE: One principle is that time should be open to revisiting, and exhibitions to re-curating. Why must certain exhibitions be

16. Charles Esche and Ann Fleming, *Be[com]ing Dutch*, Van Abbemuseum, Eindhoven, at http://www.becomingdutch.com.

17. See http://www.kulturstiftung-desbundes.de/cms/en/projekte/bild_und_raum/postwar.html.

done only once? If a show is relevant once, can it be relevant a second time, or third, or fourth time, as a way of really doing a review, or survey, of some significant question, some important moment, some interesting place? Through *Annual Report: A Year in Exhibitions*, at the Gwangju Biennale in 2008, I surveyed exhibitions that had been presented elsewhere during the preceding year. I have been thinking about how we might revisit that idea within a museum setting, inside these big rooms. I would like to install sets of these exquisite moments, to see if the public isn't best served, sometimes, by ingesting these offerings in smaller chunks rather than in one big meal.

TS: A series of platforms, like Documenta 11?

OE: Well, Documenta 11 was hugely important to me. It was where I developed quite a number of approaches that I have tried to follow ever since. I am very interested in the possibility of Haus der Kunst bringing together the idea of the museum and the idea of the open university. Not by fetishizing learning, but by treating it as an active force field of different forms of engagement around different platforms. The renovation will offer bright, new, beautiful gallery spaces, but it might also enable us to think about the building as a campus. One of the things that we admired about Chipperfield's presentation was that he was already thinking about the building as a force field of sorts, as a number of fixed spaces, and many variable ones. In order to think how we might provide an orientation within this fluidity, we have asked ourselves: what would be the essential GPS of the institution? For example, we need to construct a library, as a place for undertaking work in progress, because knowledge is open-ended and never finished; it's under permanent construction. So, Haus der Kunst has to be an institution in permanent transition. This means we have to think about active forms of learning—to really explore the principle of the symposium, to re-examine these categories, to return back to some of the classical terms, and to animate them in the present. How does one think historically in the present? For me, that's the challenge.

TS: Also, of course, how does one think about the present historically?

OE: Precisely. It's those two things, together.

TS: To be able to do that, you have to see the world as a whole, to see the connectivities between the provinces that constitute it. In effect, you want to create a kind of house of art for the world, a house of the art of the world…

OE: … based in Munich. A well-ventilated space, a layered set of platforms, open to the world, in order to show art's infinite capacity to generate surplus values.

Hans Ulrich Obrist
Curating As Medium

Hans Ulrich Obrist, a Swiss curator and art critic, is currently the co-director of exhibitions and programs and the director of international projects at the Serpentine Galleries in London, which he joined in 2006. In 1993, he founded the migratory Robert Walser Museum and began to run the Migrateurs program at the Musée d'Art Moderne de la Ville de Paris, where he served as a curator for contemporary art from 2000–2006. Since 1991, Obrist has curated over 250 solo and group exhibitions and conducted over 2,400 hours of interviews, as well as organized countless other cultural events, such as the annual Serpentine Marathon, for which he invites fifty artists, architects, philosophers, and other cultural producers to give short, consecutive presentations on a given theme. He has developed a number of innovative exhibition formats, such as *museum in progress* and *do it* (both begun in 1993); *Cities on the Move* (1997–8), co-curated with Hou Hanru; and *Utopia Station*, co-curated with Molly Nesbit and Rirkrit Tiravanija (Venice Biennale, 2003). In addition to numerous publications on artists, he has authored books on the subject of curating, which include most recently *Ways of Curating* (London: Allen Lane, 2014), *Everything You Always Wanted to Know About Curating* (Berlin: Sternberg Press, 2011), and *A Brief History of Curating* (Zurich: JRP/Ringier; Dijon: Les Presses du reel, 2008).

We spoke at the Maritime Hotel, New York, on November 10, 2014.

Terry Smith: You begin your new book *Ways of Curating* by considering whether Switzerland's insularity and its location at the crossroads of Europe make it fertile ground for curators. We think, of course, of Harald Szeemann, Bice Curiger, Adelina von Fürstenberg, and yourself, among others. You speak of Switzerland as a "polyglot culture," yet one that "does not admit new influences without a process of selection." You go on to say that, in this sense:

> There is a fundamental similarity to the act of curating, which at its most basic is simply about connecting cultures, bringing their elements into proximity with each other—the task of curating is to make junctions, to allow different elements to touch. You might describe it as an attempted pollination of culture, or a form of map-making that opens up new routes through a city, a people, and a world.[1]

1. Hans Ulrich Obrist, *Ways of Curating* (London: Allen Lane, 2014), p. 1.

This is one of your clearest, most concentrated, yet most general statements about curating. It leads me to wonder whether this would be your way of responding to the last of the "notes to self" that I listed at the end of *Thinking Contemporary Curating*: "Curate contemporaneity in art and society—past, present, and to come—critically."[2] So let me begin with these questions: is the connecting of cultures the way you understand the idea of contemporaneity? If so, how do you actually curate contemporaneity—I mean you, personally? And then, more generally, how might, or even *should*, it be curated?

CURATING CONTEMPORANEITY

Hans Ulrich Obrist: The idea that art is what living artists *do* has always been universally implicit. On a personal level, everything I have done comes out of dialogues with living artists. I grew up in the studio of artists Peter Fischli and David Weiss. At the time, I thought about Nietzsche's distinction between actual and *inactual* [Spanish, "out of date"] or *inattuale* [Italian, "irrelevant"] ways of relating to one's times.[3]

In his wonderful essay "What Is the Contemporary?" Giorgio Agamben revisits this distinction in answering the question: "What is it to be contemporary?" He shows us that the person who truly belongs to his or her own time does not coincide perfectly with it, but rather adheres to it through "a disjunction and an anachronism."[4] Being out of step with the present is precisely what enables one to fully perceive it. To me, that's the key thing about contemporaneity. I wrote a text about this for *e-flux journal* a few years ago.[5] But I'm sure you've got Agamben covered…

2. Terry Smith, *Thinking Contemporary Curating* (New York; Independent Curators International, 2012), p. 256.

3. Friedrich Nietzsche, *Untimely Meditations* [1873–76] (Cambridge: Cambridge University Press, 1997).

4. Giorgio Agamben, "What Is the Contemporary?," in *"What Is an Apparatus?" and Other Essays* (Stanford: Stanford University Press, 2009), pp. 40, 41.

5. Hans Ulrich Obrist, "Manifestos for the Future," *e-flux journal*, no. 12 (January 2012). http://www.e-flux.com/journal/manifestos-for-the-future/.

TS: To me, his essay is a brilliant evocation of much, but not all, of what it's like for all of us involved in art and thought—artists, poets, philosophers, and curators—to be in the world today. Agamben vividly conjures a sense, or really the sensibility, of a certain relatively limited range of individuals who, it is implied, feel the times most intensely, precisely in their mismatch with it. Which is why his reading has such currency in contemporary art discourse, where it seems so right that it has become a kind of a terminus to further self-questioning, a brilliant block that saves art-worlders from having to stray too far from the art world.

Of course, it is not Agamben's fault that his argument is used in this way. But it is interesting to ask why this particular argument can be read like that. One reason may be that most of his examples, such as the quotations from Osip Mandelstam's poem "*Vek*" [The Century], written in 1923, are modern in character, so he seems instinctively located in the modern era. But the real problem is that he does not try to weave his insights into a larger idea in order to understand contemporaneity as a world condition that is shared, in diverse ways, by everybody. I was somewhat disappointed because many of his earlier ideas were profound descriptions of deep, difficult-to-fathom changes in broad-scale world conditions, such as when he wrote about "states of exception" becoming the norm among governments these days, and about the relationship between the sovereign power of such governments and the "bare life" of individuals. He evoked not only the loss of freedom we are all experiencing, but most poignantly the deplorable condition of increasing numbers of the world's peoples: their in-between states, their statelessness, their perpetual migration, their provisional encampment.[6]

HUO: Perhaps the question is, to what extent can Agamben's ideas be used to better understand our contemporaneity in the

6. Giorgio Agamben, *States of Exception* (Chicago: University of Chicago Press, 2005), and *Homo Sacer: Sovereign Power and Bare Life* (Stanford: Stanford University Press, 1998).

twenty-first century? I find his comparison of our attempts to understand our condition with the perception of astral light traveling through the night sky, for example, from his essay about contemporaneity, particularly illuminating: "To perceive, in the darkness of the present, this light that strives to reach us, but cannot—this is what it means to be contemporary."[7]

TS: In one of my essays about contemporaneity, I cite Charles Baudelaire's famous "definition" from 1864: "*modernité*, that is, the transitory, the fugitive, the contingent, the half of art, the other half of which is the eternal and the immutable," and comment that his implicit promise that "a timeless art could be distilled from the random-seeming mobility of the contemporary" is no longer available to us.[8] I notice that in your *e-flux journal* essay "Manifestos of the Future" you make a similar point, saying that Baudelaire's "modern" seems to disregard "the plurality of temporalities across space, a plurality of experiences through modernity that continue to this day, and on a truly global scale," citing as examples the new centers throughout Asia and the Middle East, many of them energized by biennials.[9] Agamben addresses these kinds of changes in many of his writings, but his thinking about art and contemporaneity does not stray far from Baudelaire's.

HUO: Agamben has always been a great inspiration, but for me the real tools for dealing with our contemporaneity are to be found in Édouard Glissant's writings, which I read every day, and which have convinced me that globalization is not today's big idea. Obviously, we're not living through the first globalization of the world: the Roman Empire globalized its domain, so did Alexander the Great his. However, right now we are experiencing

7. Agamben, "What Is the Contemporary?," p. 46.

8. Terry Smith, "Introduction: The Contemporaneity Question," in Terry Smith, Okwui Enwezor, and Nancy Condee, eds., *Antinomies of Art and Culture: Modernity, Postmodernity, Contemporaneity* (Durham, N. Car.: Duke University Press, 2008), pp. 3–5.

9. Obrist, "Manifestos for the Future."

certainly the most extreme, and the most violent, moment of globalization. In Europe, for example, but also in other continents, it is manifesting itself in very strong neo-nationalist, xenophobic tendencies that reject global dialogue. Glissant's idea of *mondialité* invites us instead to negotiate everyday contemporaneity by beginning not from the homogenizing, inward-looking perspective of competing continents, but from the open, relational perspective offered by thinking of nations as strung together like archipelagos.[10] We have to engage constantly in a global dialogue that actually produces differences rather than annihilates them. That's what my shows try to do: many of them, such as *do it*, *Utopia Station*, and *Laboratorium*, are open-ended, potentially permanent, and can be made and re-made by any one who participates.[11]

TS: These are future-directed frameworks. They take the form, like a lot of early Conceptual art, of sets of instructions that when followed create futures—or, more accurately, imagined presents at a future time. What about the many different kinds of pasts that seem so powerfully present within contemporaneity, sometimes to the extent of threatening to almost fill it up?

HUO: Well, to quote Agamben for the last time, he concludes his text on the contemporary by saying that:

> ... the contemporary is not only the one who, perceiving the darkness of the present, grasps a light that can never reach its destiny; he is also the one who, dividing and interpolating time, is capable of transforming it and putting it in relation to other times. He is able to read history in unforeseen ways, to 'cite it' according to the necessity that does not arise from his will, but from an exigency to which he cannot not respond. It is as if this invisible light that is the darkness of the present

10. Édouard Glissant, *The Poetics of Relation* (Ann Arbor: University of Michigan Press, 1999).

11. The exhibitions curated by Hans Ulrich Obrist mentioned in this conversation are described in some detail in his book *Ways of Curating* (2014).

> cast its shadow in the past, so that the past, touched by this shadow, acquired the ability to respond to the darkness of the now.[12]

I understand him here as asking us to read history in an unedited way. Although, I don't necessarily mean, as Erwin Panofsky said with reference to art history, that we always invent the future with fragments of the past, and, sometimes, replace it with those fragments. I would remove the "always."

CURATING THE FUTURE

TS: The sense I am getting is that you work on questions of contemporaneity in everything that you do. Let's look at some current projects, such as the 89plus project you have curated with Simon Castets. Is that an example of "curating the future," which is a phrase that you also use? I looked at the 89plus.com online platform and saw that the concept is built around residencies. Okwui Enzewor says that residencies are major connectors, or fields, for a lot of contemporary artists, and that their requirements and limitations are reshaping contemporary practice. What's your view of the value of residencies?

HUO: Well, I am the product of a residency. Twenty-nine people visited my first exhibition—a group show called *The Kitchen Show* actually installed in the kitchen of my apartment in St. Gallen—during its three-month run in 1991. Among them were the curators Marie-Claude Beaud and Jean de Loisy, who subsequently invited me to undertake a three-month residency at the Cartier Foundation near Paris, later that same year. All of a sudden, I was liberated.

At the foundation my neighbors were the artists Shen Yuan and Huang Yong Ping, the co-founder of Xiamen Dada, who

12. Agamben, "What Is the Contemporary?," p. 53.

came to Paris for *Magiciens de la terre*, and Absalon, the Israeli sculptor who died in 1993, at a very young age. I was the curator-in-residence, and they were the artists-in-residence. We had marvelous conversations everyday. I was excited to learn about non-Western art, because at that time we were still operating inside the paradigm of Western modernism. The residency also allowed me to visit artists' studios in France. I made hundreds of studio visits, many to artists from overseas. I was in my early twenties, so this experience had a real impact.

This is why Simon Castets and I decided on residencies as a way of supporting young artists from all over the world in a more sustained way. Our 89plus project is not about predicting future creation, but rather, through panels, books, periodicals, exhibitions, residencies, bringing together individuals whose voices are only starting to be heard. So far 5,000 artists all over the world have responded to our open call and uploaded information about their respective practices to our platform. Since we started in 2013, we have also conducted onsite research in Hong Kong, Singapore, Rio de Janeiro, and Cape Town. Wherever we go, we interview local practitioners, and then develop public panels out of our conversations. This February, in Cape Town, we developed a panel for the annual design conference INDABA (meaning "business" or "meeting" in Zulu). One of the panelists, artist Bogosi Sekhukhuni, had previously never left South Africa for very long, so we invited him to do a residency in Paris where he could develop his video diary and make other work. Right now, Bogosi is working on a film about his ancestors who fought against the Boers, and his time at the Google Cultural Institute allows him access to the technology he needs for research and production. In December we are going to present his work alongside that of other artists at the Cartier Foundation in Paris in a small exhibition.[13]

13. See http://bogosisekhukhuni.tumblr.com/ and http://www.nytimes.com/2014/08/07/arts/design/89-plus-project-focuses-on-technology-obsessed-artists.html?_r=0.

TS: I see on *Rhizome* that the "Younger Than Rihanna" event in Munich for a group of 89plus artists was criticized as being a device for tracking emerging artists, precisely by inviting them to identify themselves as such.[14] Saatchi has been doing this for years, via his gallery's website. How do you respond to that kind of criticism?

HUO: It's important to emphasize that 89plus is not necessarily concerned with youth, but rather is conceptualized as a generational study of people born within a new paradigm. 1989 is a milestone: think of the fall of the Berlin Wall, the exit of the Soviet Red Army from Afghanistan after almost ten years of military occupation, and the students' insurrection in Tiananmen Square in Beijing, among other key events. It is also the year when Tim Berners-Lee wrote the coding and protocols of the World Wide Web, establishing the basis for the digital culture of today. These changes generated multiple transformations, deeply affecting all parts of life, including art and architecture.

This is an amazing generation—born after 1989, it is half of the world's population, and it is the first to grow up with the Internet. In twenty to thirty years, which is the duration we intend for the project, the participants will be mid-generation, and we are very interested to see how their practices will develop over the course of this time. We are not interested in individual artistic heroism. The big question of the twenty-first century is how to foster collective action. In the age of the Internet, the potential to join, to come to shared engagement, is there, so we ask, what would that mean in relation to display? Curating always follows art, so it is an exciting moment to be close to a new generation that oscillates between the analog and the digital. That is what we would like to understand in the next years, hopefully, through the 89plus project.[15]

14. See http://rhizome.org/editorial/2013/feb/14/younger-rihanna/.

15. See http://89plus.com and Hans Ulrich Obrist, "The future was born in 1989," *Wired*, July 31, 2014, http://www.wired.co.uk/magazine/archive/2014/08/ideas-bank/hans-ulbrich-obrist.

TS: As part of the project, you put out an open call asking for responses to the question, how does the Internet change curating? How would you respond to that question?

HUO: Many of my exhibitions have been self-organized, DIY affairs. With the Internet, you can do the same but in a very public way. Although twenty-nine people saw the show in my kitchen, my Instagram handwriting project has 92,000 followers. In 2012, on a visit to LA, I had breakfast with the critic Kevin McGarry and the artist Ryan Trecartin, who decided to download the Instagram application onto my iPhone. Ryan posted an image; people started following me. For days, I didn't really know what to do with this app. I knew I didn't want to photograph my breakfast. I didn't want to take selfies. I didn't want to document my trips, because that would reinforce the cliché of the curator as globetrotting traveler. Yet I did want to curate something in this medium.

Then, as always, the real, profound beginning was a conversation with an artist. That Christmas, my partner, Koo Jeong A, and I were on a very stormy Normandy beach with Simone Fattal and Etel Adnan. Etel wrote a poetic line on a paper napkin. I saw the beauty of her handwriting, and at the same time realized that, in the age of the Internet, there is a danger that handwriting might disappear, become extinct. So, I thought maybe I could use the Internet to start a movement to celebrate handwriting. I began to ask the artists and architects I met to give me a handwritten sentence, and now I post one every day. Yesterday, I saw Christopher Williams here in the hotel, and asked him to participate.

TS: What did he write?

HUO: Let me read it: "A good exhibition design should not need more than a drawing on a cocktail napkin to be realized." So, now I take a photograph of it, and post it. There are more than 700 sentences, so far. It will obviously lead to a book. You could say that these are my immaterial exhibitions.

PARALLEL REALITIES

TS: You commented in an interview about the 89plus project that you're interested in artists who work in two or three parallel realities. To me that implies contemporaneity, but can you expand on what you mean by this?

HUO: David Deutsch, in his wonderful book *The Fabric of Reality: Towards a Theory of Everything*, talks about the parallel realities revealed by quantum physics.[16] This notion has definitely now arrived in art, and it's fascinating to see: artists of the 89plus generation are, very often, also poets, or they work in architecture, in design, in literature, in music, in science. They do not opt for one field alone, but instead explore different parallel realities. And they use any medium to do so, from craft objects to the Internet. Many of these artists have a history within collectives or are activists. That's another part of their reality: they have a political slant to their practice. For example, Yollotl Gómez-Alvarado, a twenty-four-year-old artist from Mexico, who in a gesture of solidarity recently made sculptures out of the tiny bags of concrete that the government handed out to individual householders during the 1990s to encourage them to complete home renovations.

TS: Most of these qualities may be found in the work of Etel Adnan, whose work you are enthusiastic about. Yet she is in her late eighties.

HUO: Yes, many of the 89plus artists mention Etel as an influence. There are so many dimensions to Etel's practice; it's almost like superstring theory. She originally wanted to be an architect, actually an urbanist, but when the Lebanese civil war interrupted her studies she became one of the greatest poets of our time—Mahmoud Darwish, the Palestinian poet in

16. David Deutsch, *The Fabric of Reality: Towards a Theory of Everything* (London: Penguin, 1998).

"permanent exile," said that she has never written a bad line. Her poetry led to her plays, and incredible novels, like *Sitt Marie Rose* [1977], which is one of the ultimate books about the civil war in Lebanon. It's very salutary to read now, in relation to wars today. As well, she wrote *The Arab Apocalypse* [1989], a book of poems showing that war is the worst form of extinction. It announces many more wars to come. Her small landscape paintings, often of Mount Tamalpais, near Sausalito, in Northern California, however, are much less dark. Etel also makes public art. She has always had this dream of getting her art into the world in a Bauhaus kind of way, so she makes murals and textile works. She works with craft. She's a filmmaker.

TS: And she illustrates poetry, as we saw in the Whitney Biennial earlier this year, where a whole room was devoted to both her illustrated books and her paintings. I don't think she is exceptional for her generation, but I'd like to get at the difference between, if you like, modern ways of being contemporary and contemporary ways. How is she different from the under-twenty-fives?

HUO: Obviously, she's not using the Internet. That's the key difference, you know? She's analog. Yet, it's very interesting, actually, in that there are many, many more links than one would think between the two states. For example, I am particularly struck by the fact that poetry hasn't disappeared, that there's a whole new form of poetry in the digital age.

THE PRODUCTION OF POIESIS

TS: I think I can see why Adnan appeals so strongly to you. What stands out for me about your work overall—including your whole ongoing interview-the-world project—is that, in fact, it's curating as poiesis. "Poiesis" means more than to simply poeticize something mundane, more than to romanticize material actualities. It is a creative process that seeks to make things while at the same time provisionalizing the hardening of distinctions, working against institutional determination, introducing temporal holes into historical structures, and opening out, as you suggested before, certain parallel realities—or, at least, hinting at their possibility.

HUO: Inside this concept of poiesis is the idea of making; that's the root of the word in Greek. Curating is about making something, but never on one's own. It's always a matter of making something *with* someone else, or *for* someone else, and always in dialogue with artists. I often get asked if I am an artist, or, more generally, if the curator is an artist. The opposite is true. Art does not illustrate curating. Curating follows art. Always.

I was wondering if we could maybe explore the notion of autopoiesis in this context. Can exhibitions become capable of creating, reproducing, and maintaining themselves? The concept of autopoiesis was a direct inspiration for *do it*, for example.

TS: In the strictest sense, the analogy is not exact, because when cells, say, reproduce, they pretty much repeat themselves, and do so in the same way, unless there is an aberration, like a cancer, or a pressure for an evolutionary change of some kind. But the interesting thing in the context of exhibition making—the poiesis of the process, if you like—is that you are looking to *reproduce difference*. That's an impossible paradox, but it's what art seeks to do. Maybe curating does, too.

MARATHONS AND EXTINCTION

TS: How can we move out, as we necessarily must, from our immersion in the contemporaneity of difference? How can we move through a consciousness of our being already inside the "sixth extinction," as Elizabeth Kolbert calls it, toward the construction of a really concrete planetary consciousness that produces actual, positive connectivity, rather than continuing with the mass destruction of nature that we have initiated?[17] I believe we have to do this, rather than continue to depend on weak universalizing metaphors like ecology, or globality, or trusting that capitalism—U.S.- and Chinese-style—will deliver a variety of technological solutions while leaving everything else the same. If we are to believe Naomi Klein's latest book, *This Changes Everything: Capitalism vs. the Climate*, these supposed solutions are in fact the problem.[18] This dilemma is obviously also on your mind: you just completed the *Extinction Marathon* at the Serpentine Galleries, with an extraordinary range of participants.[19] I notice that the subtitle was *Visions of the Future*.

HUO: Well, first of all, I think that art now engages in the production of meaning, and of consciousness, within a new paradigm that is a constructive "impetus" rather than a demarcation, a rating, or a ranking. Distinctions of this kind have dominated Western thought and culture since Immanuel Kant began laying the foundations for modern philosophy in the eighteenth century, but they do not prevail in Eastern cultures. So, how can we think about that in the twenty-first century, which will not be dominated by either? How does this question play a role within any upcoming exhibition?

It may be that our European perspective is limiting our openness to experience. Perhaps display in the twenty-first century will come from other cultures, and will tend toward a holistic condition. The question of sensibility is deeply connected with physical experience. I think it is essential to recall Margaret Mead—"the eye, the ear, the smell of incense, the kinesthesia of genuflection, the kneeling or swaying to passing procession, to the cool touch of holy water on a forehead"—and to understand

17. Elizabeth Kolbert, *The Sixth Extinction: An Unnatural History* (New York: Henry Holt, 2014).

18. Naomi Klein, *This Changes Everything: Capitalism vs. the Climate* (New York: Simon & Schuster, 2014).

19. See http://www.serpentinegalleries.org/exhibitions-events/extinction-marathon.

how to have all the senses involved.[20] It might seem paradoxical, but there is a great desire for this in the digital age.

To come back to the Marathon, each of our Marathons has different rules, and different criteria, whether thematic, geographical, or spatial, and so on. The idea is very much about exploring different formats and platforms for discussing culture. The exhibition format has been questioned throughout the twentieth century, but perhaps conferences, symposia, and interviews have not yet been considered to the same extent. We often see the phenomenon of the anticipated audience: when an architect speaks, an architecture audience turns up while hardly anyone from the art world does, and vice versa. This lack of crossover is something that is also addressed by the Marathons. The people being interviewed, or presenting, are not just from the field of art—they include representatives from the fields of architecture, science, literature, and many other disciplines. It is about venturing out from art into other fields, and building bridges between them.

The *Extinction Marathon* was actually inspired by Timothy Morton's book *Ecology without Nature*, and his theorizing of "hyperobjects," such as climate change, as well as his more recent writings on queer ecology.[21] I interviewed him for the Marathon (the text is published online by DIS Magazine). He gave interesting answers to the questions you just posed. He defined ecology as the interconnection of all life forms, and indeed the interconnection of all those life forms with non-life: "It means thinking something that is boundless, yes. Everything's related, but it's boundless.... [s]o there's no center, there's no edge, and

20. Margaret Mead cited in Richard Kostelanetz, *The Theatre of Mixed Means* [1968] (London: Pitman, 1970), p. 35. She goes on to say, "For Art to be Reality the whole sensuous being must be caught up in the experience."

21. Timothy Morton, *Ecology without Nature: Rethinking Environmental Aesthetics* (Cambridge, Mass.: Harvard University Press, 2009), and Timothy Morton, *Hyperobjects: Philosophy and Ecology after the End of the World* (Minneapolis: University of Minnesota Press, 2013). See also http://www.academia.edu/1050754/Queer_Ecology.

there's no one dominant top level or there's no one fundamental bottom level. There's no middle level."[22]

To me, right now, this is the real context for curating in the twenty-first century.

TS: When I read *A Brief History of Curating*, I thought, here is someone who deeply respects his predecessors—Harald Szeemann, Lucy Lippard, Willem Sandberg, Walter Hopps, and many others—but is also clearly ambitious to add to this history through his own curatorial practice.[23] In that book, you exhibit a historical consciousness, which is different from the framework we're talking about now.

HUO: You mean, a move from a linear to a non-linear understanding?

TS: Not simply so, because both weave around, perhaps saturate, each other. I see you as increasingly trying to create around yourself a domain where there's a constant making present, or presencing, of surprising distinctions within current realties, of unexpected holes cut through historical time, and the chancy revelations of unusual places, or imaginings of elsewhere, if you like. But there is also, I will not say equally, a strong desire to always connect these differentials—differences in medium, ideas, approaches—into a kind of total, lived, curatorial open work. This is the picture I'm getting of your practice. Does it make sense to you?

HUO: Well, on the one hand, I've always been interested in the idea of "the extreme present"—it's part of the subtitle of a new book, *The Age of Earthquakes*, which I co-wrote

22. See http://dismagazine.com/disillusioned/discussion-disillusioned/68280/hans-ulrich-obrist-timothy-morton/.

23. Hans Ulrich Obrist, *A Brief History of Curating* (Zurich: JRP/Ringier; Dijon: Les Presses du réel, 2008).

with Douglas Coupland and Shumon Basar.[24] But I would also emphasize that there are always sparks from past models. There's such a staggering amnesia about exhibition history. We do need to protest against forgetting. When I met Rosemarie Trockel in 1985, aged seventeen, I told her I wanted to get as close as possible to the present of art; she told me it was important to talk to a range of people, not only artists of my own generation, or of my own time, but also pioneers in their eighties, nineties, and one hundreds, and to make sure I recorded their memories, which could be seen as a protest against forgetting. This is what I tried to do with *A Brief History of Curating*, and what I am continuing to do through also researching artists as curators. These histories were never linear, there were always many different conversations going on, and these conversations led to exhibitions.

Having many conversations, then bringing elements from them together… J. G. Ballard once told me that he thinks curating is a form of junction making. This happens in many different ways, when we remember that a curator brings objects together, as in the old tradition of the curator as a collection creator, builder, and manager, but also the newer one of the curator as an exhibition maker. And not only objects, but also quasi-objects—that is to say, objects that gain meaning or significance when used or displayed in a particular way—non-objects, such as human beings or live art, and, last but not least, Tim Morton's hyperobjects. So, for me, curating makes junctions between objects, non-objects, quasi-objects, and hyperobjects.

RESISTANCE AND CRITIQUE

TS: Many people criticize the kind of connectivity that we are trying to build as being so similar in style to the productivity and worldviews of globetrotting globalizers that it ends up being part

24. Douglas Coupland, Shumon Basar, and Hans Ulrich Obrist, *The Age of Earthquakes: A Guide to the Extreme Present* (London: Penguin, 2015).

of their world. Not *mondialité* at all, just more high-end, luxury-good, fashionable, globalized culture. They see a lot of the work done by millennials as embedded in the massive data-tracking, crowd-sourcing, and, above all, money-making operations such as Google, Facebook, and Instagram, and thus caught up in what we might call the autopoetic unfreedom that these companies are constructing inside what appears to be a zone of liberation.

HUO: We should remember that there are some important precedents for working with tech companies, such as, for example, Billy Klüver and E.A.T. [Experiments in Art and Technology] in the 1960s and 1970s. Today it is interesting to ask: what sort of experiments in art and technology do we need for the twenty-first century? A lot of artists have a very critical stance toward the whole idea of surveillance and data mining, for example, and are against companies like Amazon developing vast information archives. I think it's important to engage with these questions in the twenty-first century, which is why we did the interviews with Julian Assange.[25] It's certainly not about promoting techno-lifestyle developments as a natural condition. I think it's about the question of resistance.

TS: Your conversation with Assange was fascinating, as were his responses to the questions posed by artists including Paul Chan, Martha Rosler, Superflex, Luis Camnitzer, and Ai Weiwei. What did you take from this experience as an answer to your question about what counts as resistance, or about what could be critical in this circumstance?

HUO: Well, Daniel Birnbaum, Philippe Parreno, and I are working on an exhibition called *Resistances*, which was the

25. Hans Ulrich Obrist, "In Conversation with Julian Assange, Parts I and II," *e-flux journal*, nos. 25 (May 2011) and 26 (June 2011). http://www.e-flux.com/journal/in-conversation-with-julian-assange-part-i/ and http://www.e-flux.com/journal/in-conversation-with-julian-assange-part-ii/.

exhibition project Jean-François Lyotard was planning when he died. We think of *Les Immatériaux*, which he curated at the Pompidou in 1985, as an exhibition that bridged science and art, but it actually was mainly about quasi-objects in the context of the Internet and its superfluidity.[26] In that connection, it's interesting that Lyotard mentioned a second exhibition, one about resistance. *Resistances* is not, perhaps, a good title, as it immediately evokes a series of moral issues. But when I spoke to Philippe Parreno, who remembers a discussion where Lyotard explained his plans, I understood that he in fact meant resistance in another way. *Les Immatériaux* was an early reflection on the possibilities of the Internet age; *Resistances* would be about the opposite: the notion of resistance in our age of connections. What ultimately interests us in a film, painting, piece of music, or writing is not so much that someone directly resists the system, but that the artist accepts the challenge to think, write, paint, or film resistance in the very material of language, image, color, or sound. Parreno, Birnbaum, and I now plan to realize Lyotard's show, a show curated by a ghost, at an intriguing site: the LUMA Foundation. Art collector, producer, and patron Maja Hoffmann has invited Liam Gillick and curators Tom Eccles and Beatrix Ruf, together with Parreno and me, to form a group with her to plan this experimental art center, which will be designed by Frank Gehry, in Arles, in the marshland of France's Camargue.

REFUSALS AND ACCEPTANCES

TS: A criticism that's frequently leveled at you is that you are ubiquitous—here, there, everywhere, doing everything, whatever. Do you recognize yourself in this description?

26. See Tara McDowell, "Les Immatériaux: A Conversation with Jean-François Lyotard and Bernard Blistène," introduced by Tara McDowell, *art-agenda*, May 27, 2014, http://www.art-agenda.com/reviews/les-immateriaux-a-conversation-with-jean-francois-lyotard-and-bernard-blistene/.

HUO: Not really, as it is about both linking and delinking, I'm both attached and detached. There is certainly the impression in the art world that I accept every invitation. That is clearly wrong. It is, however, true that I do agree to a lot of things. I don't have a master plan, so I need to be out in the world, and I am willing to do a lot of public talking and many shows. I think my approach is a vertically open system, and it's important for me, each time, to learn. Whenever I'm invited to do a project, say, I get criticism, I get feedback, and I learn from it. Also, I very much believe that we learn through experiences in different geographies. I've curated the Dakar Biennale. I've curated different biennials in Asia. I've curated shows in Brazil, and in Mexico, and many other places in Latin America. Each time I go into a new context, I come out a different person.

TS: I sense that, for you, curating is a medium in which you are immersed, and that your task is to show that medium to the world, to exhibit it as a process, to show its forms, and its context. At the same time, you are driven to document every detail of this quest as it unfolds.

If this makes any sense, let me ask: what is compelling you to do this? Who is speaking to you? Are all the conversations that are happening in the world somehow addressing you, asking you to bring them together, to be the medium that connects them? Or is it just that you respond to whatever the art world asks you to do? Is there anything you actively, I suppose conscientiously, *refuse* to do?

HUO: It's fascinating that you ask this question, because I just recently spoke about this with Jeanne Moreau, the actress—

TS: Ah, wonderful. She was unforgettable in *Jules et Jim*.

HUO: She said that an actor is very much defined by the roles that he or she refuses to play. I think, in a way, it's the same with a curator. Whenever I do a show it has to enter my system with a logic that is innate to my work and that derives from my methodologies. There have been shows, dozens of shows, which I have refused to do. I've always refused to curate in the commercial sector, for example. I do not curate when works are for sale. I've never sold an artwork. In this sense, I am a very old-fashioned curator.

TS: What about art fairs? I often see publicity promoting your presence at art fairs, most recently at Art Basel and Miami.

HUO: I participate in and organize conversations at art fairs; they have featured debates and panels for a long time. But I do not curate exhibitions within them where the works are for sale. This year, Klaus Biesenbach and I organized *14 Rooms* for the Fondation Beyeler, Art Basel, and Theater Basel. It was based on *11 Rooms*, which we did for the Manchester International Festival in 2011. The show has had various iterations since then, with a varying number of works and artists, and every year we add an extra room. But it is based on live art, or works about live art, and nothing is for sale. It's more of a sketch for a future institution of live art.

Resistance comes up again here, interestingly, in the recent insistence by artists on live art, in contrast to on-screen mediation. Tino Sehgal is an obvious example, but obviously there are many, many others. In the 1960s and 1970s artists like Bruce Nauman and Joan Jonas began to work with the idea that a performance piece could actually have the same duration as an exhibition. In fact, Eugène Ionesco, the first artist I ever met, when I was fourteen or fifteen, by chance in the streets of St. Gallen, told me that his play *La Cantatrice chauve* [The Bald Singer] had been performed in Paris every night for more than thirty years. (By now, it's more than fifty years.) He said, "It is like a public artwork. It's like a sculpture. It's there everyday." In *14 Rooms* we connected a performance by Otobong Nkanga, *Taste of a Stone*, to *Touch Piece*, an earlier work by Yoko Ono, and to a secret work by Dominique Gonzalez-Foerster. What if one of these works was endowed to a museum for fifty or one hundred years? I think that would be very, very interesting. It's not about selling something. It's about supporting an artist, and it would require labor to sustain it. To me creating this kind of experience for the next century or so is a positive act.

In the 1990s, when I started working with my mentors Kasper König and Suzanne Pagé, we often had a year or two to organize an exhibition. *The Broken Mirror* was the first big show that I co-curated with König; it had an eighteen-month preparation period. But with the acceleration of art world schedules, I've been asked to do shows six months out. You can't do that to artists, basically, so I've always turned them down. That's a third refusal.

As well, there is a list, quite a list, of bigger institutions I was asked to direct over the years but decided not to. I fear that when you have a lot of institutional bureaucracy your research might suffocate. If an independent curator runs an institution, then the curator in you dies, in a way. On the other hand, if you are completely unattached, you are everywhere. Harald Szeemann made me very aware of this, because even after he stopped being the director at the Kunsthalle Bern he maintained an attachment to the Kunsthaus Zurich. I have always had a desire to have an attachment because I didn't feel that it was appropriate to be a fly in, fly out curator: you can't produce anything sustainable in that way. So I wanted, like Szeemann, to have an attachment, which I had with the Musée d'Art Moderne de la Ville de Paris during the 1990s. And then in the 2000s I felt that it was somehow important to have a deeper attachment, so I became the curator in Paris, and then, since 2006, with Julia Peyton-Jones, co-director of the Serpentine. In that role, I have office hours from Monday to Thursday or Friday, and then every weekend I do the research.

TS: You've listed many offers that you have refused, but you haven't actually said, I cannot see myself doing a show about X or Y, or in a certain part of the world, or for somebody, or in a certain circumstance, or about a particular subject. Most of us have some things we have decided that we won't do. Like work for big tobacco companies, or accept their money. So, are there any things along those lines to add to the list?

HUO: I've always believed that we need to be independent. I would not do anything that could be instrumentalized politically, by a party or a government, or by an individual. I'm reminded of the sentence "To every age its art, and to art its freedom," which is inscribed above the entrance to the artist-run Vienna Secession building.

TS: So no kind of subject matter or material or any kind of circumstance or event, apart from the ones we're talking about, that you just would refuse no matter what?

HUO: I would never do anything that is instrumental. I would always start with the artist; the artist is the center.

And I've been asked a lot to curate outside the museum world. Because I have done shows in kitchens and living rooms, companies have asked me to curate commercial kitchens. I've been invited to curate hotels and all of that. These I have all turned down, less as a matter of principle, more because it's not part of my logic. Each show has to have a necessity, an urgency, otherwise I'm not going to do it.

When I do shows outside the museum context it's because I believe that there are unexpected moments of encounter with art. As Robert Musil said, "Art can appear where we expect it least." For example, in Lina Bo Bardi's Glass House in São Paulo. So many artists, from Dominique Gonzalez-Foerster to Adrián Villar Rojas, are obsessed by Lina Bo Bardi's work as an architect that I agreed to do a show there. I would not do such a show simply because someone has a villa and wants me to curate their collection. There are lots of different reasons why art can be instrumentalized: commercially, ideologically, for someone's status, et cetera.

TS: In such cases, you would be instrumentalized as the figure of the curator. If you did it all the time, you would become the symbol of curating as such, a brand for the whole profession. Like Roger Federer endorsing watches, or champagne.

All the things on the list so far are invitations from others to which you're saying no. Let me ask: what would you refuse to do on your own volition? "I'm tempted to do this. I don't want to do it. I shouldn't do it. I could do it. Why shouldn't I do it? I won't do it." This is about your internal ethics, the source of your sense of necessity, the logic of what you want to do. "What positions will I not put myself in, for reasons I may not even know, that may be unconscious, but nonetheless there is a pattern in my refusals?" Perhaps it's not a fair question, but it is parallel, from my perspective, to the one you ask of everybody in your interviews: what is your unrealized project?

HUO: What is it in your case? What do you refuse to do?

TS: Well, I share your refusal to work in commercial settings. Not because of any distaste for that sector, except for its upper tiers. Artists have to make a living, and that's how things are organized in market economies. Of course, it is easier for me because I have had tenured jobs in universities for decades now. Yet, with such a base comes an obligation to carve out an independent voice, so you are not beholden to anyone in the system: dealers, museums, collectors, other critics, even artists. One result is that I very rarely write about individual artists, for example, not only in commercial gallery publicity, but also not in museum catalogues, even for alternative spaces. I discuss individual artists only as their work comes up within the art historical narratives I write, or within the theories about art that I develop. That's an example of a refusal to work within a form of writing that is very common, even among critics who have academic positions. For me, however, endorsing individual artists does not square with how I see the public role of someone based at a university yet engaged with the art world. It is, I suppose, parallel to your sense of yourself as a public curator. But this is not an adequate answer to my question.

HUO: Well, my work ethic forbids me from doing a lot of the things I'm tempted to do everyday. There was the crazy rhythm of the 1990s where I would be on the road 300 days a year, and now the crazy rhythm since 2000 where I run an art institution during the week, and every weekend research, fifty-two times a year, even on Christmas and New Year's. I usually don't sleep more than five hours every night. I start at six in the morning.

So, what could be the next step? What if I stopped traveling and just pulled all the strands together in one place? It would be very interesting to found a kind of Black Mountain College for the twenty-first century. Then I could invite all the artists I am interested in to focus their energies on one place. But that's for much later, maybe.

TS: I have a similar fantasy that I'm hoping to realize. My dream is to create, on each continent, what I call a "constitute," which would be a node in a worldwide network across which three things would happen. First, an ongoing, interactive conversation between people who are concerned to picture worlds on planetary scales, to understand how localities are shaped and sustained, and above all how connectivities flow between pictures and places. Second, I'd like each constitute to be attached to a university or a museum, not as a formal institute but as an organic operation. Not necessarily at a famous museum or elite university, but perhaps at a peripheral one where people would work to actually constitute a consortium of conversations within their own locality. Third, I'd like to enroll a nomadic cohort of graduate students, young artists, curators, and activists who would move between each of these constitutes and consortia. They would be required to study across this network, to spend lengthy periods at two or three different places, and to work on projects that explore connectivity, which I see as the biggest challenge to understanding our contemporaneity. Eventually, they would receive their degrees from one place, or, ideally, from every place.

HUO: It sounds wonderful.

PROJECTS TO BE REALIZED

TS: I just told you about my unrealized project. Tell me about yours.

HUO: The main project is my "Palace of Unbuilt Roads." Ever since the early 1990s, I have been asking artists, what is your unrealized project? What is the project that's too big or too small to be realized? Asking this question has been enormously productive for my curating, probably the most productive stimulus of all. But I have for years wanted to gather all of these unrealized projects into one place, you know, like a Crystal Palace of the twenty-first century. I've asked architects such as Yona Friedman, who designs spatial cities, to do models for it. With e-flux, we've developed it as an exhibition of documentation. But whenever I get close to actually realizing the project as a three-dimensional construction, it ironically falls through.

TS: Maybe it will be forever unrealized. Because perhaps it is, actually, being realized all the time in this world, but one can glimpse only fragments of it, and see them, like all exhibitions, as partially realized possibilities.

HUO: Yes, perhaps so. And then, of course, in my parallel universe, there are the unrealized conversations. Above all, the one I have not yet had with Jean-Luc Godard. I loved the exhibition that he did at the Centre Georges Pompidou in 2006, with a long title: *Travel(s) in Utopia, Jean-Luc Godard 1946–2006, In Search of a Lost Theorem.* It was a retrospective of all of his films, but also a remarkable installation, a series of rooms that became a kind of archaeology of the cinema, like many of his films. It is one of my favorite shows of all time. For me, to do a show with Godard would be a dream.

Claire Bishop

Museum Models, Radical Spectatorship

Claire Bishop is an art historian, critic, author, and professor of art history at the Graduate Center of the City University of New York. She previously taught at Warwick University, Coventry and the Royal College of Art, London. Her books include *Installation Art: A Critical History* (London: Tate Publishing, 2005), *Participation* (Cambridge, Mass.: MIT Press; London: Whitechapel Art Gallery, 2006), and *Artificial Hells: Participatory Art and the Politics of Spectatorship* (London: Verso, 2012).

We began our debate on the ideas in progress that led to her book *Radical Museology, or, What's 'Contemporary' in Museums of Contemporary Art?* (London: Koenig Books, 2013) at the National Institute for Experimental Arts, College of Fine Arts, University of New South Wales, in Sydney, Australia, on December 9, 2012. Our discussion continued through 2013 and 2014.

Terry Smith: I notice that in the title of your new book you put the word "contemporary" in quotes. Does this signal your doubts about the term itself, or about how it is used in art worlds these days? Is your concern with what it means when it names a museum, or are you arguing that what you call "radical museology" is the most contemporary kind of practice occurring in art today?

Claire Bishop: My contention about "the contemporary" is that we can draw the most useful model of it not from current art history or theory, but rather from recent museum practice, specifically that of three European museums: the Van Abbemuseum in Eindhoven, the Museo Nacional Centro de Arte Reina Sofía in Madrid, and the Museum of Contemporary Art Metelkova [MSUM] in Ljubljana. Each of them provides a partisan, politicized understanding of the contemporary as a *method*, rather than its more usual manifestation as a periodization, or as a discourse. My overall aim is to advance the art historical discussion about museums (which hasn't had much to say since the thematic versus chronological debate, circa 2000), but also to provide alternative models to the market-led character of contemporary hangs in most U.S. museums and elsewhere.

Given Europe's current regime of austerity, which has subjected public institutions to continual and extreme defunding, there is a degree of urgency to provide a constructive manifesto on the possibilities for museums. I also want to break with the pessimism of the most important critical writing on contemporary museums to date, which is dominated by tirades against spectacle and blockbuster exhibitions. Instead, it's time for a defense of inspirational new missions for the museum of contemporary art as a public institution.

At the moment, "the contemporary" as a category in both the academy and the museum tends to be understood as *presentism*: the condition of taking our current moment as the horizon and destination of our thinking. Instead, I want to propose the contemporary as an *operation*, a way of acting on the past that is informed by a set of political desires for the future. I draw upon Walter Benjamin's "Theses on the Philosophy of History," especially his idea of the constellation as a way of bringing together ideas, images, and events from the past into the present.[1] Moreover, I want to emphasize that this action is a fundamentally *curatorial* gesture.

TS: You are picturing a contention between different kinds of museums, each claiming to be contemporary, to show art of contemporary relevance, and to show the past (or parts of it) as possessing contemporary relevance. Broadly speaking, each of

1. "Historicism contents itself with establishing a casual connection between various moments in history. But no fact that is a cause is for that very reason historical. It became historical, as it were, through events that may be separated from it by thousands of years. A historian who takes this as a point of departure stops telling the sequence of events like beads on a rosary. Instead, he grasps the constellation which his own era has formed with a definite earlier one. Thus he establishes a conception of the present as a 'time of the now' [*Jetztzeit*] which is shot through with chips of Messianic time." Walter Benjamin, "Theses on the Philosophy of History" [1940], in *Illuminations*, ed. Hannah Arendt, trans. Harry Zohn (London: Fontana, 1973), p. 265.

them constellates, but not perhaps in the historical materialist way that Benjamin had in mind. Each does so differently, for different reasons, and each actually presumes a different kind of spectator. How would you describe these differences?

CB: There are basically three museum models we can turn to (and here I am indebted to the writings of Manuel Borja-Villel, director of the Reina Sofía): the modern, the postmodern, and the contemporary.[2] MoMA, New York, is, of course, the obvious example of the modern museum. It is invested in chronological history mediated through the white cube, and its destination is the modern notion of the public (that is, a universal subject uninflected by questions of race, class, or gender). By contrast, the apparatus of the postmodern museum (Tate Modern, for instance) is multiculturalism, seen in its equation of contemporaneity with global diversity; this is mediated through marketing addressed to the multiple demographics of economically quantifiable "audiences." Borja-Villel argues that a contemporary museum might instead be understood as an archive of the commons, in which the collection activates multiple, competing modernities (rather than the exclusivist narrative of modernism, or the inclusive narrative of multiculturalism). Within this framework, the work of art is seen as a transitional object, leading to radical education. The pedagogical model here is drawn from Jacques Rancière's idea of the ignorant schoolmaster.[3]

2. Manuel Borja-Villel, contribution to the conference *The Now Museum*, convened by Independent Curators International in collaboration with the CUNY Graduate Center and the New Museum in New York, March 2011. For videos of the *Now Museum* presentations, go to http://curatorsintl.org/events/the_now_museum. See also "Talk between Charles Esche, director of the Van Abbemuseum Eindhoven and Manuel Borja-Villel, director of the Museo Reina Sofia Madrid," n.d. (2012), http://vanabbemuseum.nl/en/newsletter/agenda/agenda/.

3. Jacques Rancière, *The Ignorant Schoolmaster: Five Lessons in Intellectual Emancipation* (Stanford: Stanford University Press, 1991).

Of course, when we discuss museum models we are always dealing with an ideal spectator—the one silently presupposed by the institution—rather than actual visitors in all their statistical diversity. But this way of thinking allows us to see the extent to which a museum's decisions about how to hang its collections are always profoundly ideological. When I presented these ideas recently to colleagues in other departments at my university, I was surprised to find that some of them never think about a museum's construction of meaning through the arrangement and juxtaposition of objects. It was news to them that art historians do a two-fold reading whenever we go to a museum: we look at the works, and we look at how the museum has arranged these works. We deploy two registers of looking simultaneously.

MODERNIST BEMUSEMENT

TS: Let's take up the first of these museum models of spectatorship, the modern. In your book you mention Rosalind Krauss's 1990 essay "The Cultural Logic of the Late Capitalist Museum." It is well known and rightly celebrated for its pungent attack on the spectacularization of art museums in the latter decades of the last century. It is titled in homage to Fredric Jameson's famous definition of postmodernism from a New Left perspective—his own, very specific one—as "the cultural logic of late capitalism."[4] Near the beginning of her essay is a passage that's always struck me as a very strong description of what it was like to look at works of art in museum settings during late modernity (and still is, in many places). Krauss vividly evokes her experience of visiting, in 1990, an exhibition of U.S. Minimalist, post-studio, and Conceptual works from the Panza Collection at the Musée d'Art Moderne de la Ville de Paris, in the company of the museum's director Suzanne Pagé, who curated the show.

4. Fredric Jameson, "Postmodernism, or, The Cultural Logic of Late Capitalism," *New Left Review*, no. 146 (July–August 1984), pp. 59–92, in Fredric Jameson, *Postmodernism, or, The Cultural Logic of Late Capitalism* (Durham, N. Car.: Duke University Press, 1991), pp. 1–54.

Pagé explains her effort to present the work in a sympathetic way by stripping down the museum's *deco moderne* settings, which originate from the late 1930s. It seems to Krauss that some of the neutralized rooms work well in themselves, but at one point Pagé draws her attention to the effect that she found "somehow most riveting." It is not the presentation of a particular work or even a single room installation; it is a view through a large doorway to "the disembodied glow produced by two... Flavins, each in an adjoining room." Despite the apparent beauty of this effect, Krauss undergoes an existentialist moment of horror and disgust. She is repelled by the thought that the display itself has become more powerful, aesthetically, than the actual work. I cite her conclusion: "We are having this experience, then, not in front of what could be called the art but in the midst of an oddly empty but grandiloquent space of which the museum itself—as a building—is somehow the object."[5] By using the artwork to prioritize itself, the museum instantiated what most appalled her (and Jameson) about late capitalist economic logic: its denigration of production, of skill-based work, in favor of *leveraging* what already exists into a baseless surplus fit only for awestruck, thoughtless consumption.

I share this view. But not in favor of what was then its opposite: the sense that there has to be absolute criteria for what counts as serious art, and that everything else is something lesser. Today, many late modernists—or, as I name them, "remodernists"—insist on a fractured, embattled version of seriousness, one that has maintained itself through and against the inane spectacle of postmodern art, and market-oriented contemporary art. Attention to the signs of this struggle becomes a mode of viewing that persists, although perhaps mostly, and, increasingly, only, in New York.

CB: Does the model of an individual viewer having a deep, rich

5. Rosalind Krauss, "The Cultural Logic of the Late Capitalist Museum," *October*, no. 54 (Fall 1990), pp. 3–4.

encounter with a single work of art, regardless of its context, remain at all relevant, or has a shift occurred that renders it utterly anachronistic? The ideal spectator presupposed by Krauss in 1990 remains very close to the one put forward by Michael Fried in his essay "Art and Objecthood" of 1967.[6] But today, the experiential richness of an exhibition is more curatorial in character than ever before. We look at individual works, but also at how these have been juxtaposed to resonate with each other and with the space that contains them. This change—in which the importance of the individual work of art is demoted in favor of the ensemble or constellation—was in fact implicit in Minimalism, as Robert Morris acknowledges in his "Notes on Sculpture."[7] But Fried resisted the logic of this expanded or diffused focus.

TS: There is no doubt that exhibitions are becoming more self-consciously curatorial, and that we are more aware of the museum experience as being overtly curated. This leads all of us away from the singular work of art paradigm toward the idea of an exhibition as consisting of individual works of art that, precisely because of their selection from among an array of others, and through their organization, accumulate into the curated equivalent of a *Gesamtkunstwerk*. Szeemann's idea of the exhibition as a total work of art has become almost normal these days. Indeed, the term "work of art" seems unnecessary for what is basically an artfully arranged display. The real point is that it is the exhibition—over and above each artwork within it—that is the work, and that puts us to work. The exhibition is the complex aesthetic experience that invites us to unpack it and reassemble it as we go through it. This has always been true of exhibitions as mediums, but in a low-key, background sort of way. In recent years, the exhibition has come to the foreground for a convergence of reasons. From the 1970s through to the 1990s, it was artists who re-imagined the nature of exhibitions, then

6. Michael Fried, "Art and Objecthood," *Artforum*, vol. 5, no. 19 (June 1967), pp. 12–23.

7. Robert Morris, "Notes on Sculpture, Part II," *Artforum*, vol. 5, no 2 (October 1966), pp. 20–23.

museums as a whole, more than curators. Then, during the 1990s and in the first decade of this century, a few bold and inventive curators set the agenda, or at least much of it. Most recently, however, biennials have been curated by artists, or by curators acting as, or with, artists. How does this development factor into your narrative?

CB: The intersection of curating and "institutional critique" exercised by artists such as Hans Haacke, Joseph Kosuth, and Fred Wilson in the late 1980s and 1990s is very well known, so these exhibitions don't factor into my account. That said, they remain important for legitimating a more creative and polemical type of collection hang—such as those initiated by the Van Abbemuseum in Eindhoven. And it is not irrelevant that these projects took place exactly at the time when curatorial courses were being instituted to professionalize curating. Not that there was much traffic between these two, but it indicates that something was in the air during the early 1990s.

What these installations also consolidated was a trend for inviting artists into the museum to re-hang the permanent collection, albeit in a much more atmospheric mood. Consider how de-fanged MoMA's *Artist's Choice* series appears compared to *Mining the Museum* [Wilson, 1992] or *The Play of the Unmentionable* [Kosuth, 1990]. A transitional example might be Haacke's *Viewing Matters* [1999] at the Boijmans Van Beuningen in Rotterdam, for which the artist used works from the museum's storage, re-categorizing them and shifting the taxonomies in order to expose the inner workings of the institution. Haacke, as is his wont, drew attention particularly to the provenance of particular works of art and to the sources of wealth (often heinous) of the particular collectors who donated these specific works to the museum. Yet, in another part of that same exhibition, he curated a display that was distinctly Surrealist, using the model of the exquisite corpse as his rationale. This is much less discussed, but chimes with the highly subjective line of artist-curated exhibition making that is so dominant today—a lineage in which Warhol's *Raid the Icebox* [1971] is the most salient historical precursor. In this model, the only logic holding the exhibited materials together is the artist's own taste, sensibility, and identity. We see this in a slew of recent exhibitions curated by artists from Tacita Dean to Mark Wallinger and Grayson Perry. I'm naming British examples here, because British art institutions, especially Camden Arts Centre and National Touring Exhibitions, have particularly pushed this model of artist-curated exhibition since the early 1990s.

TS: Why Britain in particular?

CB: I have a student, Natalie Musteata, who is writing her dissertation on artist-curated exhibitions, so I hope she will answer this question! National Touring Exhibitions set up their series before the Young British Artists [YBA] phenomenon of the nineties, but the latter's glorification of the artist as celebrity certainly fuelled the trend, and you can't explain the overwhelming popularity of Grayson Perry's show at the British Museum [*The Tomb of the Unknown Craftsman*, 2011–12] without factoring in the YBAs' popularization of art and artists in the 1990s. That said, we shouldn't forget other models of artist-curated exhibitions pioneered in the UK, such as those organized by Jeremy Deller, which are more invested in the politics of popular culture. Deller's *From One Revolution to Another*, at the Palais de Tokyo in 2008, was a fantastic constellation of single-room exhibitions that drew a line from the industrial to the digital revolution. It included early Soviet approaches to music, glam-rock singers, and Deller's own *Folk Archive*.

TS: The Palais de Tokyo is the current incarnation of one wing of the museum that so shocked Krauss back in 1990. Do you see its program as postmodern or contemporary? Personally, I enjoyed the ways in which Nicolas Bourriaud and Jérôme Sans transformed it into a "*site de création contemporaine*." To me, it works not least because it has, since 2002, made a point of displaying its "deconstructed" interiors as a locational signifier, which distinguishes it from any other exhibitionary space or event venue. Remember the fluster during the same period about the Musée du Quai Branly, Jacques Chirac's museum for objects from African, Asian, Oceanic, and American civilizations? All the fuss about French condescension toward the arts of peoples they implicitly regard as "primitive." Compared to that, I felt that at the Palais de Tokyo there was a certain honesty in admitting one's location within spectacle in a no-fuss yet trendy kind of way. More importantly, from a curatorial perspective, displays at the venue often succeed because of the sense they convey of having been inserted into these leftover interiors, often into just some of them, leaving the unused parts as in-between spaces, gaps within what seems like an infinity of potentialities… places for parties, raves, meetings, that in turn become exhibitionary. It is remarkable that this sense has been sustained since 2002.[8]

CB: I'm not such a fan of the Palais de Tokyo. I remember when it opened and how artfully deconstructed its squat-like interior appeared in the context of the chichi 16th arrondissement. I was quietly pleased that one of the first artists to show there, Wolfgang Tillmans, insisted on being given a clean white wall!

However, the Palais de Tokyo is not a collection-based institution, and thus it tends to present the new and affirm the zeitgeist. My contention is that the burden and responsibility of a permanent collection is precisely the part of a museum that inhibits this kind of presentism, because it makes us think in several tenses simultaneously: the past perfect and the future anterior. It is a time capsule of what was considered culturally

8. A 2013 show at the Palais de Tokyo, *Nouvelles Vagues*, invited you to follow pink markings down the stairs, then across a number of floors, through no less than twenty-one discrete exhibitions. They ranged from quite conventional surveys of, for example, women artists who had worked in Paris for important periods in their lives (Amrita Sher-Gil, Saloua Raouda Choucair, and Zarina Hashmi, among others) through installations of works that suggested a kind of psychic pathway through an imaginary noir novel (*The Black Moon*, curated by Sinziana Ravini), to works commissioned for the occasion and for the site (such as Henrique Oliveira's sculpture *Baitogogo*, which fused the concrete supports of the building with wooden tree formations, tying them into a Gordian knot). On exhibition, therefore, were the various styles of contemporary curating.

significant in previous historical periods, while more recent acquisitions anticipate the judgment of history to come (in the future, this *will have been* deemed important).

There are, however, temporary exhibition venues that are doing a great job of presenting history in a dialectically contemporary fashion. Nottingham Contemporary's *Jean Genet* [2011], for example, took Genet's anti-colonial plays, his dialogue with the Black Panthers (for whom he was an advocate and spokesman), and his writings on Palestinian refugee camps as starting points for rethinking a constellation of incendiary cultural and political events. Publications, press photos, and video interviews were placed alongside murals and posters by Emory Douglas, Black Panther Party newsletters, and works by contemporary artists equally engaged in denouncing the ongoing occupation of the West Bank. I'm also a big fan of the work of Anselm Franke at Haus der Kulturen der Welt.

CONTEMPORARY POSTMODERNITIES

TS: Let's turn to the phenomenon of re-curating exhibitions and re-imaging the museum through its own exhibitionary history. One of your examples, the Van Abbemuseum, has committed itself to doing just this as a long-term project for over a decade now. How do you view this effort? Can such reflexivity continue to work with its local and international audiences?

CB: Since the arrival of Charles Esche as director in 2006, the Van Abbemuseum has been relentlessly experimental, exploiting the full resources of the institution—its collection, archive, library, and residencies—to present a catalogue of possible ways to exhibit its holdings. I'll just cite two examples. The first phase of *Play Van Abbe* [2009–11] emphasized institutional transparency and historical contingency: "Who are these 'players' within a museum and which stories do they tell?… How does the current director present the collection? In what way does an art museum position itself—both in the present and in the past?"[9] One display, *Plug In #34*, showed works that were acquired by Edy de Wilde when he was the museum's director from 1946 to 1963, while a further display, *Plug In #50*, showed the original kernel of the museum collection: twenty-six paintings (none by major international figures) bought by Henri van Abbe in the 1920s and 1930s. *Repetition: Summer Displays 1983* re-presented a collection display curated by Rudi Fuchs during his tenure as director, thereby drawing a sharp contrast between the approaches of Fuchs and Esche in order to explore how we perceive this conservative period today. These curatorial frames rendered the displayed works subject to a double temporality: as individual voices speaking in the present, but also as a collective chorus once considered essential at a previous historical moment.

The second part of *Play Van Abbe*, titled *Time Machines* [2010], grew out of the museum's ambition to be a "museum of museums" or a "collection of collections," and showed the history of ideological display and exhibition archetypes and models. Again, repetition was a key strategy: the museum revived the project, set in motion by Jean Leering when he was director in the 1960s, of collecting reconstructions of installations and environments. In 2007 the museum commissioned a reconstruction of Aleksandr Rodchenko's *Workers' Reading Room* [1925]; in 2009 it refabricated László Moholy-Nagy's *Raum der Gegenwart* [1930], invited the artist Wendelien van Oldenborgh to reconstruct Lina Bo Bardi's exhibition display system for the Museu de Arte de São Paulo [1968], and commissioned the Museum of American Art in Berlin to remake El Lissitzky's *Abstraktes Kabinett* [1927–28]. In this way, the Van Abbemuseum offers the apparatus of exhibition display as a vehicle of historical consciousness.

9. See http://www.vanabbemuseum.nl/en/browse-all/?tx_vabdisplay_pi1[ptype]=24&tx_vabdisplay_pi1[project]=546.

TS: It has struck me recently that the repetitions, revisitations, and restagings of past exhibitions that we are now seeing might amount to a parallel with one of the most positive streams in current art history: the mapping of alternative modernities during the twentieth century. This effort has really complicated the whole Euro-American-centered narrative of modernism, by actually tracking the ways in which different kinds of art, values, and structures were created in different parts of the world as they each underwent their different modernizations—and, in some cases, continue to do so.

While I applaud this undertaking as absolutely essential, there is a problem if it is presumed that modernization was the primary goal, and the key marker, of all the inventive and significant art made throughout the world since the eighteenth century. Indigenous artists, for example, while they might renovate their traditions, were rarely modern*ists*. The same holds for most cultures in which craft traditions predominate, and in others where specific mediums have extensive histories, like ink painting in China.

Another problem with the alternative modernities project is the assumption that it is ongoing, that it encompasses the whole of the present. Rather, I would argue that these twentieth-century modernisms, traditionalisms, neo-traditionalisms, and indigeneities actually feed into the multiplicities of difference that constitute contemporaneity. Modernisms today are a vital if anachronistic part of one of the currents of contemporary art. Some artists have always understood this: thus the group IRWIN in Ljubljana, with their key concept of retro-avant-garde, an understanding of counter-historicizing, or instant self-historicizing, which they arrived at during the breakup of Yugoslavia. Do you think that parallel perspectives are emerging in curatorial practice now, in the repetition of breakthrough exhibitions such as *When Attitudes Become Form*?

CB: The fad for re-installing entire exhibitions could be seen as a belated historical appreciation of a creative phenomenon that was almost unrecognizable, let alone analyzable, the first time around. But I would not call this "retro-avant-garde." IRWIN's use of anachronistic sources in their paintings of the 1980s was a particular response to the political (and aesthetic) impasse of the post-Tito era. Unable to move forward, the only solution was to move sideways and revisit the past—not by drawing on any old material, but on the most ideologically charged imagery of nineteenth- and twentieth-century art. The reconstruction of *When Attitudes Become Form* at the Prada Foundation in Venice seems more about exorbitant experimentation for its own sake—especially when you consider the architectural incommensurability between the Kunsthalle Bern and the palazzo Ca' Corner della Regina. The experiment was not uninteresting, but I don't think it needs to be repeated.

TS: The repeat strategy has had a profound effect on exhibitionary practice throughout Central Europe especially, as a direct outcome of intense collaborations between artists, artist groups, curators, and curatorial collectives. How do you see it playing out in the museum practice of, say, Zdenka Badovinac in Ljubljana?

CB: Badovinac's work at the Moderna galerija and MSUM in Ljubljana makes her, in my view, one of the most thoughtful and courageous museum directors in Europe. We should start by acknowledging that the whole question of how to display art history in Slovenia is very fraught, since the country only gained independence in 1991. The museums, therefore, have to reconcile two conflicting projects: the desire for nation-state representation, and the obligation to hold their own in a globalized, contemporary art world insistent on transnational (or even post-national) cultural production. The government would like both museums to face West in narrating the art of former Yugoslavia (since there was artistic communication with Austria and Italy throughout the Cold War), but Badovinac is insistent on also facing East, to the Soviet Bloc, with which there was less contact, but whose ideological context was more comparable to the Slovenian situation.

I think there are two points to note about MSUM, the contemporary art branch at Metelkova. The first is that its entire display is organized around thematic categories relating to overlapping temporalities: "ideological time" (the socialist past), "future time" (unrealized modernist utopias), "time of the absent museum" (when artists compensated for the absence of a developed art system by self-organizing), "retro time" (when artists began to self-historicize), "lived time" (body and performance art), "time of transition" (from socialism into capitalism), "war time" (the conflicts of the 1990s), "dominant time" (present-day global neoliberalism), and so on. Contemporary art is staked as a question of *timeliness*, rather than as a stage on the conveyor belt of history. And as at the Van Abbemuseum, MSUM privileges art driven by a commitment to emancipatory traditions; there are, for example, no big-market players in the collection (no Damien Hirst, Matthew Barney, or Jeff Koons).

The second point is Badovinac's response to the dramatic cuts in cultural funding exercised by the Slovenian government. The museum has dealt with this by *repeating* the presentation of its inaugural collection display, *The Present and Presence*, in a slightly expanded and revised form. *The Present and Presence—Repetition 1* [April–October 2012] justified this repetition in a devastating five-point manifesto.[10] The museum has subsequently rehung *The Present and Presence* two more times: *Repetition 2* [October–November 2012] and *Repetition 3* [January–June 2013], focusing on movement and the street, respectively. This strategy is a radical, obdurate way to make reductions in cultural funding evident to the public.

10. See http://www.mg-lj.si/node/856.

THE CONTEMPORARY COMMONS

TS: Where does the idea of the commons fit now, in terms of kinds of spectatorship? Is the concept a quantitative or a qualitative one? Around the world, in all sorts of contexts, there are a growing number of spectators—individuals, groups, participants—whose continual visits to local and other museums, art spaces, and performances keep enriching their experience of art, its histories, and its possibilities, and whose engagement with art is well-informed, multi-faceted, and includes critical participation. The three places you mention are doing their critical exhibitionary work, very much with the participation of their relatively small numbers of informed spectators. But the spectacularization of culture has also led to massive numbers of people attending very well-known art museums, shuttling through them, cameras flashing, in quantities that sometimes seem to threaten the physical capacities of the works, the buildings, and the staff.

Some museums are responding by trying to address both types of spectator at once, to become places for the high art experience *and* sites where social and personal values may be interrogated and transformed. Thus Tate Modern director Chris Dercon's idea of having three drivers within the museum: Tate Curatorial, Tate Learning, but also Tate Exchange, a kind of open site for cultural transformation. He wants, somehow, to operate all three of Borja-Villel's models—modern, postmodern, and contemporary—at once, and on a scale commensurate with the vast attendances at that museum. This is a very contemporary ambition, a kind of mad leap into contemporaneousness, letting the chips fall where they may.

CB: I don't know so much about Dercon's tripartite mission for Tate Modern, but I have reservations about the centrality of corporate sponsorship to Tate Exchange (which is underwritten by BP). The language on the Tate's website is one of innocuous appreciation—albeit updated to reflect digital participation. The real question for me is, if the BP Tate Exchange is a "driver," then where is it heading? The first Tate Exchange collaboration featured a teacher from South Korea collaborating with children and teachers from Puerto Rico, Japan, and Turkey. Why these four countries, and to what ends are they collaborating? The rhetoric is entirely one of "fun" and "adventure" and '"creativity." It's completely depoliticized, leaving one to suspect that the ideological motivations are a renewed form of Western imperialism. (Certainly this is reflected in the Tate's unselfconscious desire to be a global art museum, with forty percent of its exhibition budget now dedicated to art from Africa, Latin America, and the Middle East.) Tate Exchange strikes me as the school-kid version of the New Museum's Museum as Hub initiative, by which that institution gains all the cultural cachet of being "global," while participating organizations in Egypt, Mexico, Lebanon, Seoul, et cetera remain the off-shore suppliers of outsourced content.

TS: Manuel Borja-Villel's conception of the contemporary museum as an "archive of the commons" is one that you find strongly suggestive. How do you see it operating at the Reina Sofía? How might it work elsewhere?

CB: Although still a work in progress at the Reina Sofía, I think it can be seen in the ways in which the museum acquires and catalogues works of art—through, for example, collaborating with Red Conceptualismos del Sur, a research network founded in 2007, which attempts to preserve local histories and the political antagonism of Conceptual art practices produced under the Latin American dictatorships. Cooperation with this network necessarily influences how the museum acquires work from this region. Rather than buying up artists' archives wholesale, like Tate in Latin America or Viennese institutions in Eastern Europe, the Reina Sofía devises new ways of operating. For instance, the Chilean group CADA [Colectivo de Acciones de Arte, 1979–85] recently offered their archive to the Reina Sofía, lacking confidence that a Chilean institution could preserve it. The museum hired two researchers to catalogue the archive and worked to ensure that an institution in Chile would house it, in return receiving an exhibition copy of all materials for their archive.

The work of CADA consists primarily of performances, actions, and interventions, so the material remains of their process are documentary. As Boris Groys has observed, today the line between the work of art and its documentation is negligible; indeed, most of the time we are looking at what he calls "art documentation"—because the art actually happened elsewhere, and earlier.[11] This documentary status increasingly defines the most politically engaged art of the late twentieth century. So, in order to redefine itself as an "archive of the commons," the Reina Sofía is attempting to legally re-categorize certain works of art as "documentation." This re-categorization serves to increase accessibility—for example, the public can go to the library and handle "art documentation" alongside publications, ephemera, photographs of works of art, correspondence, prints, and other textual materials. The museum is thereby reframed as a collection available to everyone because documentation is not a question of national property, but a universal resource.

TS: In your book you argue that recent critical thinking about contemporary art has failed to come to terms with the changes that are occurring in art and in the world. Can you specify how, and why?

CB: I'm making a point about art history, rather than critical theory. The former remains rather locked within the discipline when compared to the kind of adventurous cross-disciplinary work we see in major exhibitions like *Animism*.[12] Along with

11. Boris Groys, "Art in the Age of Biopolitics: From Artwork to Art Documentation," in *Art Power* (Cambridge, Mass.: MIT Press, 2008).

12. *Animism*, Haus der Kulturen der Welt, Berlin, 2012, curated by Anselm Franke. See http://hkw.de/en/programm/2012/animismus/veranstaltungen_68723/veranstaltungsdetail_71987.php.

Susan Buck-Morss's work on "global art history," your theorizations of contemporary art and contemporaneity have been hugely useful for me—indeed, they are what really set in motion a lot of the thinking about the contemporary that I and others are currently doing.[13] But in general, contemporary art history, despite being the biggest boom area in the academy, is still churning out monographs on artists active in the 1960s and 1970s—both the usual suspects and lesser-known figures. Very few Ph.D. students seem willing to look at art as part of a broader cultural phenomenon, to be more adventurous, and to think creatively across disciplines. Perhaps this is simply too much to ask of graduate students, but I hope that we can start to shift this mentality.

In tandem with this, art fairs and galleries are equally preoccupied with resuscitating yet more minor, overlooked, or forgotten figures from the 1960s and 1970s. This is not to say that a minor figure can't provide perspective on this period—look at Branden Joseph's fantastic book on Tony Conrad.[14] More frequently, however, we see the same old monographic formulas being trotted out. It's the constellation question again: how can you mobilize an artist's work to tell new stories?

TS: It reminds me of the 1970s, when everyone became obsessed with the 1850s and 1860s in Paris.

CB: Back then there was a political reason: understanding post-1968 politics meant going back to mid-nineteenth-century France.

TS: And, specifically in terms of art, going back to the conflicted beginnings of modernism was essential if we were

13. Susan Buck-Morss, *Dreamworld and Catastrophe: The Passing of Mass Utopia in East and West* (Cambridge, Mass.: MIT Press, 2000), and *Thinking Past Terror: Islamism and Critical Theory on the Left* (London: Verso, 2003).

14. Branden Joseph, *Beyond the Dream Syndicate: Tony Conrad and the Arts After Cage* (Brooklyn: Zone Books, 2008).

to work our way out of its ending without falling into the trap of "anything goes," which was postmodernism's huge mistake. Is something similar occurring in "contemporary art" now?

CB: The flurry of questions around "the contemporary" a few years ago certainly indicated a need to take stock and find consensus regarding a term that has become institutional and ubiquitous. But I don't think there's any necessary reason why contemporary art has to keep returning to the 1960s and 1970s, given that its essential features derive from the historic avant-garde. It's probably just an Anglo-centric attraction to the glory days of New York (hey, no languages necessary for this dissertation!), fuelled by political nostalgia for 1968.

Which brings me to articulating the difference between your understanding of contemporaneity as a state of affairs (the clashing and asynchronous co-existence of multiple modernities) and my own understanding of the contemporary as a dialectical method or operation, potentially applicable to all periods. Rather than claiming that many or all times are present in each historical object (as per Georges Didi-Huberman), we need to ask *why* certain temporalities appear in particular works of art at *specific* historical moments.[15] Furthermore, this analysis is motivated by a desire to understand our present condition and how to change it.

TS: The concept of contemporaneity operates in all of the registers that you mention, and then some. It highlights the co-temporality of differences as a condition that is always potentially present in world being, always in specific ways at particular times and places, and in individual artworks or collective practices. This gives historians, and art historians, a different set of tasks than those offered by nationalist narratives, or accounts of art's autonomy, which preoccupied us during the modern era; now, our first job is to identify and articulate these temporal specificities.

15. Georges Didi-Huberman, *Devant le temps: Histoire de l'art et anachronisme des images* (Paris: Editions de Minuit; Critique Edition, 2000).

I also claim that, in recent times, the contemporaneousness of irreconcilable difference has become the most evident, paradoxical aspect of our shared worldwide condition, displacing and reconfiguring the modernities and not-modernities that initially constituted it, and which are being rapidly rendered anachronistic, in art as elsewhere. Our challenge is to be exact about how the many different kinds of art producers, enablers, and consumers are dealing with this situation. Step one: stop generalizing about "contemporary art" and "the contemporary" as if they are unitary phenomena. Step two: go, as you say, to the specifics. But the really important step is number three: show how the specifics operate within the overall world situation, how they reveal it, and how they might contribute to changing it for the better.

CB: I agree with much of what you're saying, but I think the main difference between us is a relationship to post-Marxism. The examples I am taking my lead from are all overtly leftist, meaning that they have a particular investment in rebooting the legacy of communist thinking. Moreover, it is this political commitment that motivates and produces institutional experimentation. (This is why I doubt that their methods can be imported to museums like Tate or MoMA unless there is a radical change of leadership in those institutions.) My book *Artificial Hells* concerns the way in which specific political affiliations (most frequently on the left) gave rise to participation as a privileged artistic form; to an extent, the new book on museums continues this project.[16] The idea of dialectical contemporaneity is underpinned by the (often elusive) theories of Walter Benjamin, and as such aspires to be a method potentially applicable to all historical periods. I find the politics of your account to be more liberal than leftist, but correct me if I'm wrong.

16. Claire Bishop, *Artificial Hells: Participatory Art and the Politics of Spectatorship* (London: Verso, 2012).

TS: "Liberal"?! That description would come as a surprise to those who have closely followed my work since the late 1960s, as it does to me now. But whatever *I* think drives my individual consciousness, we are all of us (as Marx demonstrated in 1859) primarily social beings, so I have to wonder, what is it about my presentation of these issues that would prompt such a (mis)reading?[17] If you are referring to my larger project—i.e., thinking through the ontology of contemporaneity, the ethics of co-temporal difference, and the geopolitics of planetarity—then all such labels are a narrowing, to put it mildly. Indeed, to me, the left-liberal-right distinctions make sense only as shorthand for coalitions of convenience with conventional social democratic politics. Orientators such as "post-Marxism" are weak signifiers, on a parallel to "postmodernity." These are placeholders that have, for a generation now, pleaded for time to come up with a better modernism, a more equitable, less authoritarian, unbureaucratic modernity, a utopia that will not fail us. Meanwhile, all over the world, the reactionaries, the fundamentalists, and the security seekers have morphed to fill the vacuum, with ever more disastrous consequences. By working against this grain, I think the projects you describe present criticality in their circumstances *and* are prefigurative of a kind of world being that has to be more worldly *and* more internally differentiated than anything Marx was able to conceive, or Marxism able to elaborate.

ESCAPE TIME

TS: Let's conclude by considering a counter-example, a recent, widespread mode of curating that we have not yet discussed. It takes up the current thirst for "pastness," but it amounts, in my view, to an effort to turn art's back on the demands of contemporaneous difference. While you and I (in our

17. Karl Marx, *A Contribution to the Critique of Political Economy* [1859], preface, in Karl Marx and Frederick Engels, *Selected Works* (Moscow: Progress Publishers, 1968), pp. 180–84.

different ways) might take the dispositions of power in the past to have had actuality and necessity, and to understand them as bearing heavily on the present, there is clearly a thirst out there for the consciously non-historical, or even contra-historical. Some exhibitions emphasize the a-temporality of art, its time-transcendent values; they dream of a pure "land" of art. For example, as we speak here in Sydney, Jean-Hubert Martin has just finished curating the exhibition *Theater of the World*, at the Museum of Old and New Art, Hobart, in which he brings together items from David Walsh's, the museum's founder, collection of Saatchi-style YBAs with items from the ethnographic collections of the Tasmanian Museum and Art Gallery. This kind of show continues the trend of exhibitions Martin has curated, from *Magiciens de la terre* [1989] to *Artempo: Where Time Becomes Art* [2007]. It is always enchanting to wander around settings such as the Palazzo Fortuny, and some conjunctions can be stunning, but usually the connections made are those of formal coincidence across the centuries, or generalizations about the universality of human emotions. To me, these shows embody a desire to escape the challenges of contemporaneous difference, to take off for eternity, in the name of the timelessness of art. What do you think? What's your take on these kinds of shows?

CB: I'm not particularly interested in such shows, although they can offer a seductive aesthetic frisson if you're in the mood. It seems to be telling that—with the exception of *Magiciens de la terre*—it is always private collectors supporting these exhibitions, and they have a strong curatorial hand in their conception and staging. This is true at the Museum of Old and New Art, and at the Palazzo Fortuny in Venice. Insel Hombroich near Düsseldorf is another collection where Western and non-Western works are shown together in pristine white cubes, with no labels and no information. For me, these come under the rubric of the collector-curator, as distinct from the artist-curator.

TS: That makes me think of Ydessa Hendeles from Toronto, who collects works not only for her private collection but also to create temporary exhibitions in her own museum. These exhibitions often travel to other museums, or commercial galleries, where they have a character somewhere between an imported show and an installation. Hendeles calls them "curatorial compositions," and many are strikingly inventive. Just last month, she accepted the label "artist" for one of these compositions. Merges such as this seem indicative of the post-institutional critique moment within curatorship.

CB: Well, this underlines an important point: the constellation isn't itself automatically a political mode of re-writing, because there are also extremely subjective, highly aestheticized modes of constellation making that can actually be quite regressive.

TS: Exactly. It isn't always a critical activity. After all, as Benjamin showed us, the Parisian arcades were constellations of a sort: intense concentrations of capitalism's fantastical, inventive energy. Now, they barely cling to life on the borders of the city's tourist districts. But they still draw visitors, such as me, when we wish to indulge nostalgic feelings about modernity as contemporaneity's antiquity.

Zdenka Badovinac

Continuities and Ruptures in Museums of Modern and Contemporary Art

Zdenka Badovinac has been director of Moderna galerija, Ljubljana, since 1993. In 2011, she launched the Museum of Contemporary Art Metelkova, in the Metelkova district of Ljubljana, of which she is also director. She has curated numerous exhibitions presenting both Slovenian and international artists, notably the exhibition *Body and the East: From the 1960s to the Present* (Moderna galerija, Ljubljana, 1998; Exit Art, New York, 2001); the first public display of the Arteast 2000+ Collection, *The Art of Eastern Europe in Dialogue with the West* at Moderna galerija (2000); and a series of Arteast exhibitions, mostly at Moderna galerija, including *Form-Specific* (2003); *7 Sins: Ljubljana–Moscow* (2004; co-curated with Viktor Misiano and Igor Zabel); *Interrupted Histories* (2006); *Arteast Collection 2000+23* (2006); *The Schengen Women* (2008); and *NSK from Kapital to Capital* (2015). Her other major projects include *unlimited.nl-3* (de Appel, Amsterdam, 2000), *(un)gemalt* (Sammlung Essl, Kunst der Gegenwart, Klosterneuburg/Vienna, 2002), *ev+a 2004, Imagine Limerick, Open&Invited* (Limerick, 2004); *Democracies*, for the Tirana Biennale (2005); *The Museum of Parallel Narratives* (Museu d'Art Contemporani de Barcelona, 2011); and, with Snejana Krasteva and Bojana Piškur, *Grammar of Freedom/5 Lessons* (Garage Museum of Contemporary Art, Moscow, 2015). She was Slovenian Commissioner at the Venice Biennale from 1993–97, and again in 2005, and Austrian Commissioner at the Bienal de São Paulo in 2002.

We spoke at the Moderna galerija, Ljubljana, on August 23, 2013.

Terry Smith: I am very struck by the way that you have installed the "permanent" galleries of the Moderna galerija, here in Ljubljana. Like most museums, the building consists of a static series of rooms with a rather traditional ground plan, but you have arrived at what I think is a unique solution to the problem of showing art historical continuity and change within modern art. I am especially impressed by how you have tackled the problem of local specificity and internationalism, or, to be more direct about the power differentials, the exchanges between peripheries and centers—so complex and contentious during modern times, now perhaps even more so. You call your solution "the museum of parallel narratives." To me, it suggests a model that other museums might consider following. As well, you are director of the Museum of Contemporary Art Metelkova [MSUM], where you show work from Slovenia, from this region, and from elsewhere in Europe and around the world, but in another kind of way, one that I also think is very innovative, and highly suggestive for museums of contemporary art everywhere. I hope that we can discuss how you arrived at both these models, but can we begin with the situation here in the late 1980s, early 1990s? This was the time just before the breakup of the former Socialist Federal Republic of Yugoslavia [in 1992]; it was a critical moment for art in this region, and seems to be a pivotal crucible for your curatorial thinking.

TRAUMA TIME

Zdenka Badovinac: Let's talk about trauma. The biggest traumas for people involved in art in the time of socialism were, firstly, the unrealized ideals of communism, and, secondly, isolation—the lack of any consistent international, or internal, cultural policy. The post-war avant-gardes were marginalized and mostly worked in groups or in some kind of collective way to supplement institutional support. (Except in Albania, which was virtually a prison; in Romania, which was ruled by a very severe regime; and also in Russia, where exhibitions and events were organized in private apartments, by artists like Nikita Alexeev, or away from the centers, in remote areas of the countryside, by the Collective Actions group, for example.) The events organized by institutions mostly focused on building national myths. Nevertheless, things in Yugoslavia were quite open and vibrant. The Biennial of Graphic Arts in Ljubljana, founded by the Moderna galerija in 1955, was explicitly international. There were other international art, music, and theater festivals and biennials in Zagreb and Belgrade. There were also many youth and student culture centers, where non-official art found its place. One of the most notable was the Student Cultural Center [SKC] in Belgrade, which collaborated with artists such as Joseph Beuys and Art &

Language. In Zagreb, the Museum of Contemporary Art, which had an important international collection, was pretty receptive to new tendencies in art.

Despite these positive initiatives, most innovative and radical artists felt excluded and had to find their own way of operating and entering into international dialogues. In Zagreb, the renowned group Gorgona (formed in the early 1960s) published an "anti-magazine," so called to distinguish it from the usual art journals. Each issue was actually an artist's book, produced by a group member or an international artist. Josip Vaništa, the group's leader, made the first issue in 1961—two years before Ed Ruscha published his *Twentysix Gasoline Stations*, generally considered the first artist's book. Some very eminent international artists, such as Victor Vasarely, Dieter Roth, and the playwright Harold Pinter, participated in this project. In Ljubljana, several artists' initiatives in the 1960s and 1970s, like the OHO group, had good international connections, leading to, for instance, Walter De Maria visiting Ljubljana and OHO being included in the *Information* show at MoMA in 1970. Harald Szeemann thought about including OHO in Documenta 5, but refrained from doing so in the end, because their work was after all too different from Western Conceptualism. In Belgrade, Marina Abramović started her international career in the 1970s, then, in 1979, Goran Djordjević sent out a letter that initiated an international strike of artists.

International connections grew even stronger during the 1980s. Neue Slowenische Kunst [NSK] in Ljubljana made the idea of entering the international art world on an anti-Western-hegemony platform the basis of their aesthetic concept, which also functioned as a strategic tool for international communication. For me this was very important. In the late 1980s and early 1990s I learned more from artists than from my museum predecessors or colleagues. When I started serving as the director of the Moderna galerija in 1993, the new state had only just formed, and there was no official international policy—

it was one of my best periods precisely because of that. An old trauma became an advantage.

TS: So, you are saying that a positive, constructive challenge within the larger trauma of the breakup of the former Yugoslavia was the excitement of helping to construct a new phase of Slovenian culture, now that it was its own nation-state?

ZB: From 1945 to 1991, Slovenia was one of the six republics in the former Yugoslavia. At that time, the Moderna galerija here in Ljubljana was simply the main institution in one of the republics—in fact, you could say Slovenia was a province within a larger province. The central institutions were in Belgrade (now in Serbia). But even they did not have really important or comprehensive international collections that could narrate the development of international modern art.

My generation of curators, which entered the museum field in the late 1980s, still shared the idea of Yugoslavia as a society that wanted to be both integrative and outward looking, so of course we wanted to work more internationally. I would especially like to mention my dear colleague Igor Zabel, a curator at the Moderna galerija from 1986 until 2005, when he passed away.[1] We shared the same experiences and the same dreams, so to speak, and we were both closely associated with the strong community of artists of our generation. We started organizing small-scale international exhibitions at the Moderna galerija, mostly of prominent Western artists, who were more and more interested in presenting their work in our part of the world, in synch with the West's increased interest in Eastern Europe. When the war in the Balkans broke out, we turned to asking ourselves about the role of art and its institutions in such circumstances.

1. Igor Zabel, *Contemporary Art Theory*, ed. Igor Španjol (Zurich: JRP/Ringier, 2010) is a collection of Zabel's essays very relevant to the situation under discussion here.

Consequently, our focus shifted to our local social, political, and cultural context, and to emancipatory artistic traditions.

TS: That's fascinating because, in thinking of the 1980s, it's clear you're wrestling with a contradiction. You are part of a generation of curators, artists, and critics who are obviously internationalists, in a modern way, rather than contemporary globalists, as some people are thinking of themselves today. They have forgotten that the power of modern and avant-garde art was always its disruption of local power structures and its reach for connectivity with like-minded artists elsewhere. For my generation, even in faraway Australia, that kind of modernist internationalism necessarily opposed the narrow nationalisms that led to fascism and to national socialisms in Europe. Yugoslavia, as an idea, was intent on resolving that contradiction by creating a kind of intra-national culture that was also international in outlook. Then, in 1993, in the shadow of that history, you were given the job of actually creating elements of the culture of a new nation. This was an invitation to enter the land of paradox, I imagine. No wonder Slavoj Žižek is so fond of the parallax as a metaphor for the situation we have found ourselves in since those days. You published an amazing essay of his about these issues in 1993.[2]

ZB: Like elsewhere in this region these days, many people in Slovenia want to go back to what they imagine the nation was like before socialism, before the wars, even before representative governments. This is the dream of the conservative nationalist. NSK provided one of the most important instances of artistic deconstruction of the growing nationalism in the 1980s. By using the German language, which was not only the language of Nazism, but also a hegemonic language of the Austro-Hungarian

2. Slavoj Žižek, "Why are Laibach and NSK not Fascists?" *M'ARS*, vol. 3, no. 4 (Ljubljana: Moderna galerija, 1993), in Laura Hoptman and Tomás Pospiszyl, eds., *Primary Documents: A Sourcebook for Eastern and Central European Art since the 1950s* (New York: Museum of Modern Art, 2002), pp. 285–88.

Empire, they suggested that fantasies about pure nationalism inevitably lead to totalitarianism. (In addition, one of NSK's constituent groups, a music and multimedia group, took as its name "Laibach," the German name for Ljubljana, evoking strong public outrage, especially among the older generation who had experienced the German occupation during the Second World War. The other two constituent groups of Neue Slowenische Kunst are the visual arts group IRWIN and the Scipion Nasice Sisters Theater; subsequently they together formed the design group New Collectivism.)

NSK also utilized another extremely important strategy: eclecticism—finding ways of surviving with whatever resources you can lay your hands on. This is characteristic of the art of a small nation. It *is* traumatic to be forced to be eclectic, but it can also be an advantage if you heighten awareness of the basic insanity of playing with incompatible elements.

TS: Yes, I learnt a lot about that from Miško Šuvaković's chapter in Aleš Erjavec's book *Postmodernism and the Postsocialist Condition*.[3] There were related but different strategies throughout Central Europe, and also in Russia, Cuba, and China.

Yet, at the time, "postmodern" was the term used for most of these practices. "Post-avant-garde" reaches back—as it were *through* postmodernism—to the historical avant-gardes of the early twentieth century in Western Europe. Do you mean that for NSK and others, repeating the core strategies of the historical avant-gardes was, however futile, the only option, albeit in a context that had changed so much that doing so might seem absurd? This is what Ljubljana in the 1980s and 1990s looks like now: a time for paradoxical gestures inside a parallax universe.
ZB: It is important to understand NSK's critique as a postmodernist mixing of signs without a clear statement; this

3. Aleš Erjavec, *Postmodernism and the Postsocialist Condition* (Berkeley: University of California Press, 2003).

was even their political position. Here I want to mention Rastko Močnik's definition of alternative culture in Slovenia in the 1980s as the materialistic side of postmodernism. Postmodernist strategy, says Močnik, is a historical replay, while alternative culture is a transfer of the postmodernist principle to contemporaneity.[4] When NSK artists refer to national traditions, or when they quote from art history, they always do so from a precise critical position related to the present.

TS: This is a useful distinction, as it addresses the change from postmodernist strategies, so critical in this region during the post-socialist moment, to the challenges of dealing with our current condition.

I wonder how the IRWIN group's use of icons relates to this transition? Perhaps their goal is to discourage thinking in terms of inevitable historical progression by appealing to a practice that seems transhistorical or, at least, transcendent? Their works, their installations and performances, look like assemblages of icons, but actually work as anti-icons, because, I think, they disperse the concentrated singularity of how an icon requires you to see it.

ZB: You are right in the sense that it is not enough to approach an IRWIN icon as a discrete artwork. In 1996 the group picked out six images that were recurrent in the interactions between them and adopted those as their icons. The element of repetition is important here in my view, especially if their icons are understood as Orthodox icons, which have been painted in exactly the same style for centuries. There has been no modernization in icons, and the icon painter does not count as an author.

TS: A practice of repetition, almost like the ritual of religious observance?

4. Rastko Močnik, "Postmodernizem in alternativa," *Extravagantia* (Studia humanitatis, Minora, 1) (Ljubljana: ŠKUC, Znanstveni inštitut Filozofske fakultete, 1993).

ZB: Repetition becomes extremely important in the context of the Eastern European trauma of lacking a shared, collective narrative. To create histories you need to build a referential field. So you need icons. You recall Hal Foster's description of *Les Demoiselles d'Avignon* as *the* iconic work of modern art?[5] The painting is crucial to modern art's primitivist relationships to non-Western art, but it has also become an iconic image simply by being repeated so often in the historical narrative of modern art's evolution. But in the East, and in other non-Western contexts, there was no infrastructure that would enable repetition of this kind. Our history could not be built in this way.

TS: Which means that every work made outside the Western narrative is—or was, because we are talking about modern art here, not the contemporary condition—provisional, in the sense that it had to keep repeating itself in order to have a chance of establishing itself as historical. Is this what you mean by the trauma effect?

ZB: For me, trauma principally relates to the lack of proper infrastructure. As for IRWIN, you should always keep in mind that their work references the absence of a local art system, an established system of local references. From that point of view, their motifs, which they have been reproducing with variations for thirty years now, can be said to create a kind of self-reliant stability, their own narrative, their own planned history.

TS: Over the last twenty-five years, you and your artist-curator collaborators have established an iconic narrative, one that has eclipsed all other stories, as far as I can see. The counter-narrative proposed through this museum, the Moderna galerija, culminates in a room of work by IRWIN, and resumes at the Museum of

5. "At once eccentric and crucial, *Les Demoiselles d'Avignon* (1907) is the set piece of the Museum of Modern Art: a bridge between modernist and premodernist painting, a primal scene of modern primitivism." Hal Foster, "The 'Primitive' Unconscious of Modern Art," *October*, vol. 34 (Autumn, 1985), p. 45.

Contemporary Art Metelkova, with work by the same group. All the 1980s groups that we've been speaking about become the bridge and, in effect, a kind of platform, for subsequent Slovenian art. Is this positioning inspired by the retro-avant-garde principle of behaving as an avant-garde *after* the end of the historical avant-gardes?

THE MUSEUM OF PARALLEL NARRATIVES

ZB: Actually, there were very strong post-war avant-garde movements both here and in the so-called Soviet Bloc where Socialist Realism was early on replaced by modernism. (This was perhaps also due to the fact that Yugoslavia split from the Soviet Union in 1948 and developed its own unique model of socialism called "self-management.") So our idea was to build a collection of art with emancipatory potential from our own process of subjectivization. That was crucial for building our narrative.

This emancipatory potential lay at the core of NSK's interest in pre-war avant-gardes, although its interest in local traditions was more about the future than about the past. In this context the slight differences in the terminology used by the NSK members become significant. Dragan Živadinov of the Scipion Nasice Sisters Theater, for example, prefers the term "retrogarde" rather than "retro-avant-garde" to present his—and NSK's—work as the antithesis of the avant-garde. For Živadinov, "retrogarde" refers at least as much to the future as it does to the past; this is art that sees itself as somehow realized in the future. This has been a characteristic trait of his art since the early 1980s. He defines his performances as informances, as signs, as information, as the genes of something that will be born in the future with the help of his art, technology, and science. It is the same with IRWIN's icons, which are a form of self-generating institutional critique. It is as if they are saying that they don't need an art system because their art is building the ground for its own future.

TS: Can you describe how you incorporated this type of institutional critique in your museum?

ZB: Since the beginning of the 1990s we have been developing our own model, which we describe as "anti-hegemonic." Using the Moderna galerija's collection we actually present two different understandings of autonomy: one that has evolved through the inner logic of the art object and individual subjectivization, and another that results from the process of collective subjectivization and the performative role of art and its institutions in society. We show how they diverge for the most part, but, at other times, also clash or mix. We have incorporated our own local artistic traditions in the process.

Of the resulting two paths through our displays, one is propelled by modernism; it is sequenced in a linear fashion, and is called "the line of continuity." I will try to describe this "line" so that readers can imagine the experience of moving through the rooms, beginning with a long gallery that presents Impressionist works by Rihard Jakopič, Matej Sternen, Matija Jama, and Ivan Grohar. Next we have the Expressionist painters who gathered in the Young Artists' Club, such as France Kralj, Tone Kralj, Božidar Jakac, Ivan Čargo, Lojze Spazzapan, and Franjo Stiplovšek. Subsequently we show the impact of German Neue Sachlichkeit [New Objectivity] on artists such as Veno Pilon. This leads into the second large room in the sequence, where we show the works of Slovenian artists from the 1930s who became known as the Independents: sculptors Zdenko Kalin, Karel Putrih, France Gorše, and Tine Kos; painters Stane Kregar, France Mihelič, Zoran Mušič, Maksim Sedej, Marij Pregelj, and Gabrijel Stupica; and many very good photographers. These artists really came to the fore soon after the end of the Second World War, some of them with abstract works. Then we have a large room devoted to modernism in the 1950s and 1960s, which leads into another large space for the Art Informel of Janez Bernik, for example, then the Neo-Constructivist sculptors, whose work parallels Minimalism and Kinetic art. Finally, we track the new abstraction of the 1970s through artists such as Tugo Šušnik and Gustav Gnamuš, and in the last room we present New Image, or revived figurative, art, which was prominent in the 1980s.

TS: As we walked around, I noticed that the walls in each space are treated in a distinct way. This is certainly not a sequence of white cubes. Can you say a little more about how you subtly change the basic format of the installation in each space?

ZB: Well, the New Collectivism group designed the rooms, and each is related to the kind of environment and conditions that the works were made for. For instance, the Impressionist paintings were intended for private rooms, so the works hang at different levels, and next to plants. A more subtle touch is that the wallpaper, which from a distance looks like something you might find in a bourgeois home of the period, is actually patterned with dots based on Impressionist theory—when you look at it more closely, you realize that it demonstrates how the eye perceives color, so it is a comment on the style itself. In the same room we document the establishment of the first public gallery in Slovenia, which marks the beginning of the modern art system here, and which was initiated by one of the Impressionists, Rihard Jakopič, whose works hang in the room.

The color of the walls in each room differs slightly. Of course, during the 1930s and 1940s, public museums and artists were aware of the white cube ideal, but it was not widely adopted until after the Second World War, when the Moderna galerija opened and the most important Slovenian modernist painters began thinking of themselves as artists making art for the abstract space of a modern museum. At the same time, don't forget that these were state-sponsored artists. The most renowned of them, such as Marij Pregelj, Gabrijel Stupica, and Drago Tršar, were privileged, one could almost say, sheltered by the state. They worked under excellent conditions—beautiful studios, professorships at the academy, and career privileges and recognitions. They got commissions for public art, mosaics, sculptures. Their art was neutral in terms of social or political critique. This created a climate in which artistic autonomy became self-evident and was accepted by society at large, in this way also serving the state, which wanted to show itself as modern. To emphasize this status we introduced a subtle line along the walls of that room, reminiscent of typical socialist interior design in the homes of that period. You will know it from Kabakov's installations; he uses these lines often. In our exhibition rooms, this line disturbs the neutrality of the white cube.

TS: So, you have gradual changes along the line of continuity. What about the other route, that of ruptures?

ZB: "The line of ruptures" links a set of smaller spaces, along the main central wall of the museum. Each one totally differs in style and design from the next and from the continuity rooms. Each is a singularity, you might say. First, there is a reconstruction of the *Trieste Constructivist Cabinet*, a famous exhibition held in 1927, collectively organized by a group led by August Černigoj. Next you enter a room of works by artists who joined the anti-fascist Partisan resistance during the Second World War: drawings, prints, posters, sculptures, paintings, and photographs. Then there is a major installation by OHO, which was very active locally and internationally during the 1960s, before it withdrew from the art system in 1971. Finally, there is the NSK room, the last "interruption" in our history of modernism, and also the terminus of both lines. So, you could say that parallel avant-garde and post-war avant-garde traditions have been created: a "tradition" of ruptures. It comes to a stop here, in the Moderna galerija, but it also points visitors toward our Museum of Contemporary Art Metelkova.

Of course, we also have spaces we use for monographic shows and other types of exhibitions related to the history of art in the twentieth century and to our collection. For example, we are currently staging a retrospective of Gabrijel Stupica, as well as exploring the theme of realism.

TS: Yet, in walking through all of these spaces, I sense that the line of ruptures is at the heart of the Moderna galerija's ethos.

ZB: You may have this feeling because that line, by continuing in the Museum of Contemporary Art Metelkova, occupies more space. We present it as the more important tradition for the concepts presented at Metelkova, for this moment of contemporary art, rather than as the absolutely more important. At the same time you should think about the two lines as about two parallel traditions that co-exist. It is true that, in the past, the line of continuity was privileged and the line of ruptures marginalized, but we do not want to go to the other extreme now. What we want to point out—for the first time in the life of our institution—is that there was something else besides the orthodox modernist line. It is also our point of departure for explaining our authentic interest in contemporary art.

AUTHENTIC INTEREST

TS: "Authenticity" is a loaded term, particularly in the context of debates within Europe about national belonging. What do you mean by it, specifically? How do you measure authenticity?

ZB: I wrote about this in 2010.[6] I was inspired by the argument of Luc Boltanski and Eve Chiapello, who showed how globalizing capitalists absorbed the counter-cultural spirit of the 1960s and the radical critiques of the 1970s to create the new spirit of capitalism.[7] Marx posited art as a model of unalienated work, of an authentic mode of life, but these capitalists took the ideals of freedom, authenticity, personal autonomy, creativity, and so on and made them the motors of new kinds of businesses. In order to develop a critique against this incorporation, and to get back

6. Zdenka Badovinac, *Avtentični interes*, ed. Petja Grafenauer (Ljubljana: Maska, 2010). Forthcoming in translation as *Authentic Interest* (New York: Independent Curators International, forthcoming, 2016).

7. Luc Boltanski and Eve Chiapello, *The New Spirit of Capitalism* (Paris: Gallimard, 1999; London: Verso, 2005), especially chapter 7, "The Test of Artistic Critique."

to an earlier understanding of art's potential, we need to redefine authenticity for the contemporary situation.

So, my understanding of authenticity relates more to performative than to descriptive characteristics. It lies in the active social and political interest that artists took in their specific local circumstances, and it is the line of ruptures that displays this interest. Of course, this doesn't mean that other artists were not active, or that they passively mirrored Western styles, but their art was less engaged in their immediate social situation. The avant-gardes of the 1920s were very critical of the local art system as a temple of bourgeois art. The Partisan artists were deeply involved in the struggle for national liberation. OHO's actions proposed an alternative to socialist or bourgeois subjectivities. By over-identifying with totalitarianism, NSK mirrored the inconsistencies of socialist ideology. So, "authentic" basically means active in a specific space and time, taking a stance toward local and global society.

TS: Actually, the Partisan room is a rare, if not unique, room. Mostly, even in places like Poland, you see such art in history museums. The only parallel that I can think of is Cuba's National Museum of Fine Arts, which has rooms of art from the 1960s, but that's a revolution achieved, and anyway they organize the displays around art historical categories and time periods.

ZB: Yes, I'm sure we are rather unique in that. Today, we could compare art of the anti-fascist resistance to contemporary art with a participatory or activist character. The Partisans devised many initiatives to encourage people to write, draw, and sing. They wanted to awaken the creativity of the masses, as a way of giving people an active position in society, and, more concretely, as a way of encouraging resistance to the German occupiers. So, it was like a broad cultural front that supported the resistance and led to a new society after the war.

TS: How does the idea of rupture apply in this case, when the goal of these Partisan artists was the opposite?

ZB: In most cases, Partisan art was a continuation of Socialist Realism, but we need to understand each moment as form-specific. We can also think of rupture from the point of view of the singularity of an international style, of how it behaves in a specific context. So, for us, authentic interest was resistance against uncritically following the dominant—okay, Western—styles that are shown in the line of continuity. Therefore, resistance was not about replacing such styles with authentic art, but with an awareness of the power relation between the center and the margin.

TS: Yes, I understand that dynamic. But it evokes the nationalism paradox again, because you have just said, basically, that the thinking and the practice of all the artists in the line of continuity—all Slovenian artists—is mainly Western in character: mediums, attitudes, styles. Then you say that the interruptions are more authentic, truly so. But they, too, use Western forms, ideas, procedures...

ZB: Even if we agree that these are Western forms, ideas, and so on, they behaved totally differently in the Eastern context. And our contemporaneity started when this behavior became a conscious part of an artwork, when artists no longer understood their style as simply universal. I defined this attitude as "form-specific" in an exhibition of the same name [2003]. What makes art form-specific is the way it understands itself, the way it is used and perceived locally. None of the local traditions that I've described here were pure in any essentialist or nationalistic way. At the same time we can say that some of them were more engaged than others in the struggle against local bourgeois art systems, against the imperialist aspirations of bigger European nations toward our nation of two million people, against global or Western cultural domination.

My point is that neither of the display lines is more important than the other in absolute terms; in fact, we can't think of one without the other, without the antagonism between them, or, better, the dialectic between them. It is just that the line of ruptures somehow seems more relevant for contemporary artists today, precisely because of its broader interest in society at large, not only in Slovenia.

TS: I hear you saying that your schema has two contemporary resonances, one actual and historical, the other relating to our present concerns. First, the ruptures—the artists of the 1920s avant-garde, the Partisan resistance fighters, the OHO group, the 1980s retro-avant-garde—are examples of historical interruptions within an overall modernist development, breaks that expose the different kinds of art that were being made at the same time. Meanwhile, in the main rooms, a more even, although still quite dynamic, set of flows and exchanges goes along its modernizing way. Second, the contemporary relevance of the ruptures is that they prefigure the current situation, in which everything is rupture, continuity with the past seems mostly anachronistic, and the prospect of continuity into the future seems to shrink every day. Have I understood you correctly?

ZB: Yes; of course, every future is not a simple result of its past—it also has its own contemporaneity. In this respect, contemporaneity is a rupture already. And there are also ruptures in the modernist line, in terms of oppositions to previous styles, but here we are not talking about the inner logic of art. We can think about contemporary ruptures in terms of anti-neoliberal, anti-commercial, anti-corporate, and anti-dominant cultural positions in the West.

TS: As well as the paths we have talked about, it is possible to walk through the rooms in a strictly chronological way, so that you go from a phase of modernism through a rupture then through another phase until the next rupture, all the way to the NSK terminus. Looked at in this way, the ruptures could also be seen as a set of four avant-garde moments within the larger narrative, but, really, my sense is that, say, the Constructivists were doing something different than the Independents, the Partisans did not have a big impact on the abstract artists of the 1960s and 1970s, nor did the Conceptualists on local New Image painting. On the other hand, looking back from NSK to the earlier ruptures, you certainly sense a strong, if broken, lineage.

ZB: Exactly; there was little direct dialogue between the artists, or if there was, the relations were antagonistic, critical. For example, you can find the statement "a painting is a luxury" in the room of the Constructivists, in reference to the contemporary painters in the previous rooms.

POST-WAR AVANT-GARDES

TS: Okay. That leads us to Peter Bürger's theory of the experimental art of the 1960s as being a repetition of the strategies of the early twentieth-century avant-gardes, but without their social and political agendas—a "neo-avant-garde," he calls it. This idea does not seem particularly relevant in Eastern and Central Europe after the collapse of communism, precisely because the social and political pressures of the situation, however attenuated, remained crucial. They will continue to be, unless, or until, the region becomes entirely neoliberal, which a lot of people wish for, but I doubt will happen—at least, I hope that it will not.

ZB: I agree; that's why we don't use the term. We talk about post-war avant-gardes rather than about the neo-avant-garde. The term "post-war" defines a concrete time period and the struggles within it. This is similar to the way we use the term "contemporary art." For me, the post-war avant-gardes end with the 1980s; after that time I use the term "contemporary art" to name the continuation of the same tradition of active artistic positions.

TS: I am struck by how many museums in Northern Europe, the Baltic states, and Scandinavia are historicizing this distinction between art of the immediate post-war period and contemporary art, usually art since around 1989. They absolutely prioritize the work of artists who are now engaged in revisiting art that was made in their country or region during the 1960s and 1970s.

ZB: That's understandable. In all Eastern European countries, the new generation of artists is interested in local traditions that are of relevance to their respective practices. And these traditions encompass far more than just dissident art. In the territory of the former Yugoslavia, for instance, there is strong interest in Partisan art; the self-management socialist system; the Non-Aligned Movement; unique modernist projects, such as the Croatian group Exat 51; socialist modernist architecture and urban planning; modernist public art; and socialist monuments. A lot of art today clashes with the newly re-written official histories that are trying to erase or downplay the emancipatory aspects of our socialist heritage. David Maljković, Tobias Putrih, and Darinka Pop-Mitić are some of the artists working along these lines, and they are not at all part of this dissident narrative that Western critics expect from contemporary Eastern European art.

EASTERN BODIES

ZB: *Body and the East* [1998] was the first Eastern European exhibition that we organized, and it was also the first contemporary re-historicizing exhibition in our region.[8] *After the Wall* at the Moderna Museet in Stockholm followed a year later.[9] One of my main concerns in *Body and the East* was to present art from the 1960s up to the end of the 1990s that somehow repeated the patterns and behaviors from its social and political contexts and thus made those contexts visible. For me, it was of paramount importance to stage the first Eastern European exhibition with art that spoke directly in the first-person narrative, without

8. The exhibition was held at the Moderna galerija, Ljubljana, in 1998. See Zdenka Badovinac, *Body and the East: From the 1960s to the Present* (Cambridge, Mass.: MIT Press, 1999).

9. David Elliot and Bojana Pejic, eds., *After the Wall: Art and Culture in Post-Communist Europe* (Stockholm: Moderna Museet, 1999).

translation, so I chose art that used the body as its primary material.

TS: In Europe after the Second World War, the body as a medium—obsessed with trauma, a kind of inner Holocaust—was a huge subject for artists, for obvious reasons. It is a theme that is repeatedly rehearsed by artists all over the continent. In Poland, it's incredibly strong: Tadeusz Kantor, for example, staged performances showing dismembered or misshapen bodies to wide audiences. But I don't see that so much here, in Slovenian art.

ZB: Slovenian performances in the 1960s and 1970s were not about self-torture, but rather about the universal inner human core, and in the 1980s about assuming different personas. I could not avoid presenting the traumatic experience of the body in socialist society, but I was interested in the problematic question of translating specific experience. This is directly related to another question: what goes missing in translation when presenting Eastern European art? These two questions were crucial for me in thinking about *Body and the East*. The answer to the first question was that there is no absolute presence in body art per se. There is never an absolute coincidence between the action and the perception, because there is already a social construct embedded in the viewer's mind. Interpretation is therefore already a part of the actual act. However, I must say that, at the time, Marina Abramović would not have agreed with me about this.

TS: No, and even less nowadays, because she's seeking a totally visceral response, the sense that the spectator and the artist are absolutely in the same moment, right there—that nothing intervenes between them.

ZB: As I wrote in the catalogue, many artists in the West tortured their bodies. What was specific to our region was that, in the very act of self-mutilation, artists repeated the social experience of isolation or control. For example, when Tomislav Gotovac ran naked in the streets of Belgrade and Zagreb, he was arrested and put in jail, because his act immediately acquired a political dimension. As public performances were not permitted in Romania, Ion Grigorescu recorded himself on film, either with photography or video, which became, in this first instance, his only "audience." In fact, Katherine Verdery says Romanians experienced a meaningful self only in relation to an enemy. We could say something similar about other Eastern European artists; they constantly re-created an enemy in their performances. In her work *Rhythm 0* [1974], Abramović passively allowed the audience to use a range of objects on her semi-naked body. The gestures in the West may have been similar, but their meaning was different. This relationship of similarity and difference and these issues were my main interest then, and still are today, in whatever I do.

THE MUSEUM OF CONTEMPORARY ART

TS: Let's talk about the Museum of Contemporary Art Metelkova [MSUM], which is some distance away from historic center of the city, where the Moderna galerija is located. It is housed in the former barracks of the Yugoslav People's Army, which was squatted in from the early 1990s, becoming a famous "autonomous social center"; now, it is a complex with arts spaces, offices, clubs, bars, and a large open courtyard in the center. Entering MSUM, you walk through spaces that are filled with activity—a bookstore, videos, temporary installations, performances, and talks. The upper floors take us on an archival journey that begins at the retro-avant-garde moment, and pushes forward through the many directions that have been pursued since then. At this point you understand that there are two layers occurring simultaneously, or, better, contemporaneously: a reflexive yet distributed history of contemporary art since the 1980s hovers on the two upper floors, above a concentrated dose of one aspect of the legacy of that history, as it is occurring now, which is shown on the ground level as a temporary exhibition.

You have made some interesting statements about the character of a contemporary museum as distinct from a modern or even postmodern one. One was in an essay in *e-flux journal*, in

2009, called "Contemporaneity as Points of Connection." Let me remind you of what I think is the key passage:

> If the museum of modern art served certain universal paradigms, a master narrative, and the hegemonic goals of the big Western institutions, then the museum of contemporary art must serve the needs of local spaces so that they can enter as equals into dialogues with other spaces. In order for conditions to be at all possible for designing a museum of contemporary art as I describe it here, local spaces must determine their own work priorities, which cannot be universal. The pursuit of these principal objectives is necessary if a given space is to rid itself of backwardness and provincialism and become truly timely, and not merely concurrent with the West. The museum of contemporary art must make possible the perception of art as it has developed in various contexts.... It must also be a museum of history, a museum of a diversity of narrations and their presentation.[10]

This is, I take it, the model for Metelkova. Can you specify your approach to contemporaneity in the museum in more detail?

ZB: For me, the contemporary art museum has a position that is "active," in the sense that it questions the hegemonic view of what is contemporary, and it demonstrates that the tradition of ruptures is both foundational and continuous. That's why I think that we are not a postmodern museum. The postmodern museum is about pluralism, while the contemporary art museum is about taking a clear position, about breaking with the dominant interpretations of freedom, creativity, democracy, et cetera.

Accordingly, we present different narratives, often together with their narrators, the artists. We don't speak in their name or

10. Zdenka Badovinac, "Contemporaneity as Points of Connection," *e-flux journal*, no. 11 (December 2009). http://www.e-flux.com/journal/contemporaneity-as-points-of-connection/.

on their behalf; they are there, *in* their stories. I coined the term "self-historicization" to describe art practices in which artists do the work of historians and archivists, with regard to the specific local traditions that contextualize their work. For example, IRWIN defined their own genealogy of local traditions in a late 1990s version of their wall installation *Retro-Avant-Garde*, which is both an artwork and a historicizing tool that incorporates their influences and contexts into an organized system.

TS: What about the really strong research aspect of these works?

ZB: There are now three generations of artists either presenting archives as their artworks or historicizing artistic traditions. We start in the 1970s with, for example, Polish artists Zofia Kulik and Przemysław Kwiek, working under the name "KwieKulik"; Hungarian artist György Galántai; and Slovak artist Július Koller, to mention just some who compiled the best-known and most relevant archives that can also be used for serious research into their specific local conditions. They just accumulated materials relating to the work of their colleagues, exhibition records, examples of censorship, documents from the education system, and the like.

The second generation is that of the 1980s. When NSK was established in 1984, the three founding groups took on different roles. IRWIN assumed the role of chronicler using their medium, painting. Their recent project on the historicization of Eastern European art, entitled *East Art Map*, can't be properly understood without knowing their early concept of self-historicization.[11] An interesting example of the third generation of artists, which formed in the late 1980s and early 1990s, is Janez Janša, Janez Janša, and Janez Janša, three artists who each officially took the name of Slovenia's then prime minister, who was very right wing. Their appropriation of his name was a critique of his autocratic leadership. One of their best-known subsequent works is called

11. Group IRWIN, *East Art Map*, at http://www.eastartmap.org.

Mount Triglav on Mount Triglav [2007], which reviews the local tradition of collective practices through re-interpreting IRWIN's 2004 re-enactment of OHO's 1968 performance *Mount Triglav*. Crucial to all three groups of artists was the significance of Mount Triglav (meaning "three-headed mountain") as a Slovenian national symbol. Three members of the OHO group had "enacted" Mount Triglav by draping black fabric over their bodies so that only their heads jutted out. Their action was carried out in the center of Ljubljana. IRWIN chose the same location for their re-enactment of the performance, but intended it primarily for the camera. The material dimension of their work—a well-produced, nicely framed photograph—underscored the under-represented status of art projects from the 1960s in the history of Slovene art and the absence of a developed art market, as well as relayed interest in a professional and standardized presentation of art. The three Janezes were photographed in a similar manner, wrapped in a black cloth, but on the mountain itself. They then published this photographic documentation in three main Slovenian dailies (*Delo*, *Dnevnik*, and *Večer*). Repeating history in an artistic action underscores the previously marginalized tradition as well as the loss of the original meaning, which disappears through reproduction, creating a performative history.

TIME IN THE CONTEMPORARY ART MUSEUM

TS: I want to discuss the multiple times that co-exist within the very idea of contemporaneity, and how they might shape the contemporary art museum. In 2011, you wrote a valuable statement titled "The Museum of Contemporary Art and Its Time" in the little handbook *Glossary of the Present and Presence*, which is itself a great example of a discursive intervention—pocket size, full of sharp and critical glosses on various buzzwords. Anyway, the statement reads:

> The museum of contemporary art differs from the museum of modern art not only with respect to the time periods that they cover—here in fact they can overlap (the tradition of

> modernism remains alive today, while contemporary art also includes the history of this art). In contrast to the modern art museum, the museum of contemporary art is further characterized by a critique of the construction and universal application of linear time, and, consequently, also [offers] a critique of the modernist understanding of quality.

Then, after citing Boris Groys, as we all must these days, you add:

> For the continued growth of the contemporary art museum, it seems important to underscore antagonisms rather than conceal them in the guise of a diverse pluralism. We must ask ourselves, then: Which antagonisms in particular should the museum of contemporary art be interested in? One of the main antagonisms that affects the museum of contemporary art is the antagonism between local and global time. The time of the museum of contemporary art can be described as the interaction between, on the one hand, local time and space a nd, on the other, the processes of globalization that are increasingly forcing us to adopt a measurable understanding of time and space.[12]

What I find really interesting about the idea of these different times is that, at MSUM, you don't present just two—local and globalized—in battle with each other. Rather, you identify no less than eleven kinds of time that are, more or less, tempo-spatially co-existent.

ZB: Yes. We begin with the distinction between "the present" and "presence," or what most people mean by "the contemporary"—unthinking ways of being in the present, without any distinctions as to the different kinds of time—compared to actual, lived difference, that is, what is called "contemporaneity." So, we recognize all these different kinds of time, which I can briefly summarize for you.[13]

12. Zdenka Badovinac, "The Museum of Contemporary Art and Its Time," in *Glossary of the Present and Presence*, ed. Igor Španjol (Ljubljana: Moderna galerija, 2011), pp. 86–87.

13. Full descriptions may be found in Tamara Soban and Igor Španjol, eds., *MG+MSUM* (Ljubljana: Moderna galerija, 2012).

There is "lived" or "literal time," which we see in time-specific works, from the performances of Marina Abramović to the installations of Serbian artist Raša Todosijević. "Future time" interests artists in our region as something from the past to be realized in the future.[14] NSK founder Dragan Živadinov, together with Dunja Zupančič and Miha Turšič, initiated *Noordung 1995::2045, Biomechatronic Projectile* in 1995 as a way of researching the conditions of creativity in a state of post-gravity. The fifty-year time span of this project will enable them to employ the latest developments in science and technology in their performances, which are to happen every ten years. Opposed to this is the punk attitude of "no future," a kind of anti-time, a refusal of progressive time that was adopted by many artists in the 1980s, most emphatically by the band Pankrti. Then, there is "war time"; the war in the Balkans marked the beginning of our contemporaneity. Now, war happens everywhere, all over the world, so contemporary time is always war time. In this section, we show photographs taken during the ten-day war for Slovenia's independence in 1991, and Jenny Holzer's *Lustmord* piece from 1993–94, which relates to rape during the war in Bosnia and Herzegovina. "Ideological time" was the rule during the Cold War period. Its relation to individual life is shown, for example, in the monumental photographs of Braco Dimitrejević's *Casual Passer-by* series, which he has being making since the 1960s, or in Mladen Stilinović's *Red Era* installations [1973–90].

This leads us to what we call "dominant time," the time that globalization demands that we conform to. Dan Perjovschi's drawing on the entrance to MSUM illustrates this, not only in its title: *In 1990 we spoke about freedom, now we talk about money*. Resistance to this dominant time takes many forms. We call one of them "creative time": switching off, evasion, playfulness, inner-directedness—a self-portrait installation by Mirosław Bałka

14. Inke Arns, "Avant-Garde in the Rear-View Mirror: From Utopia under General Suspicion to a New Notion of the Utopian," in *7 Sins: Ljubljana–Moscow: Arteast Exhibition* (Ljubljana: Moderna galerija, 2008), p. 18.

introduces this quite substantial section. "Time of the absent museum" is probably the largest section, however. It is full of the self-historicizing and collective works we talked about earlier. To me, it's a specific Eastern European version of institutional critique in that it calls for art institutions where there are none, and starts to build them in a critical way. This is related to "retro time," which we discussed when we spoke about IRWIN's *East Art Map* and the performance by Janez Janša, Janez Janša, and Janez Janša. Another example is Kazimir Malevich's *The Last Futurist Exhibition* in Belgrade and Ljubljana in 1985 and 1986, respectively. Finally, there is "time of transition." To us, this is a bitter irony because it is a term often used in political discourse to describe our shift from socialism to capitalism, from a status of being "outside" Europe to being "inside" it in the sense of being a part of the European Union, with all its economic and political implications. But, fundamentally, nothing much has changed, at least not for the better.

TS: That's a very powerful, and contemporary, way to launch a museum! Straight into the multiple times of contemporary life, showing all the various temporalities, how they are moving at different speeds, yet through the same overall historical time.

MUSEUM FUTURES

TS: In recent years, new museums of modern and contemporary art have opened all over Eastern and Central Europe. The focus seems to be on international contemporary art, what I call the "first current" of contemporary art. Piotr Piotrowski told me that he had to leave the directorship of the Zachęta [National Gallery of Art] in Warsaw because the board and the city wanted it to be a kind of neoliberal contemporary art space. Is that spirit manifesting in Slovenia and elsewhere in the region? How do you see yourself working with or against it?

ZB: It's worse than that. Maybe in Poland it's different, because Poland is doing well economically at the moment. But here, after

Yugoslavia split up, many new problems surfaced, and economically we are still not doing well. In Zagreb they opened a very large museum, just a few years ago, with a great collection and 160,000 square feet of exhibition space. (We have just over 100,000 square feet over two buildings, to give you some sense of comparison.) But it soon became obvious that the building is simply too big and they are already having problems maintaining it.

In Ljubljana we are lucky to have renovated this building, the Moderna galerija, and to have a new building at Metelkova. Yet our economic situation is difficult, too. Metelkova opened toward the end of 2011. At the beginning of 2012 we were informed that there was no money for the program. So, we decided to repeat the same exhibition with which we opened the museum, and we have made serial repetitions a part of our program. Through them we aim also to draw critical attention to the ever more quickly changing roster of exhibitions and other art events today, to the excessively fast and excessively superficial consumption of intellectual content, and equally to the importance of re-reading.

We do the best we can with the money we have, but we don't pretend to be okay, and we want to make the conditions of our work transparent. Our conditions are our content. We want our exhibition rooms to describe a concrete space and our concrete problems. That's the idea of the contemporary art museum as I see it, which is very different from the white cube, because the white cube doesn't concern itself with the outside world; it's an abstract space.

Contemporaneity is a condition that demands that we take an active role in it. Interruptions actually entail "being the enemy of your own time," as Agamben points out.[15] I think this is not too far removed from what you've been saying in your books.

15. Giorgio Agamben, "What Is the Contemporary?," in *"What Is an Apparatus?" and Other Essays* (Stanford: Stanford University Press, 2009), p. 40.

TS: Yes, it is very close—for me, this defines curating contemporaneity, curating from inside its antinomies, making them manifest in the museum, as you do in yours.

ZB: Another requirement of contemporaneity is that museums of contemporary art open a dialogue with the rest of the world, and fight for conversation on an equal basis. For this reason, a museum has to articulate the symbolic capital that it brings to the international dialogue. And this symbolic capital is not only the art tradition the museum represents, but also its own self-reflexive position.

If you compare this current situation with previous times here in Eastern Europe, you'll see that our time is more concerned with the past than ever before. So, we—curators, artists, and theorists—have become aware of how important it is to go back to our own traditions. It's not about nationalism; it's about local-to-local dialogues, about a comparison of different experiences instead of everybody trying to speak one universal language.

That's why we initiated L'Internationale—a confederation of six European art institutions—together with the Museum of Modern Art, Antwerp; Museo Nacional Centro de Arte Reina Sofía, Madrid; Van Abbemuseum, Eindhoven; SALT, Istanbul; and Museu d'Art Contemporani de Barcelona, Barcelona. We connected so as to build an international family that is based on similar urgencies, and thus to avoid falling prey to the new-old hegemonic initiatives. Everything is increasingly about understanding contemporaneity as a point or moment of connection, where different urgencies from different contexts can come together. We are finding partners, not only in Eastern Europe, but also all over the world. To me, this is a turn that is not simply geopolitical, but refers instead to different, let's say minor, positions in different contexts. Together, we are trying to build new conditions.

Mami Kataoka

Phantoms of Asia; Curating According to What?

Since 2003, Mami Kataoka has been the chief curator at the Mori Art Museum in Tokyo, where she has curated, among other exhibitions, *Lee Bul: From Me, Belongs to You Only* (2012), *Ai Weiwei: According to What?* (2009), *Sensing Nature: Yoshioka Tokujin, Shinoda Taro, Kuribayashi Takashi—Rethinking the Japanese Perception of Nature* (2010), *All About Laughter: Humor in Contemporary Art* (2007), *Roppongi Crossing* (2004), and *Ozawa Tsuyoshi* (2004). Between 2007 and 2009 she was the international curator at the Hayward Gallery in London, where she curated *Laughing in a Foreign Language* (2008) and co-curated *Walking in My Mind* (2009). From 1998 to 2002 she was chief curator at Tokyo Opera City Art Gallery. She has curated numerous exhibitions at venues around the world, most recently iterations of *Ai Weiwei: According to What?* at the Hirshhorn Museum and Sculpture Garden, Washington, D.C. (2013), and the Brooklyn Museum (2014). She served as joint artistic director of the 9th Gwangju Biennale (2012), and guest curator for *Phantoms of Asia: Contemporary Awakens the Past* at the Asian Art Museum of San Francisco (2012).

Our conversation took place at the Mori Art Museum, Tokyo, on August 3, 2013.

Terry Smith: In a recent lecture you mentioned three key events in the history of modern Japan: the 1868 Meiji Restoration, the end of the Second World War in 1945, and 3/11—the Tohoku earthquake and tsunami of March 11, 2011, which led to the Fukushima nuclear disaster. The first two are also major markers of change within Japanese art, and perhaps 3/11 will become one as well. Many writers take the years around 1989 as marking changes in the world at large that accelerated the shift from late modern to contemporary art—in Europe, obviously, but also in China because of the Tiananmen Square massacre, in South Africa with the end of apartheid, and in Cuba due to the landmark Havana Biennial of that year. Political markers do not apply in the same ways in the United States, but market ones do. In Japan, the late 1980s signal the beginning of the "lost decades" for the economy. What was the impact of this decade on the periodization of art history in Japan?

Mami Kataoka: My objective in choosing those three dates in the history of Japan was to identify moments when society underwent major changes and to ask: what were the responses of artists to the resulting circumstances?

But 1989 was also significant. It marked the end of the Showa era under Emperor Hirohito [December 25, 1926, to January 7, 1989] and the beginning of the Heisei era under the current emperor. During the Showa era Japan enhanced its modernization and Westernization, as well as embarked on a nationalist path. It also experienced the Second World War, followed by rapid economic growth in the 1960s and 1970s. The Tokyo Stock Exchange reached its highest value ever on the last day of December 1989, after which Japan's "lost decades" began. So, the end of the Showa era somehow symbolized the country's shift from a time of growth and progress to one of slowing down and pausing.

Post-war economic growth had raised awareness of the social necessity (or, at least, the economic usefulness) of "the arts and culture." Many museums, theaters, and concert halls were built during the 1970s at the prefecture level (Japan's equivalent of states or provinces), a trend that still continued after the 1990s—indeed, it persists today. Major cities such as Yokohama and Nagoya inaugurated museums, and the first public museum of contemporary art opened at Hiroshima in 1989.

In the field of international contemporary art, *Magiciens de la terre* opened in Paris in June 1989, and in the same month the Japan Foundation began a United States tour of *Against Nature: Japanese Art in the Eighties*, an exhibition that traveled to seven museums and university galleries. In 1990, the exhibition *A Primal Spirit: Ten Contemporary Japanese Sculptors* was shown at the Los Angeles County Museum of Art. There had already been some cultivation of audiences for Japanese art in Europe during the 1980s through historical survey shows such as *Reconstructions: Avant-Garde Art in Japan 1945–1965* [Museum of Modern Art,

Oxford, 1985] and *Japon des avant gardes, 1910–1970* [Centre Georges Pompidou, Paris, 1986]. And we could further interpret the two shows in the U.S. as signs of Japan's rising economic influence, and perhaps also as a counter-move against the "Japan bashing" that had began to appear in some popular media in the West. So, we could also take 1989 as a turning point in terms of the infrastructure of the art industry.

TS: Does that give us a date for saying that art in Japan became contemporary?

MK: No, the beginning of contemporary art in Japan dates from an earlier moment. Art historian Reiko Tomii argues that:

> ...the area of practice called *gendai bijutsu* (literally, "contemporary art") was firmly established by 1970, as distinct from the modern practices of *Nihonga* (Japanese-style painting) and *yoga* (Western-style painting), which date back to the late nineteenth century. This local development was accompanied by an art discourse that articulated the significance of *gendai* (the contemporary), as opposed to *kindai* (the modern or modernity). As the concept of *kindai* was deemed to have "collapsed" (*hokai*), the concept of the avant-garde (*zen'ei*) also lost its relevance, and was replaced by *gendai bijutsu*. This shift was not only prompted in part by the local political situations around 1970, but also underscored by a heightened sense of international contemporaneity (*kokusaiteki dojisei*) in art, which resulted from more than two decades of conscious interfacing with the outside world, typically Euro-America.[1]

There are even earlier precedents of exchange going back to the 1920s and 1930s, and beyond, when Japanese artists traveled

1. Reiko Tomii, "Historicizing 'Contemporary Art': Some Discursive Practices in *Gendai Bijutsu* in Japan," *positions*, vol. 12, no. 3 (2004), pp. 611–41. http://shinku.nichibun.ac.jp/jpub/pdf/jr/JN2103.pdf.

to Europe, especially to Paris, to study. Some made their way to the U.S. in the 1950s, including Yayoi Kusama, who went in 1957, Fluxus artist Ay-O in 1958, and Yoko Ono in 1959. This current continues to this day.

Included in the "more than two decades" of contact that Tomii mentions are early post-war movements such as the Experimental Workshop (*jikken kobo*), the interdisciplinary collective activities in Tokyo from 1951–57, and the Gutai Art Association, founded by Jiro Yoshihara in the Kansai area in 1954 and continuing until the early 1970s. In 1949, the Yomiuri Newspaper Company initiated the Yomiuri Independent Exhibition, an annual open-submission show, which in the 1960s became a vehicle for anti-art and happenings. European Art Informel was introduced to Japanese audiences in 1956, by the *Exposition internationale de l'art actuel*, organized by Asahi newspapers and held at the Nihonbashi Takashimaya department store. French critic and curator Michel Tapié became aware of the post-war Japanese art movements during his first visit in 1957, and subsequently promoted this work, especially Gutai, in Europe. Tapié organized the World Contemporary Arts Exhibition at the Bridgestone Museum of Art in Tokyo, in October 1957. In the same year, the National Museum of Modern Art in Tokyo organized exhibitions such as *15 Vanguard Artists* and the First Tokyo International Biennial Exhibition of Prints, while the Museum of Modern Art, Kamakura, organized *Contemporary Arts of Japan after World War II (1945–1960)*, in 1964.

One of the earliest examples of a contemporary art museum in the country was a private initiative, the Nagaoka Contemporary Art Museum in Niigata Prefecture, which opened in August 1964. It was funded by Komagata Jukichi, the founder of a local bank, the Taiko Mutual Bank, and lasted until around 1979. A number of privately funded art spaces showed international contemporary art. Among these were the Seibu Sezon Museum [1975–99], the Hara Museum of Contemporary Art [1979–], the Sagacho Exhibit Space [1983–2000], the ICA

Nagoya [1986–90], and the Touko Museum of Contemporary Art [1988–91]. After 1990, however, with the exception of the Hara Museum, these private (or corporate) initiatives were slowly overtaken by the public museums set up by regional governments. In this sense, too, we could say that 1989 marked a turn toward the institutionalization of contemporary art in Japan. Of course, it all depends on how you define "contemporary art," but you can see that the awareness of "international contemporaneity" has quite a history in Japan.[2]

CURATING MODERN ASIAN ART

TS: What you are describing resonates with how art historians are interpreting the worldwide shift from modern to contemporary art, underway since the 1970s, as a series of local developments. It is becoming evident that the overall change happened in complex, uneven, distinctive, but connected ways within the cultures of the various regions of the world, within art worlds in cities everywhere, and even in the work of individual artists. In some places, of course, it is still occurring, and in some others, it has yet to occur. It seems to me that independent curators, and some museum-based curators, have been at least as active as university-based art historians in this enterprise, perhaps more so. I would be interested in your view on how curators in Japan have tackled this task, or how they have tracked this change in Japanese art. Can one see it happening elsewhere in Asia, and in Asian art, and can one even generalize in this way? Are path-finding exhibitions such as the wonderful *Tokyo-Berlin/Berlin-Tokyo* show that I saw here in 2006 part of an overall program of research, collecting, and collection display that curators in Japan, and throughout Asia (as in Europe and the U.S.) are undertaking?[3] Could you talk about Japan first, and then Asia

2. For an overview, see John Clark, *Modern Asian Art* (Honolulu: University of Hawaii Press, 1998), and subsequent publications by the author, as well as his bibliography of modern and contemporary Asian art at sydney.edu.au/arts/art_history_film/documents/BIBFINAL2005.pdf.

3. *Tokyo-Berlin/Berlin-Tokyo* (Ostfildern: Hatje Cantz, 2006). Curatorial teams: David Elliott, Fumio Nanjo, Mami Kataoka, Mami Hirose (Mori Art Museum), and Peter-Klaus Schuster, Angela Schneider, Alice Laura Arnold, Gabriele Knapstein, Andres Lepik, Ludger Derenthal (Staatliche Museen, Berlin).

more generally, as I know that you are fond of Okakura Kakuzō's aphorism "Asia is one."

MK: Yes, Okakura's statement, made in 1904, is well known, and is still resonant for us. Let me quote his opening paragraph. You can see that he puts this idea as a singularity, and then as a contrast:

> Asia is one. The Himalayas divide, only to accentuate, two mighty civilizations, the Chinese with its communism of Confucius, and the Indian with its individualism of the Vedas. But not even the snowy barriers can interrupt for one moment that broad expanse of love for the Ultimate and Universal, which is the common thought-inheritance of every Asiatic race, enabling them to produce all the great religions of the world, and distinguishing them from those maritime peoples of the Mediterranean and the Baltic, who love to dwell on the Particular, and to search out the means, not the end, of life.[4]

The art critic Yusuke Nakahara explored this difference in the 10th Tokyo Biennale, *Between Man and Matter*, which was shown at the Tokyo Metropolitan Art Gallery in 1970, and regarded as one of the first significant international contemporary art exhibitions in Japan. Participating artists included Carl Andre, Daniel Buren, Christo, Jan Dibbets, Luciano Fabro, Barry Flanagan, Jannis Kounellis, Mario Merz, Bruce Nauman, and Richard Serra, along with Japanese contemporaries such as Koji Enokura, Susumu Koshimizu, Hitoshi Nomura, and Jiro Takamatsu. Of the forty artists included, twenty-seven were from overseas. It was quite a comprehensive comparative exhibition of Arte Povera, Minimal art, Anti-Form and Mono-ha, and it exemplified the "international contemporaneity" (*gendai bijutsu*) I referred to earlier. Prior to this exhibition, there were a number

4. Okakura Kakuzō, *The Ideals of the East with Special Reference to the Art of Japan* [1904] (Albany, Calif.: Stone Bridge Press, 2007), p. 9.

of comparative historical exhibitions as early as the 1960s, including *Mutual Influences between Japanese and Western Arts* in 1968 and *Contemporary Art: Dialogue between the East and the West* in 1969, both at the National Museum of Modern Art in Tokyo.

If we see the U.S. and Europe as centers, and Japan as a peripheral location, it is important to note that artists and curators in this country have always been aware of contrasts and comparisons, similarities and differences. When a person in the West talks about contemporary Asia, the emphasis tends to be on rapid cultural change and economic growth contrasting with some generalized idea of the "eternal values" that are presumed to have existed in Asia's past. The production of contemporary art from Asia has been mostly discussed from art market–related perspectives, with insufficient focus on the histories of the modernities and the development of public art spaces within each country and the region as a whole. Many artists have engaged in the struggles between modernity and tradition, in the loss of connection with nature caused by new lifestyles and the urban landscape, or in identity issues and post-colonial theories. This seems to parallel the struggles that Japan has been going through for more than 150 years. People still discuss the current overall situation, and what we mean by "fine art" (*bijutsu*)—a term that was adapted from the German words *Kunstgewerbe*, "handicraft," and *Bildende Kunst*, "fine art," when Japan was invited to participate in the Vienna World Fair of 1873. It is an imported concept, based on the understanding of a dichotomy between the East and the West. But it does not have to be that way.

Recently, in terms of rapid growth, many people have noted a gradual shift from China and India to Southeast Asia more generally. Actually, Japan is uniquely positioned in comparison to the rest of Asia. We were one of the first non-Western countries to modernize in the late nineteenth century. We have consciously built a culture based on the co-existence of modern or Western thinking with traditional Japanese thought. In terms of Japan's relationship with Asia, there have been two major initiatives.

One is the Fukuoka Art Museum, which, since 1979, has been building cultural exchanges between East, Southeast, and South Asia. Every five years, starting in 1980, it presented *The Asian Art Show*, a survey of contemporary art from the twenty-one countries in the region. In 1999, it changed its name to "the Fukuoka Asian Art Museum" and replaced *The Asian Art Show* with the Fukuoka Triennale, for which it is now renowned. The other major initiator is the Japan Foundation, founded in 1972, which established the ASEAN Cultural Center in 1990 (called "the Asia Center" from 1995 to 2004). It has over the years supported numerous collaborative exhibitions and arranged conferences to promote international exchange in the Asian region.

However, when it comes to comparative studies of different modernities in Asian curatorial practices, we must say that they have only just begun. *Cubism in Asia: Unbounded Dialogues*, a touring exhibition and symposium organized by the Japan Foundation in 2006, was an exceptional project in this context. Featuring around 130 works from eleven countries, it investigated how artists over the years in various parts of Asia have responded to the Cubist movement. The show was first presented at the National Museum of Modern Art, Tokyo, before traveling to the National Museum of Modern and Contemporary Art in Seoul, and the Singapore Art Museum.[5]

Today in Asia, a new generation of collectors has appeared, and a market is rapidly forming. It seems that a new system, or conception, of contemporary art is becoming visible; in this context, the development of a new art precinct in Hong Kong, for example, is exciting. At the same time, I have noticed some eagerness among younger generations to revisit the history of their contemporaneity, and of modern and contemporary art. They say it is not about creating an alternative art history because there is no master narrative yet. When it comes to exhibiting the histories of the visual arts of our region to international audiences,

5. *Cubism in Asia: Unbounded Dialogues* (Tokyo: National Museum of Modern Art, 2006).

however, we are in the early days. The Asia Art Archive, for instance, is building an essential resource for research into this history. It recently launched the digital archive of artist and teacher Roberto Chabet [1937–2013], who led the emergence of Conceptual art within the Philippines during the 1960s.

PHANTOMS OF ASIA

TS: Your exhibition *Phantoms of Asia: Contemporary Awakens the Past*, which was shown at the Asian Art Museum of San Francisco in 2012, was organized around four themes: (1) "Asian Cosmologies: Envisioning the Invisible"; (2) "World, Afterworld: Living Beyond Living"; (3) "Myth, Ritual, Meditation: Communing with Deities"; and (4) "Sacred Mountains: Encountering the Gods." You argued that "Asia is not a timeless construct," but rather an ever evolving concept that can "awaken a new awareness of our existence in this world."[6] How is this the case, philosophically, and how did you indicate this curatorially, in the ways you displayed the works within the museum?

MK: I was interested in revisiting Okakura's idea that "Asia is one," while being aware that it could be interpreted as an ultra-nationalistic statement. I wanted to see if, beneath the modernizing surface, any unconscious pan-Asian cultural current persisted in people's minds or in their cultural DNA. Okakura was stating the position of Advaita, the Indian philosophy of non-dualism. In my mind, this connected with the ideas of Tetsuro Watsuji, the Japanese philosopher, and particularly his book *Climate and Culture: A Philosophical Study*, in which he argues that climate—understood in the broadest sense, as both natural *and* cultural setting—is a significant factor in determining human

6. Mami Kataoka and Allison Harding, press release for *Phantoms of Asia: Contemporary Awakens the Past* (exhibition at the Asian Art Museum of San Francisco, 2012), May 2012, http://www.aaa-a.org/2012/04/30/phantoms-of-asia-contemporary-awakens-the-past/.

nature.[7] Accordingly, he identifies three basic climatic types—monsoonal, desert, and meadow—as corresponding to different world cultures. The monsoonal climate extends through most of Asia, which is, as a consequence, distinguished by its receptivity and subservience. In this fluid, mostly humid and rainy zone, people have developed a different relationship to nature in comparison with the West, where the temperate meadow climate encourages them to radically transform and exploit its resources.

This led my thoughts to ancient Indian cosmology and on to diverse religious traditions. From these perspectives, nature is almost synonymous with the cosmos or the universe; it gives people an awareness of the invisible realm, of pure energy, and a vast spatial sensibility, which encompasses the afterlife as well as the ability to embrace plural values and elements. So, instead of defining Asia as something opposed to the West, and instead of looking at Asia as a post-colonial region locked into a sense of delayed development, I wanted to look at a much deeper cultural history. In this syncretic culture, how could contemporaneity be perceived in a positive way?

The Asian Art Museum of San Francisco is a perfect place to pursue this curatorial approach because it has one of the largest historical collections of Asian art in the West. I asked curators at the museum, who are all scholars specializing in different Asian countries and regions, to suggest works from the collection that would resonate with the contemporary works that I wanted to introduce to the museum. In the temporary exhibition galleries, I showed both historical and contemporary works freed from their national and regional affiliations, or historical categories. In the permanent galleries, I added a few contemporary works to each of the seven Asian regions into which the collection is divided.

7. Tetsuro Watsuji, *Climate and Culture: A Philosophical Study*, trans. Geoffrey Brown (Tokyo: Printing Bureau, Japanese Government, 1961). Based on transcripts of lectures given from 1928 to 1929 and first published in 1935 in Japanese. See also Bruce B. Janz, "Watsuji Tetsuro, *Fudo*, and Climate Change," *Journal of Global Ethics*, vol. 7, no. 2 (August 2011), pp. 173–84. http://www.academia.edu/2446287/Watsuji_Tetsuro_Fudo_and_Climate_Change.

The resonances between the works were not purely formal: they suggested connectivities beyond time and space. By doing this, I hoped to offer a fresh look at the historical collection, to show it as something still "alive" today. To show, for instance, that Buddhist sculptures can still be found in temples similar to the ones from which the museum's examples were taken, and that they are therefore still objects of worship in contemporary life. The exhibition expanded into the museum's public areas, and outdoors as well.

TS: Do you see your ambitions in exhibitions such as *Phantoms of Asia* as akin to those of Jean-Hubert Martin in his exhibitions since *Magiciens de la terre* and up to *The Theatre of the World* at the Museum of Old and New Art in Hobart [2012–13]?

MK: *Magiciens de la terre* was far more ambitious, in terms of the number of artists and countries it covered, and, of course, in its subsequent impact on the development of critical discourse and curatorial practice since 1989. Being aware of Tate Modern's thematic collection displays, and of the historical contextualization of diverse contemporary art practices in museums in different parts of the world, I did not consider *Phantoms* as any more ambitious than other exhibitions presented by curators elsewhere today, but I share director Jay Xu's advocacy of new approaches to the Asian Art Museum's historical collection.

Certainly, it is not common to combine spirituality and syncretic cultural development with contemporary art practices. But I have noticed recently that a number of other exhibitions, not limited to Asia, explore new possibilities in different regions through deploying pre-modern perceptions of the universe. In this sense, I was very much interested in *The Theatre of the World*, which is currently on view at La Maison Rouge, in Paris. Although I haven't been able to see it yet, this exhibition's non-linear format seems to represent an enormous liberation from the periodization and regionalism imposed by *Magiciens de la terre*, enabling us to consider human civilization, or the essential nature of human consciousness, in a more anthropological way.

TS: You have stated that you wish to promote a kind of shared consciousness that points us beyond East versus West, West versus East binaries toward a kind of dynamic equilibrium between these and other oppositions. Do you see your exhibitions as demonstrating this equilibrium, or as contributing toward its eventual achievement by showing the richness, depth, and evolutionary adaptability of the specifically Japanese, and more generally Asian, values manifest in Japanese and Asian art?

MK: I am not sure if I wanted to consider the *Phantoms* exhibition as a manifesto. And I am not sure if I am envisioning some sort of Asian-inspired spiritual evolution. It was just a very small action to demonstrate a possible model of multiple elements and values co-existing in all their complexities and contradictions, including the past and the present, the historical and the contemporary. We can still learn so much from pre-modern understandings of the universe, without denying what human civilization has achieved or without aiming to reverse hierarchical power structures. In the end, the goal was not to demonstrate Japanese or Asian values, but more to revisit what modernity left aside or excluded, and to reconsider the universal structure of our own existence from a larger, more inclusive viewpoint.

It was only natural for me to take ancient Japanese perceptions of nature as a point of departure, and to try to extend that line of thought into a pan-Asian spatiality. Prior to *Phantoms of Asia*, I curated *Sensing Nature: Yoshioka Tokujin, Shinoda Taro, Kuribayashi Takashi—Rethinking the Japanese Perception of Nature* in 2010 at the Mori Art Museum, which explored how the innate human ability to sense nature, generally, and the Japanese view of nature, specifically, persist in our urbanized and modernized world. At the Mori, I have also asked how these views are reflected in contemporary art and design practices.

The more I explore these questions, the more the idea of "contemporary art" seems very narrow and limited. Okakura once said, "We classify too much and enjoy too little. The sacrifice of the aesthetic to the so-called scientific method of exhibition has been the bane of many museums."[8]

TS: *Phantoms of Asia* was shown only in San Francisco. There may have been practical reasons for it not traveling. Would you show it in Japan?

MK: *Phantoms of Asia* didn't travel partly because it was specifically made in conjunction with the collections of the Asian Art Museum. However, the concept of investigating a possible dialogue between contemporary artists and the works from different museum collections is one that could travel to many parts of Asia and beyond.

SPECTACLE AND NECESSITY

TS: There do seem to be interesting differences between the kinds of art being made in different centers within Asia. In Japan, as you said, there has been a very careful and at times extremely subtle dialogue between traditional and modernizing cultures for over 150 years now. We see this in all the arts, perhaps nowhere more successfully than in the work of Japanese architects. Since the war, a varied and widespread exhibitionary infrastructure has been built, rivaling that anywhere else. Then, during Japan's "lost decades," China experienced an explosive opening to market capitalism and globalizing cultures. Chinese artists became aware of developments in art and thought elsewhere in the world at the moment when spectacle art and spectacle culture were being emphasized in Europe and the U.S. The most obvious examples being, perhaps, the Young British Artists and the American postmodernists. So, we have the very strange

8. Okakura Kakuzō, "Art Appreciation," in *The Book of Tea* [1906] (Hong Kong: Charles E. Tuttle Company, 1956), p. 86.

phenomenon of a country with a relatively scarce background of modern art producing a vast amount of contemporary art within the international art circuit—indeed, it is not uncommon in China to hear local artists claiming that the whole phenomenon is a Western fiction, the invention of foreigners or, at best, of overseas Chinese artists.

The parallel in Japan is Takashi Murakami, who entered the scene at the same point, although artists in this country don't seem to feel the same need to emphasize the bifurcation into nationalists and internationalists that is common in China. Nevertheless, the legacy of what I call "retro-sensationalism," which seemed to dominate art practice during the 2000s, is evident everywhere—in the shop at the Mori Art Museum, for example—although I believe its impact is fading fast. And there are many more interesting artists at work within this region today.

Could I bring you back to the idea that 3/11 marked a third turning point in Japanese life and culture, including art? This idea is certainly embodied in the Japanese Pavilion at Venice this year, and was at the core of the prize-winning Japanese contribution to the Architecture Biennale in Venice last year. How do you see the changes that have moved art in Japan forward from what we might call "the Murakami effect"?

MK: There are number of artists who engage critically with current social and political conditions in Japan. In the current exhibition at the Mori Art Museum *Roppongi Crossing 2013: Out of Doubt*, which is the fourth edition of our serial survey of Japanese contemporary art, we have contextualized works that respond to 3/11 both directly and indirectly, with earlier works and those that are not necessarily socially or politically engaged.[9]

9. See *Roppongi Crossing 2013: Out of Doubt* (Tokyo: Mori Art Museum, 2013), especially Mami Kataoka, "In Search of Something Fundamental—Beyond Complexity, Contradiction and Ambiguity," pp. 230–41. The exhibition *Roppongi Crossing 2013: Out of Doubt* was held from September 2013 to January 2014; see more at http://www.mori.art.museum/english/contents/roppongix2013/.

In her 2012 woodcut print *Prison NUKE FISSION 235*, Sachiko Kazama investigates how post-war nuclear energy policy in Japan was formed through diplomatic relations with the U.S. She depicts President Eisenhower and five Japanese politicians of the 1950s as six electrons, referring to the moment when our country started to use atomic power. Her works are shown in dialogue with those of Genpei Akasegawa. His satirical parody *manga* series *Sakura Illustrated* was made in 1970–71 for *Asahi Journal*, a major weekly magazine at that time, and touches on the U.S.-Japan Security Treaty, the return of the Okinawa Islands, and other political issues. We are also showing paintings made by Hiroshi Nakamura during the time he participated in the Reportage painting movement of the 1950s, as well as some of his works from the 1960s. His art evinces the post-war chaos of Japan's quest for a new model of society, in defiance of U.S. military power. Not least, the exhibition includes works from the renowned ant farm series by Yukinori Yanagi, which take the form of national-flag sculptures made out of colored sand that are inhabited and ultimately destroyed by ants, thereby literalizing the changing political map of the world, as well as the confusion after the end of Cold War.

Takashi Murakami, Mariko Mori, Yoshitomo Nara, and many other artists of their generation were shaped during the post-war era, at a time when popular culture was being developed into an industry, and *anime* programs were being shown on television. Murakami's concept of Superflat is easily understandable as a product of that time. During the globalization of the 1990s, young artists faced issues about identity and cultural specificity; Murakami created an international brand that responded to these questions. But he has also produced works in response to the recent natural and manmade disasters. As I mentioned, people today are more aware of socio-political issues, including the unsolved problem of Fukushima. While these run the risk of being overshadowed by "Abenomics," the short-sighted policies of the current neoliberal government, and by the public celebrations leading up to the 2020 Tokyo Olympics, the objective perspectives of some of the younger generation artists are certainly giving me hope.

TS: It seems to many observers that the new museums and cultural zones in Asia and the Middle East are primarily expressions of the global spectacularization of culture, which the visual arts have served in a major way. The numbers of people visiting art exhibitions in Western countries grew and grew in the middle of the last century as culture and cultural exchange became crucial to the class identity of the rising middle classes, then again in the 1980s, and since, through filtering the massive concentrations of wealth within economies dominated by globalization. For museum people, this has not been simply a matter of quantitative development, although sheer numbers are crucial. It has mainly been about building local nodes that can capture and concentrate the flow of global exchanges. Until recently, Bilbao, for example, was not one of the foremost cultural or capital cities of Europe, unlike nearby Santiago de Compostela, which is one of the great religious pilgrimage sites of the world. In an effort to attract tourists, the city wagered on art and architecture, and their gamble paid off—the Guggenheim Bilbao remains one of the smartest responses by a local authority to the challenge of leaping over national frameworks to create an international attraction. Many previously provincial cities, and previously peripheral nations, are now seeking to make the same kind of leap.

Spectacularization is today also evident in Dubai, Doha, Hong Kong, and Shenzhen, where cultural zones are being created, and amazing museums are being built. Some contemporary artists are being offered vast amounts of money to produce very big works of art; some of them have declined these offers. Imagine Francis Älys producing a massive, great, monumental work—it just doesn't fit with the consciousness of such an artist. Increasing numbers of younger artists work in very critical, participatory, relational ways—they also can't, and won't, produce museum monuments. It's going to be a huge challenge to

actually fill these amazing environments, like M+ in Hong Kong, with work that's going to be strong enough to survive in the space, make a critical contribution, and attract repeat visitors.
MK: I believe that each society has different needs at different times. There is a very fine line between providing what is necessary and creating a situation of unbalanced supply and demand. And there is an unresolved contradiction between the critical and revolutionary nature of contemporary art and the popularization or spectacularization of art institutions and art events. For art institutions in the West, and new institutions in the emerging regions that are just trying to catch up with the scale of what the West has achieved, the challenge will not only be to sustain these giant buildings and organizations. In emerging regions, there are still not enough experienced audiences with a real understanding of the history of modern and contemporary art. Many cities are beginning with what they can see, which is a building, before cultivating the invisible infrastructure and a real sense of the necessity of art within a community. For curators striving to maintain criticality of the status quo, and to show the revolutionary nature of much modern and contemporary art, the demands of the sustainable institutional model can be onerous. However, this is what we need. If curators don't experience any sense of dilemma, they are probably not in a good situation.

Allan Kaprow once said, "[Art] is for all beings, but in actual practice it is available to those who seek it out: the artist and a few friends. And maybe that's okay."[10] I often think about this statement.

CURATING WITHIN ECONOMIC EXPANSIONISM

TS: We have been exploring some of the consequences—for artists, curators, and art participants—of the seemingly exponential growth of the visual arts exhibitionary complex, in Asia particularly. Looking at the situation globally, this complex

10. Allan Kaprow, 7 *Environments* (Naples: Studio Morra, 1992), p. 26.

seems to have moved on from the interaction between bricks and mortar institutions (such as museums) and temporary exhibitions (such as blockbusters and biennials) toward a dispersal into events and relationships that can happen whenever and wherever—including, increasingly, online. Do you also see this change, and what do you think about it?

MK: As museums expand, they require increased marketing, fundraising, and audience development. Many biennials—which are also closely related to the identity building of their host regions/local governments—require the promotion of the local tourist industry and are expected to have a reciprocal economic impact. Within these larger perspectives, contemporary curators are expected to make spectacular, joyful, and entertaining temporary exhibitions. While bearing these goals in mind, curating should be based on a vision of how we can relate artworks produced today to the larger histories of human civilizations, and how works from a specific locality can be related to conditions in other parts of the world.

In some ways, these complex demands are more easily met if the museum has its own collection, because then one can present the same works through diverse perspectives and contexts. For this purpose, during the process of collecting and acquiring, museums have to have a firm view of both local and international histories and developments, and be clear about how they relate to each other.

One of the essential roles of contemporary art is to critically question the status quo in search of universal truths. While the answers can take the form of extraordinary experiences, positive surprises, and both physical and intellectual spectacles, these questions have to be addressed according to institutional and personal positions and statuses, social and political contexts, or history. The challenge for the contemporary curator is how to develop audiences that share such critical thinking.

When it comes to online media, my feeling is that it will take much more time, probably longer than my lifetime, for Internet platforms to provide a physical experience equal to that offered in the exhibition space. For instance, online it is super difficult to appreciate large installation works that require apprehension through looking, hearing, smelling, touching, and feeling the air around them. On the other hand, online media offer significant possibilities for archiving, for providing accumulated knowledge, and for sharing information. I think online media and real exhibition experiences should supplement, rather than compete with, each other.

ARTISTS AS CURATORS/ CURATORS AS ARTISTS

TS: The most influential impact on the exhibitionary strategies of contemporary curators seems to be the example of artists who, since the 1970s, have made exhibitions of their own work, and of the work of close colleagues. Many independent curators, following Harald Szeemann's lead, and some based in institutions have since then made exhibitions *as artworks*. Is this a temporary convergence of what are basically distinct practices, or does it suggest a deeper transformation of both art making and curating?

MK: In Asia we still sometimes find museum directors who are themselves artists. Where there has been no infrastructure for contemporary art—no public institutions, no galleries and alternative spaces of the kind that the West has developed over many decades—curatorial decisions can still be very personal. As a natural consequence, among the initial group of artists emergent in each generation, the ones who happen to be good at writing, managing, and presenting the projects tend to play a curatorial role. For instance, in Myanmar, where there is very little infrastructure for contemporary art, Moe Satt, a young performance artist, has curated and managed the "Beyond Pressure" Festival of Performance Art there over the last few years. Or in places like Indonesia, the Philippines, Malaysia, and some other regions, artists or artist-curators have been playing significant roles in the past decades. In fact, Patrick Flores made an exhibition within the 2008 Gwangju Biennale on this theme, introducing four pioneering figures in Southeast Asian art, artists who, for a time, in response to local necessities, turned toward curating: Raymond Albano from the Philippines, Redza Piyadasa from Malaysia, Apinan Poshyananda from Thailand, and Jim Supangkat from Indonesia.

Today, with thousands of new artists emerging in every corner of the world, it has become impossible for any curator to keep track. It was never possible, actually, but until recently there was certainly the expectation that an international curator should know all the important artists, and curators are still under the constant pressure of not knowing enough or not visiting enough biennials. Yet, in the end, any biennial, and every temporary exhibition, has to be curated through the curator's personal connections and subjective knowledge and even taste, or vision. If we consider curating as contextualization out of an enormous amount of choices, according to specific themes, and what sometimes seem rather forced acts of connection, then I agree that some exhibitions could be seen as their curators' *artworks*. Although, perhaps when we say that an exhibition has become a curator's artwork, or medium, we are simply implying that it is too subjective.

And yet, the global information age has, paradoxically, led to a necessity for relative and plural histories. There is no master narrative, and what we thought was standard history has had to be constantly revisited, and revised, to include unwritten, unspoken sides of the story. This is very much the role of contemporary art, which invites us to take critical views toward what we instinctively believe, and works against any sort of status quo. Contemporary curating needs to be creative and take a critical stance, which once again makes the practice extremely artistic. In this sense, we could call curatorial work "creative," but only when it evinces a deep understanding of artworks and their social and cultural contexts. There is a distinct line between theory-driven curating and curators inspired by direct contact with artists and their thinking. These two potentially colliding directions must be embraced within one curatorial practice.

Curating informed by deeper understanding and thought has become increasingly important at a time when the expanded museum world means that the number of exhibitions is increasing dramatically. It is not a case of curating "just anything." We need to curate out of significant meaning and necessities.

ACCORDING TO WHAT?

TS: Was this your motivation for curating the exhibition *Ai Weiwei: According to What?*, which is touring the U.S. at the moment? Ai is certainly well known as a freedom fighter—in my view, this is his significant creative contribution—but when his works are isolated and read as sculptures, they come in for some criticism. How did you deal with this issue curatorially, especially in a venue such as the Hirshhorn Museum in Washington, D.C., the premier U.S. institution for showing modern sculpture?[11]

MK: I feel that it is no longer valid to interpret Weiwei's works entirely through the visual information they provide. The exact same sculpture could have a completely different meaning according to its context. While *Ai Weiwei: According to What?* borrows its title from a work by Jasper Johns that, in turn, refers to Marcel Duchamp, my curatorial challenge was how to interpret Weiwei's formally Minimal works through his cultural, historical, social, and political context. For instance, one of the major pieces in this traveling show is called *Straight*, and consists of thirty-eight tons of steel rebar. At first look, it resonates well with Richard Serra; however, as soon as we learn that these rebars are originally from Sichuan, where insufficient structural

11. Kerry Brougher, Mami Kataoka, and Charles Merewether, *Ai Weiwei: According to What?* (New York: Prestel, 2012).

engineering caused the destruction of school buildings and the deaths of more than 5,000 children during the 2009 earthquake, the work starts to convey the memories of its materials. Articulating the impact of his work only in terms of its forms and compositions is therefore quite misleading. On the other hand, at the Hirshhorn Museum, where they collect and display first class Conceptual and Minimal sculptures, I was able to work with their curator to re-select the displays of the permanent collection sharing the same floor with Weiwei, so that a formal dialogue could take place. This is the very interesting part of Ai Weiwei's practice—while he shares a conceptual language with many Western artists, he is deeply engaged with his own locality in terms of materials, production, and socio-political conditions. One cannot really separate his art and life, or his art and politics. Again, we shouldn't classify too much.

TS: Given the recent interest in the history of curating, do you think it is possible to discern changes in the nature of the visual art exhibition at the level of the *container* (white cube to black box to event space to digital platform) and at the level of exhibitionary *style*? When I say "style," I am thinking of the remodernizing of everything that occurs at the Museum of Modern Art, for example, in contrast to the ahistorical, transcendental modes in *Artempo*, or to the post-colonial challenge in many of Okwui Enwezor's exhibitions. Many shows designed by Hans Ulrich Obrist prioritize participatory/experiential spaces, while other curators, such as Mayo Thompson, are out-there activist. Surprisingly few are online, crowd-sourced, but perhaps that kind of energy is consumed by sheer self-fashioning. Anyway, these are just some of the tendencies in play at the moment. Perhaps there is a typology of contemporary exhibitions that are responding to contemporary world conditions. I wonder about their impact on the inherited *formats* of the art exhibition: surveys of schools, groups, or single artists, of art mediums, of themes, or of times, places, or periods. What do you think?

MK: It is true that the notion of the container of the visual art exhibition has been expanded from the conventional white cube to performance sites like the Tanks at Tate Modern, as well as to temporary venues, private houses, or into cyberspace. It is the same for the various styles you mention. Probably, this is not a shift but a diversification of the framework of possible curatorial models. Exhibition sites and formats are multiplying, splitting off into new growths, just as biological cells do. This kind of subdividing could surely include the exhibitionary exploration of regional or micro art histories, as well as themes within art.

We should certainly make more comparative exhibitions along the lines you have suggested, but there will also be a need to find a story that can be told to the general public, who won't be interested in micro-histories and the details of subdivisions. Contemporary curators need to take a vertical view that deepens various understandings of artistic practices and of the histories of art's past and present. But they also need to have a horizontal view, to reach out to wider regions and broader publics. The fundamental point is that, whatever and wherever the show, the exhibition should reflect or reveal the deeper meaning and condition of the universe.

TS: Is that the main purpose of contemporary curatorial thought and practice? My answer to this question goes along similar lines: to seek to grasp the challenges of living within contemporary conditions, to work with artists and others who share this aspiration, and to curate experiences in which participants may exercise the kinds of creativity required by their contemporaneity. Surely, this is the kind of work that works of art, and exhibitions, should be doing in a globalized world?

MK: It's very important that you have set out a larger view about what is really going on in all kinds of curating in *Thinking Contemporary Curating*. However, for me, if an exhibition, or the artworks it presents, questions the fundamental issues related to our lives, or life on Earth, or universal thinking, then this is more important than thinking about the method or types of exhibitions as such.

I think one of the important things about contemporaneity is to have different viewpoints in one body and one brain—to have a very intimate specific view, and simultaneously a universal view. I think that contemporary art can present the diverse values of contemporary social conditions, which could be interpreted as the horizontal structure of a universe that embraces different or conflicting elements, in contrast to the vertical or pyramid structure, as represented by lists of the world's one hundred best artists or one hundred best art institutions, or the "Power 100" people in the art world. We need to shift our awareness from the order and priority of individual existing elements toward how those elements exist and relate to each other, how we achieve a state of equilibrium.

From this perspective, the concept of contemporaneity you have been articulating could be understood on a broader scale to include human beings, nature, manmade things, and more. My answer to your question is therefore that the purpose of contemporary curatorial thought and practice is to take an expanded view of the history of human beings on a global scale, and to share it with everyone.

Mari Carmen Ramírez

Brokering Identities: Translating Latin America

Since 2001, Mari Carmen Ramírez has been the Wortham Curator of Latin American Art at the Museum of Fine Arts, Houston, and is founding director of its International Center for the Arts of the Americas. Arguably the leading curator in her field, she was previously curator of Latin American art for the Jack S. Blanton Museum of Art at the University of Texas at Austin (1988–2001) and director of the Museo de Historia, Antropología y Arte at the Universidad de Puerto Rico, Río Piedras campus (1985–88). Ramírez has curated numerous exhibitions, including *Contingent Beauty: Contemporary Art from Latin America* (2015); *Antonio Berni: Juanito and Ramona* (with Marcelo Pacheco, 2013); *Carlos Cruz-Diez: Color in Space and Time* (2011); *Joaquín Torres-García: Constructing Abstraction with Wood* (2009–10); *North Looks South: Building the Latin American Art Collection* (2009); *Dimensions of Constructive Art in Brazil: The Adolpho Leirner Collection*; *Hélio Oiticica: The Body of Color* (2006–7); *Gego, Between Transparency and the Invisible* (2005–7); *Inverted Utopias: Avant-Garde Art in Latin America* (with Héctor Olea, 2004); *Heterotopías: Medio siglo sin-lugar: 1918–1968* (with Héctor Olea, 2000); as well as a segment of *Global Conceptualism: Points of Origin, 1950s–1980s* (1999).

We spoke at Independent Curators International, New York, on September 20, 2014.

Terry Smith: Let me begin by asking about the initial motivations of your curatorial work, which I believe were to question Latin American essentialism. That is, the idea prevalent in North America, in Europe—and even in various people's minds in South America—that certain shared features in the art made in the region distinguish it from art made anywhere else. I am thinking of the usual suspects: "fantasy," "escapism," "celebration," the metaphors of the tropics mixed with revolutionary politics and extreme realism, plus crazy iconographies from many cultures, indigenous and colonial legacies, and, of course, an always surprising mix of mediums. You have consistently worked against these simplifications by focusing on actual artworks, and on the contradictory forces at play throughout the Americas. We are talking together following your participation yesterday in a conference related to the Guggenheim Museum's effort to build up its collection of art from the region, as exemplified also by their current exhibition of recent acquisitions: *Under the Same Sun: Art from Latin America Today*. The title alone tells us that the stereotypes cling on. I want to explore how you have worked, curatorially, within the complexities of this situation—in the U.S., in the broader region, and, especially, as a broker between the two.

Mari Carmen Ramírez: Well, I think we have to start from the fact that I am Puerto Rican, and, even though I am a U.S. colonial subject—Puerto Rico is still, arguably, the last colony in the West—my identification from the beginning has been with Latin America.

The idea of straddling two different—even antagonistic—cultures has been a defining aspect of my life since childhood. And, not surprisingly, it has also left a profound imprint on my professional life. In fact, if there is any phrase that captures my professional trajectory, and my resistance to assimilation into any one dominant culture, it is "between two waters" (the title of a book of essays I am working on). Moreover, when I studied at the University of Chicago, during the late 1970s and early 1980s, I did not see myself as an American but rather as a Puerto Rican; that is, as someone who was there to absorb knowledge and then go back home to produce something different. In fact, I left in 1985 to become director of the Museo de Historia, Antropología y Arte at the Universidad de Puerto Rico—an institution that at the time was the closest thing to an art museum in San Juan. In Chicago I was immersed in theory, particularly the debates about post-structuralism, Marxism, gender, and cultural studies that marked this period. When I returned to the U.S. in late 1988, to take up a curatorial job in Austin, I was surprised to find that the issue of multiculturalism was suddenly at the core of the political debates of the time. The "culture wars" were in full swing and there was a great emphasis on *identity politics* and the role that Latinas/os, blacks, gays, and women were called upon to play in this new framework. Everyone was fighting for a space in the political spectrum, and, simultaneously, coalitions of all kinds were being formed.

On a personal level, I felt a lot pressure to stake out an explicit stance, which I wasn't necessarily ready to do. There was a big difference between spending your childhood and teens in the barrios of New York or Chicago and my own experience growing up on "the island," which often felt like a self-contained world of its own, immune to the pressures of the outside world (a condition of isolation for which Puerto Rican writer Antonio Pedreira coined the term "insularismo"). In spite of having grown up in a colony, I have never seen myself as an *oppressed* Latina; racism and discrimination are serious issues but never justified the meaning and the purpose of my discourse. So, when—immediately after my arrival in Austin—someone proposed that I run for the College Art Association [CAA] board (soon afterward, I was elected), I accepted that charge not as a token *Latina*, but on behalf of the broader community. It was at this time that I took up the cause of "Latin American and Latino art," which defines my personal and professional commitment until today.

BEYOND THE FANTASTIC

TS: Your influential essay "Beyond 'the Fantastic'" tackles these issues, and especially what you call "the framing of identity" in U.S. exhibitions of Latin American art.[1] Gerardo Mosquera used the former phrase for the title of his 1995 collection of contemporary art criticism from Latin America, in which your essay appears.[2]

MCR: Writing "Beyond 'the Fantastic'" was my attempt to really make sense of that whole scenario I just described. Actually,

1. Mari Carmen Ramírez, "Beyond 'the Fantastic': Framing Identity in U.S. Exhibitions of Latin American Art," *Art Journal*, vol. 51, no. 4 (Winter 1992), pp. 60–68 (ICAA Digital Archive 1065386).

2. Gerardo Mosquera, *Beyond the Fantastic: Contemporary Art Criticism from Latin America* (London: International Institute of the Visual Arts; Cambridge, Mass.: MIT Press, 1996).

I gave the first version of it as a paper at a session that Shifra Goldman organized at the 1990 CAA meeting, here in New York. Aracy A. Amaral, Luis Camnitzer, Shifra, and myself were among the presenters. It became a historic event because it was one of two panels on Latin American art ever organized at CAA, which at the time was an extremely conservative organization (the other panel was convened by Jacqueline Barnitz). Almost a thousand people from the Latin American art community—artists, critics, curators, collectors—gathered in one of the big ballrooms at the New York Hilton to listen to our papers and participate in a heated discussion about the issues at stake. That tells you something about the timeliness and political momentum that guided those debates.

My paper was a critical response to the widespread "boom" in exhibitions of Latin American art in the U.S. during the 1980s, such as *Art of the Fantastic: Latin America, 1920–1987*, at the Indianapolis Museum of Art [1987]. Both in terms of scale and ambition, these exhibitions were unprecedented. They not only showcased important examples of the art produced in Latin America but sought to encompass the region *as a whole* while in the process attempting to define its "essence": that is, those elements that separated this art from that of Europe or the United States. I was really surprised that these shows focused on such exoticized notions of the art produced in Latin America; my argument underscored the irony of mislabeling an "off-center" production as "eccentric." The main problem was that they were organized by North American curators who were lacking in any kind of expertise or authority in this field. Most of them did not even know Spanish or Portuguese, a limitation that seriously hampered their ability to communicate with artists as well as consult archives and other primary sources. As a matter of fact, the figure of the Latin American art curator was nonexistent at the time: that is one of the reasons for such a cultural gap.

A second key problem involved the limitations of multiculturalism that I, as well as others, also criticized throughout that period. "Multiculturalism" implied that, in order to achieve mainstream recognition, each cultural group or each person had to act out a specific, recognizable identity. The exhibition *The Decade Show* (which took place in 1990 at the Studio Museum in Harlem, the New Museum, and the Museum of Contemporary Hispanic Art) tried to offer a *revisionist* reading of the art of U.S. racial and ethnic minorities through a kind of collaborative team-based curatorial practice, thus sharing themes across each of the three venues. Yet, despite some of the groundbreaking features it introduced, the show presumed that we were all desperately knocking on the door of the North American mainstream, and the featured artists were obliged to hang their own identity on their lapels: here we are, I'm the African-American, you are the Native American, this is the woman, this is the Puerto Rican, and so on.

TS: You say in your essay that these exhibition strategies "suffered from their reliance on the mainstream for approval and legitimation of their points of view," and that what was needed instead was "more specifically-focused exhibitions that allow for in-depth analysis of particular movements or groups of artists, as well as the establishment of comparative frames of analysis."[3] In other words, the same frameworks usually accorded to the so-called objective study and exhibiting of Euro-American art. And what you have been working to do ever since.

MCR: The key issue at stake is that due to their colonial history, Latin American countries, for the most part, have had very little relationship to each other. Their sights have always been set on the North, either Europe or America. Joaquín Torres-García's 1936 inverted map and axiom "Nuestro norte es el sur" [Our North is the South] implies a rebuttal of this colonial position. From this point of view, it is important to recognize that the notion of Latin American art as a field of study and collecting

3. Ramírez, "Beyond 'the Fantastic': Framing Identity in U.S. Exhibitions of Latin American Art," p. 67.

was an idea that originated here in the United States, during the 1930s and 1940s. Indeed, what took shape during these early decades comes directly from the Museum of Modern Art—from Alfred H. Barr Jr. and others, and later on from Nelson Rockefeller—as part of a plan to construct a sphere of cultural interchange in parallel to the economic and political sphere of influence that was created during the Second World War. The idea was to collect art from the entire region in an "objective," positivistic manner, quite distinct from the utopian way in which the Latin American artists and intellectuals understood their rich and contradictory semi-continent.

TS: Can we try to distinguish the two viewpoints more precisely? I noted that in a footnote to your essay "Brokering Identities" of 1994 you say, "[t]he term Latin America itself, as we know, is homogenizing and ultimately useless," basically because of "the diversity and complexity within and between the societies and peoples it tries to encompass."[4] That's a huge charge against it.

MCR: The term "Latin America" was introduced by Carlos Calvo in France in 1862 as a means of implementing the imperial ambitions of Napoleon III; ambitions that began with the 1864 invasion of Mexico. Since then, there has been a consistent attempt to think of the art of the region in transnational, continental terms: "Latin" by French interests, "Hispanic" according to the Spanish mother nation, and finally "pan-American" to fit the North American involvement in the region. The identification of a common ground for political and cultural realities was an ongoing concern for those who saw their vested interests affected by a fragmented continent. This unifying, if not homogenizing, condition provided the basis for the longing for integration and the so-called search for identity that has branded

4. Mari Carmen Ramírez, "Brokering Identities: Art Curators and the Politics of Cultural Representation," in Reesa Greenberg, Bruce W. Ferguson, and Sandy Nairne, eds., *Thinking About Exhibitions* (London: Routledge, 1996), p. 35

the Latin American image since the nineteenth century. Our *pensadores*—intellectuals and politicians like the Mexicans José Vasconcelos and Alfonso Reyes—created a long-running, living discourse around what it means to pose the question of a single entity: Latin America. This is the idea of the region as an open question, for people in the area, and for the world at large.

In contrast—in fact, in overt opposition—the idea of "Latin America" that emerged in the United States was saturated with the momentous impact of Mexican Muralism. As you know, for better or for worse, Mexico has been like an ingrained otherness in the North American imagination. For North American intellectuals and artists, Mexico was a kind of cultural utopia. Writers such as Anita Brenner in *Idols Behind Altars*, photographers Edward Weston and Tina Modotti, political activists such as Bertram Wolfe who wrote on Diego Rivera, all traveled to Mexico and became involved in the revolution. It is undeniable that there are very, very strong links and quite complex relationships with Mexico. This is evident even when you look at Alfred Barr's famous diagram of the historical progression of modern art—a torpedo tipped, surprisingly, by Mexican artists.

TS: Yes, he drew it for the Trustees to illustrate the ideal shape that the permanent collection should take, covering art from the early nineteenth century up to 1950. Actually, he drew two, one in 1933 and another in 1941, but they both have "Mexican" or "Mexico" as the leading force in art since the 1920s.[5] MoMA gave Rivera the second one-person show there, after Matisse. I tracked the economic and political connections underlying this in my book *Making the Modern*.[6]

5. See Sybil Gordon Kantor, *Alfred H. Barr, Jr. and the Intellectual Origins of the Museum of Modern Art* (Cambridge, Mass.: MIT Press, 2002), p. 366, illus. 77.

6. Terry Smith, *Making the Modern: Industry, Art, and Design in America* (Chicago: University of Chicago Press, 1993), p. 207.

MCR: Barr and many of his collaborators were genuinely trying to understand the dynamic of modern art in what was uncharted art historical territory. This became evident in the published proceedings of the symposium "Studies in Latin American Art," held at MoMA in 1945, and led by scholars such as Barr himself and Grace L. McCann Morely.[7] Among the seminal questions they posed were: what is Latin America? What does it mean to make Latin American art? Is it possible to unite the art of all of these countries? Why has this art been excluded from collections in the U.S. until now? These were the same questions being debated in many of the countries of the region.

It was not until 1979, when Sotheby's inaugurated a specialized auction for Latin American art, that circumstances in the United States really began to change. The auctions stimulated a market and exhibition boom. The full impact of these developments, however, was not fully consolidated until after 2001, when museums, beginning with the Museum of Fine Arts, Houston, entered the playing field of Latin American art. This was the signal for major museums (LACMA, MoMA, the Guggenheim, and, most recently, the Metropolitan Museum of Art) to sanction Latin American art as an indispensible part of the story of twentieth-century art. The academic establishment was the last to follow suit. Until a few years ago, the only specialized courses of study in our area were those offered at the University of Texas at Austin, and by Edward Sullivan at New York University. Now, for better or worse, there is a proliferation of programs. There are ten, perhaps twelve, universities offering undergraduate or graduate degrees or some kind of "concentration" in Latin American art, and about eighty dissertations underway, in the U.S. alone.

7. See the following papers presented at the symposium: Alfred H. Barr, "Problems of Research and Documentation in Contemporary Latin American Art" (ICAA Digital Archive 833746), and Grace L. McCann Morely, "Contemporary Regional Schools in Latin America" (ICAA Digital Archive 833729).

TS: Right now? That's amazing. And I would guess that just about every one begins from the question, what is Latin American about art from South America, the Caribbean, and the Latino/Latina diaspora? You describe "Latin American art" through instances of curators and museums approaching it, but what about the conceptual apparatus they were using?

MCR: Well, as I said before, they had a reductive notion of what Latin America was all about, which is why they were fascinated by the figure of Frida Kahlo, with her iconography of personal suffering ("suFrida") and her magical realism. The literary boom of the 1960s, headed by García Márquez's *One Hundred Years of Solitude* and the like, also had a lot to do with reinforcing the idea of a continent where "magic" was part of everyday reality. This view, of course, is very far from what the boom writers intended but was easily marketable to mass audiences.

The only modernist movement that allowed a window for engaging Latin American art (or any kind of art based on difference or "the other") was Surrealism. The principles and internal logic that guided Cubism, Futurism, Dada, geometric and non-objective abstraction had no room for artistic expressions of otherness. Moreover, there was an actual, historical connection between the leaders of Surrealism and Mexico. Both Breton and Artaud developed close relationships with artists like Diego and Frida, as well as with local writers and artists, when they traveled there in 1937–38. Even before that, Wifredo Lam and Roberto Matta had also participated in Surrealism. All of these factors paved the way for the fallacious construct of the "fantastic" to emerge a few decades later.

TS: This construct *required* exotic others, and approached them primarily through strange, inverted, hybrid, outrageous, and unconscious metaphors.

MCR: That's exactly right. But this interpretation, of course, did not match my broad, decades-long understanding of the contribution of the Latin American avant-garde, particularly of complex artist-theoreticians like Joaquín Torres-García, David Alfaro Siqueiros, the Brazilian *antropofagos*, Xul Solar, Grupo Madí… the list goes on. It did not even really apply to the highly experimental Mexican Muralists, who, at the time, were misclassified as Social Realists.

THE AVANT-GARDE PARADIGM

MCR: My art historical grounding in European modernism was, however, the starting point for my approach to Latin American art. From the beginning my passion was the phenomenon of the avant-garde, which developed strong roots in Latin America. Since the 1900s, artists from all over the continent went to Europe to study with the likes of André Lhote and Fernand Léger. Some of them, such as Rivera and Torres-García, significantly contributed to important movements such as Cubism and Constructivism. Eventually, they returned to their countries of origin and through the incorporation of vernacular elements transformed what they had learned in Europe into something else. So for me, the best way to approach the phenomenon of the avant-garde in Latin America is by means of a dialogical model that takes into account the dialectics of assimilation/transformation—what Mário de Andrade and the Brazilian modernists (quite ingenuously) coined as *antropofagia*—that is, artistic or cultural "cannibalism of the sacred enemy."

This is where the central thesis of *Inverted Utopias* originated. Co-curator Héctor Olea and I were convinced that the artists featured in the exhibition had not only engaged innovative art forms, but, more importantly, had generated original thinking about art in the continent. Héctor stressed the idea of the artist as theoretician by including ninety-two documents (from manifestos to essays, from polemical pamphlets to political leaflets) in the catalogue. For example, Hélio Oiticica's research into autonomous color in the late 1950s—manifest in his *Spatial Relief* [1960–61] and *Nuclei* series [1963–64]—stems from his readings of Kandinsky, Klee, and Mondrian, among others, as well as his incorporation of elements from vernacular Brazilian culture. In fact, this is the modernist Oiticica that his *poète-maudit* promoters tirelessly try to negate by means of his late, anti-art positions. This dialogic process—one that applies to modern art all over the world—does not demean his or other local avant-garde production, just the opposite: it enriches our understanding of his art as a more complex, layered, and nuanced process. The nature of our avant-garde contribution to modernism is duly implied by Héctor's essay title: "Versions, Inversions, Subversions."[8]

TS: I love the way Gerardo Mosquera describes this dilemma. He says, "Latin American art is going through an excellent period at the moment, precisely because it's ceasing to be Latin American art. It is about escaping from one's own trap, as well as from a distant one."[9] The local trap, he says, is the identity neurosis that Latin American culture has suffered as a result of the multiplicity of its origins. "We're always asking ourselves who we are because it's difficult to know. So the danger, then, becomes the postmodern one of coining a cliché of Latin America as a kingdom of complete heterogeneity."[10] That's the opposite side of the reductive essentialism we have been talking about. You've been saying right from the beginning, yes, it is hard to know who we are, but we have this whole long tradition of people thinking about exactly this issue, and their enormously subtle, continual, open-ended understanding of our heterogeneity creates a specifically Latin American kind of coherency. It's not a matter of either/or.

MCR: Exactly. Let's face it: the starting point for everyone working in this field is the fact that this whole notion of "Latin America" or "Latin American art" is nothing but an operative

8. Héctor Olea, "Versions, Inversions, Subversions: The Artist as Theoretician," in Mari Carmen Ramírez and Héctor Olea, *Inverted Utopias: Avant-Garde Art in Latin America* (New Haven: Yale University Press; Houston: The Museum of Fine Arts, Houston, 2004).

9. Gerardo Mosquera, "Del arte latinoamericano al arte desde América Latina" ["From Latin American Art to Art from Latin America"], *ArtNexus*, no. 48 (April 2003), pp. 70–74 (ICAA Digital Archive 1065622).

10. Ibid.

construct encompassing the artistic production of more than twenty countries. If there is one single trait that identifies Latin America, it is precisely the neurotic questioning that takes place at both the continental and national levels: does Latin American art exist? If so, how can it be defined? What does it mean to be Peruvian in that context? To be Colombian, or Argentinean? Is it, as Borges wrote in *Ulrica*, "an act of faith"? Indeed, as part of the International Center for the Arts of the Americas [ICAA] book series *Critical Documents of 20th-Century Latin American and Latino Art*, we published a 140-document, 1,160-page book on this subject that stands as objective proof of the never-ending, cyclical nature of these debates.[11]

The coordinates of this "operative construct," as Guy Martinière named it, have been invented and re-invented by each generation or cultural group as an antidote to the uneven position of Latin America with respect to the rest of the so-called First World.[12] Therefore, those of us working in this field say, we're conscious that there is no such thing as "Latin American art," but we're obliged *to operate within this construct* that has come to represent such unreachable complexity and vast contradictions. We recognize that worrying about it will not lead us anywhere, so, let's put it aside and deal with the issues that the art itself is positing.

However, beyond labels and classifications, it is also important to recognize that today the term "Latin American art" is not just an artistic or geographic referent but has come to identify an intellectual field, in the theoretical sense posited by the French sociologist Pierre Bourdieu; that is, an intellectual platform that has its own laws, agents, and intrinsic dynamics. In this sense, it refers us to a series of practices, problems, and paradoxes that have been developing, with ups and downs,

11. Héctor Olea, Mari Carmen Ramírez, and Tomás Ybarra-Frausto, eds., *Resisting Categories: Latin American and/or Latino?* (Houston; ICAA/ The Museum of Fine Arts, Houston; New Haven, Yale University Press, 2012).

12. Guy Martinière, in his 1978 dissertation; see also Olea et al., *Resisting Categories*, pp. 164–77. Cf. ICAA Digital Archive 838531.

throughout the entire twentieth century. For better or for worse, these learned practices serve to properly frame the type of curatorial work that we are all engaged in.

THE IDENTITY WARS

TS: Looking back, my sense is that you arrived at this position in steps and stages, right?

MCR: Sure, because what I tried to do was to make sense of the role that I, myself, was playing in that specific 1980s/1990s context of identity politics. After assessing the power dynamics at play, I realized I was being called upon not so much to make sense of Latin American art, but to insert artists from the region into the broader arena of the mainstream, or the establishment.

TS: Today, the focus is no longer simply on shows about art from this or that South American or the Caribbean country; it is on the interrelationships between them and the United States, the whole Latino/Latina immigration. Their shared histories of colonization, and the expanding U.S. sphere of influence, both still resonate, the latter hugely so. But you say that there's not necessarily a natural alliance between all Latinos. You're very conscious of differences, for example, between Latin America and Latino/Latina experience and art. Can you spell these out?

MCR: When it comes to Latinos in the United States—the major groups are Chicanos, Puerto Ricans, Cuban-Americans, and more recently Dominicans—you're talking, basically, about displaced peoples. This situation is very difficult to define because every group claims a distinct nationality, but its idea of nation is more conceptual, or ideological, than factual. Puerto Ricans go back and forth between New York and the island in the *guagua aérea* [air bus], but their minds remain on the island, remembering Puerto Rico as a nation that never existed, or imaging one that might be. Some Chicanos in many areas of the South of the United States come from families that long precede the arrival of *gringos*. Many of them believe in a utopia called "Aztlán," a mythical imaginary nation that precedes the Aztec times. This hodge-podge of displaced peoples and nationalities remains adrift in the United States and in a contentious relationship with U.S. culture because they refuse, for the most part, to assimilate. Latinos have always resisted the melting pot notion that prevailed in this society until the 1980s, but paradoxically *they are*, in practice, basically Americans.

So, when a Latino comes into contact with someone from Latin America, there's a conflict because they don't recognize each other. A classic case is Chicanos and Mexicans; Chicanos are for the most part not accepted in Mexico, there's a strong bias against them. They are seen as people who left, who have nothing to do with Mexican culture; there are class issues, racial issues, and everything implicit in the word "exclusion." And yet, both are drawing from the same historical culture, and, ironically, the Chicano's Aztlán "construct" aligns them with the Chichimecas, and other native civilizations coming from the North (Bering Strait).

If the big issue at the crux of the debates around multiculturalism in the 1980s was how to maintain a *separate* identity while remaining part of this society, then the project for the near future is to figure out how to chart the relationships between the successive waves of immigrants who have made the U.S. their permanent residency. This is an urgent (albeit extremely challenging) task that is becoming even more complex because of the far greater influx of people from all over Latin America during the past twenty years.

TS: Which exhibitions have tried to map these relationships?

MCR: There have been numerous surveys focused on individual groups such as Chicanos, Puerto Ricans, Dominicans, or the Caribbean as a whole—for example, *Infinite Island: Contemporary Caribbean Art* [2007] at the Brooklyn Museum, and the mammoth

Caribbean: Crossroads of the World [2013–14] at El Museo del Barrio. But in general, no show has seriously tackled the broader phenomenon of Latino art or, even more importantly, the relationship between U.S. Latino and Latin American art. Historically, the first mainstream show to engage Latino art in any way was *Hispanic Art in the United States: 30 Contemporary Painters and Sculptors*, organized by the Museum of Fine Arts, Houston, in 1987. However, like most other surveys of Latin American art of the period, it ended up producing a host of new stereotypes. This show was followed by *Ante América* [1992]—organized by the Banco de la República in Bogotá and curated by Gerardo Mosquera and Carolina Ponce de León—an exhibition that coincided with the celebrations of the Fifth Centennial of the "discovery" of America and provided the most provocative statement to date on this topic. The most recent attempt to engage this budding field was *Our America: The Latino Presence in American Art* at the Smithsonian American Art Museum [2013–14]. This show set out to engage the Latino contributions to American art since the mid-twentieth century, when this community emerged as an ascendant minority in the U.S. Despite its serious scholarship, the exhibition fell short because it limited its selection of works to the museum's rather small collection of Latino art.

As with Latin American art, part of the problem with Latino art lies in the lack of specialized curators and an infrastructure to support research in this emergent field. For the most part, Latino art does not feature in art history programs. Instead, students interested in this field have to register in English or American studies. It's crazy, no? There are signs, however, that this situation is beginning to change. The Smithsonian has added several Latino art positions to their curatorial ranks, and other museums are beginning to seriously consider it a legitimate field of study and collecting.

For my part, I am currently working with Chon Noriega and Pilar Tompkins Rivas on an exhibition project for *LA/LA*, the second edition of the Getty-sponsored Pacific Standard Time, titled *HOME—So Different, So Appealing*. The show, which is being organized by LACMA and the MFAH, will investigate how artists from these broad constituencies have approached notions of public and domestic space, displacement, immigration, and homeland from the 1950s until today.

THE ROLE OF THE CURATOR

TS: A key argument in your essay "Brokering Identities" was that the curator had become a primary agent of change in art worlds, more than intellectuals, such as critics.

MCR: Yes, the curator operating as curator and not as art critic or art historian was at the time a brand new phenomenon in the playing field of Latin American art. Gerardo Mosquera [Cuba], Olivier Debroise [Mexico], Paulo Herkenhoff [Brazil], Marcelo Pacheco [Argentina], and myself were part of the first generation for which curating became a conscious professional choice. Most of us had backgrounds in art history, and some—like Gerardo, Paulo, and Olivier—also engaged in art criticism. However, we were indeed among the first to recognize the critical potential of curatorial work; that is, we envisioned it as an intellectual practice and were convinced that you could *transform* people, spaces, and institutions through this type of agency. Insofar as it lay outside academia and, in most cases, outside the museum, curatorial work embodied a very dynamic practice full of risks as well as conceptual and logistical challenges; yet this is precisely what made it so enticing.

As I traveled in Latin America during those years, when people asked, well, what do you do? and I answered, I'm a *curadora* [curator], they thought I was a *curandera* [witch doctor]. There was really no tradition for this type of work in our countries, and very little understanding of what it entailed. Before us, the most influential people in Latin American art were art critics like Marta Traba or scholars such as Walter

Zanini. In addition to being the most prominent art critic of her generation, Traba directed the Museum of Modern Art in Bogotá and organized exhibitions all her life, yet she was not considered a curator. Walter Zanini was director of the MAC USP [Museu de Arte Contemporânea da Universidade de São Paulo], and also artistic director of two biennials in the 1980s, but he was thought of more as a scholar and critic. Certainly, there were a number of people who did what we would call today "curating"—in Brazil alone I can think of Frederico Morais, Aracy A. Amaral, and Roberto Pontual—but they did not think of themselves as curators.

The figure of the institutional curator in charge of public collections was also very rare in Latin America where—with the exception of Mexico—most countries lacked fully developed museum infrastructures. In 1988 I was the *only* curator of Latin American art associated with an institution—in this case, the Archer M. Huntington Gallery [now the Jack S. Blanton Museum of Art] of the University of Texas at Austin. And even then, it could be argued that, regardless of my job description, my charge was very different from that of other U.S. museum curators. Insofar as I was dealing with an unsanctioned emerging field, my job involved bringing art from one continent to the other while in the process functioning as cultural mediator, broker, translator. Every artist or work that I chose had to be justified in terms of how its "difference" fitted into the broader framework of a mainstream modernism that, as I explained before, had no category to assimilate it. It was a very different kind of role than the research, collection building, publishing, and connoisseurship implied in other curatorial roles.

TS: I see a parallel to the ways that Okwui Enwezor thinks about his work during this period. It's done in the name of, and for, others. It was not, initially, driven by careerist ambition, by any sense of yourself as a "star" or "super" curator.

MCR: Yes, you are completely right! Over the last fifteen-plus years, we have seen a significant transformation in the role and function of curatorial practices. In fact, the curator has not only emerged as a catalytic agent of artistic and social practice but the *métier* itself has become assimilated into mainstream culture. The term appears everywhere, from fashion to food to eyewear; it has been popularized.

At the risk of sounding old, I would argue that as a result of this sort of mainstreaming the critical edge essential to curatorial practice—at least in the sense in which my generation understood it—has for the most part gone. Nowadays it is all about the market and the establishment. Ironically, many of these changes have to do with the professionalization of these practices. Back in the 1990s, we had to invent our work as we went along, to fly by the seat of our pants. Unlike today, when young curators go to school to learn how to be curators, there was no available road map. We were all self-made curators driven by a sense of mission and struggling to survive in extremely challenging contexts that involved everything from economic precariousness to extreme violence. That's what made it so exciting!

TS: Since the 1990s, at least, art worlds everywhere have been shaped by the broader change in world geopolitics and economies that some call "globalization" but that I prefer to see as a massive, worldwide, always uneven, and locally specific transition to transnationality. The consequences for art practice are something many curators are very aware of, and this awareness changes the exhibitions they make. How do you see your curatorial efforts in this context?

MCR: You have to remember that in my case, in the 1990s, I was still operating in a marginal field: Latin America, ufff! My archives are full of the letters of rejection I received whenever an exhibition I organized at the Huntington was offered to other U.S. museums. Even now, despite the successful reception of the exhibitions and publications we have generated at the ICAA over the last fourteen years, it is still impossible to get important museums in New York or on the East Coast take up something we have done. Thus far, it's never happened.

TS: That's an internal provincialism, one that still operates. Ridiculous. In "Brokering Identities," you talk about the strange economy that this produces, about Latin American art entering the mainstream of discussion within the United States only as long as it remains marginal. Twenty years later, this power structure still operates, now on a worldwide scale, so you get a strange category, the "marginal international." Despite the fact that the most interesting and innovative art is being generated in what used to be the peripheries, and is spreading everywhere, in the old, modern art centers of the world there's a constant striving to take back central power, to recover positions of dominance. In the last decade or so, however, it seems to me that markets rather than museums have been the main drivers of this.

MARKETING LATIN AMERICAN ART

MCR: Well, initially, the markets promoted the stereotype of the fantastic. However, when they realized that a number of us were tearing that construct down, they switched to promoting Concretism, or Constructive art more generally. And now, ironically, we are faced with the situation that Concrete and Constructive art have become the new "marketable" canon for Latin American art—this was unthinkable twenty years ago! Of course, this situation cannot be attributed solely to the marketplace. It is the result of a complex process in which collectors, auction houses, markets, and curators—including myself—have actively participated, and which has at the same time led to a better understanding in the U.S. of the range and scope of the art produced throughout Latin America.

But, to the extent that the unequal axis of exchange persists, a critical issue remains—one that is not going to change until Latin America is in a position to "legitimize" art on its own terms. This is an arduous process that will probably take several generations to materialize. Gerardo has very brilliantly pointed out that, despite the expansion of the international circuits, Latin America is still only providing artists for the global shopping mall.[13] We're not in a position to empower an artist from Germany; to say, come exhibit in Argentina, and it will make your career, or at the very least, will insert you into another, valuable circuit. The visual arts infrastructure is still uneven and precarious. Institutions that can play such a role are nonexistent, with the exception, perhaps, of the Bienal de São Paulo.

TS: What about an artist such as Francis Alÿs? To me, he would not have the resonance that he has internationally had he not been a Belgian transposing himself to Mexico City and making art out of that circumstance.

MCR: That's true, but I would argue that the reason why he has had such resonance is that he has been assimilated as if he *were* a Mexican artist. So, I guess you can say, yes, Mexico has legitimized him, but part of this validation implies that he appears in all of these international exhibitions as a Belgian-Mexican artist. There are, indeed, a number of other artists who have made their international careers from Mexico; this group includes Melanie Smith [Great Britain] and Thomas Glassford [Texas, U.S.].

INVERTED UTOPIAS

TS: Your major exhibition in recent years, co-curated with Héctor Olea, was *Inverted Utopias: Avant-Garde Art in Latin America* at the Museum of Fine Arts, Houston, in 2004. The inspiration seems to go right back to what we began discussing, that is, your commitment to the avant-garde as the most interesting kind of modern art. How did the idea for this exhibition come about?

13. Mosquera, "From Latin American Art to Art from Latin America," note 9.

MCR: I was a passionate student of the avant-garde in Europe and in Latin America from the point of view of the visual arts, but also always in contact with literature and other forms. That was what brought Héctor Olea and I together in 1992. He's Mexican, but lived in Brazil for nearly twenty-five years. An architect by training, he is also an experimental writer who became very involved with the Concrete Poetry movement (particularly with Haroldo de Campos). He was the "trans-creator" of the latter's poetic prose into Spanish, as well as the official translator of Oswald and Mário de Andrade's anthropophagous writings. The first conversation we ever had was, essentially, wouldn't it be great to do an exhibition that brought together the visual and the literary avant-gardes? That conversation started a lifelong partnership.

By then I had already organized my first big exhibition at the Huntington, a survey co-curated with Cecilia de Torres on the work and legacy of El Taller Torres-García, the applied arts workshop founded by her father-in-law, Joaquín Torres-García, in Montevideo in 1942.[14] I also did a number of other shows, but the opportunity to do the kind of mega-exhibition that Héctor and I had in mind did not come until 1997, when I received an invitation from the Museo Nacional Centro de Arte Reina Sofía in Madrid to participate in their monumental *Versiones del Sur* project. This was a series of five concurrent exhibitions organized to celebrate Spain's renewed ties with Latin America in the new millennium. During the 1980s and early 1990s a number of exhibitions in Europe had revisited the topic of the historic avant-garde movements, but Latin America was invariably absent. I immediately thought: the avant-garde in Latin America, a big exhibition! That was the starting point for *Inverted Utopias*.

TS: It's fascinating to compare your total lack of hesitation about the avant-garde in Latin America to perspectives in Australia and

14. Mari Carmen Ramírez, ed., *El Taller Torres-García: The School of the South and Its Legacy* (Austin: University of Texas Press, 1992).

other settler colonies, such as Canada, New Zealand, and South Africa, where the presumption up until the 1970s was that avant-garde art occurred only in the metropolitan centers. These were artistic colonies so distant, so relatively small and so dependent—and, it has to be said, so English—that every effort to bring about major change seemed to fall short or collapse into compromise. Yet, in the 1960s and 1970s, throughout these art worlds, metropolitan and provincial, an intense desire to transform art in profound ways arose. The goal was less to come up with a very good imitation of what was happening in Europe or the U.S. and more to create an originary kind of art that would change the nature of Art per se, all over the world, everywhere and forever. That's what the idea of the avant-garde meant then. But there seems to be a very clear distinction between the circumstances in those settler colonies and the situation for artists from many Latin American countries.

MCR: Evidently, the process was the same in other parts of the world that had been subjected to Western colonial rule. The impact of the avant-garde in many of these places translated into a longing for new forms of art through which artists could break away—if not from the economic, then at least from the cultural and political status quo. The key issue all along has been, how do you frame these rich, peripheral—here and there ungraspable—manifestations of the avant-garde? Héctor and I argue that the original parameters of the avant-garde were translated, turned upside down, and even undermined by the specific terms and conditions prevailing in Latin America.

TS: Yet that kind of distinction does open up the question of differences *within* Latin American art, between certain countries on the continent and in the region, with respect to their capacity to generate an avant-garde. You received criticism for concentrating on the major powers—Brazil, Argentina, with Uruguay as a close outlier—and for downplaying a lot of figurative art, as well as ignoring indigenous art.

MCR: Well, all criticisms stem from a specific point of view; we tried to encompass several. Thus, there are several points to consider in answering your question. Firstly, in Latin America, as Néstor García Canclini and others have convincingly argued, modernity was at best an *uneven* if not an *unfinished* project. As a result, not all countries had the cultural or institutional infrastructure to support the development of advanced forms of art. Basically, avant-garde groups emerged in large cities in the major countries, those with large economies that were actively pushing toward modernization or where a revolutionary process had established a new political system, as in the case of Mexico and Cuba. In this context, Brazil, Argentina, Uruguay, Venezuela, and even Cuba produced a plethora of avant-garde artists and movements. By contrast, in Mexico the drive to avant-gardism was bogged down by the hegemonic, extremely concentrated legacy of Muralism that already by the 1930s had become consolidated into a state-promoted, "official" movement. This process not only froze the original movement's experimental thrust, turning it into hard-core nationalist rhetoric, it also tended to erase or, even worse, marginalize artistic manifestations that did not conform to the official model. While we acknowledged these differences in the 586-page catalogue, our aim was to focus on those artists and groups who had really contributed to a creative re-reading of the avant-garde model in a conscious way; that is, all the writers and artists who had written manifestoes, staked out positions, and were theoretically pushing the limits of art beyond the traditional categories of painting, sculpture, drawing, et cetera. We made the case that the Latin American *contributions* were not merely a regional eccentricity, but a far-reaching phenomenon that enriched the broader project of modernism.

Secondly, I have to say that the criticism regarding the non-inclusion of figurative or indigenous art is not accurate, since both modalities were very well represented. Relevant works in the former category included, for example, those in the "Play and Grief" constellation, by artists like Antonio Berni,

Beatriz González, León Ferrari, Luis Felipe Noé, and Juan Carlos Distéfano. Similarly, the "Universal and Vernacular" constellation featured works in the second category by Vicente do Rego Monteiro, David Alfaro Siqueiros, Francisco Matto, and the artists of the School of the South. In each case, however, the motifs were filtered through the lens of avant-garde experimentation. As Holland Cotter put it, these proposals are not only interesting, they also "destabilize received standards of pictorial order."[15]

TS: The avant-gardists you highlighted produced significantly distinctive innovations that were not only comparable to those in Europe and then, later, those in the United States, but also, sometimes, happened earlier and were more interesting. What are the most striking examples of this to you?

MCR: Who else thought through the shaped canvas before the Grupo Madí [Gyula Kosice, Carmelo Arden Quin, and Rhod Rothfuss] in 1945? They were operating in a marginal context, the River Plate, yet were fully aware of what had happened in Europe up to that point and were looking to insert themselves into that narrative. During the 1950s and early 1960s, Carlos Cruz-Diez and Hélio Oiticica were among a handful of artists worldwide who theorized color as an autonomous entity unfolding in space and time. Tucumán Arde, founded in 1968, was a groundbreaking group of artists who abandoned art to become, basically, political and collective organizers, and create "unionist happenings" as a strategic stance to question both a brutal military dictatorship and an official art milieu or marketplace serving its own interests.

TS: Another obvious difference between *Inverted Utopias* and earlier shows was its lack of emphasis on iconic Latin American figures such as Rivera and Kahlo, Roberto Matta, and others. Do you not see them as avant-garde artists?

15. Holland Cotter, "Ready to Rumba! Latin Political Art Sets Utopia on Its Ear," *New York Times*, August 27, 2004.

MCR: Well, as you know, every exhibition involves strategies, both curatorial as well as political. Héctor and I were very conscious that we were making a powerful statement that involved not only staking a unique position but also going against the prevailing values of the market. As we discussed earlier, Rivera, Matta, and Kahlo had suffered from over-exposure since the late 1970s and 1980s, and, together with Lam, they became a Latin American stereotype. I think Matta was a great artist who worked within the broad parameters of the avant-garde. Kahlo, on the other hand, is a unique case: contrary to what the market would have us believe, she is the exception and not the rule. Observing her entire production, she was very uneven and overall not a great painter. However, she was able to translate her very particular circumstances and suffering into an extraordinary iconography, to draw from vernacular sources, and create a very unique artistic language. For the purposes of *Inverted Utopias*, however, that was not enough, since there were so many other unknown yet authentically innovative proposals, experiments, theories, and aesthetic contributions waiting to be brought to the fore. The "inversion" in the title stems from Héctor's introduction to the documents, where he wrote that "*Inverted Utopias* is thus a provocation rather than an evocation."

TS: My sense is that the Latin American avant-garde never coalesced into the ongoing, self-superseding tradition that we (retrospectively) believe to have evolved in Europe, but that there were clusters and groupings in certain countries, and moments when artists came up with better work—more adventurous, innovative, suggestive—than that being produced anywhere else at that time. Sometimes, this provoked a critic to interpret the work in a strikingly original way—for example, Ferreira Gullar's idea of the non-object.[16] I have argued for a long time that this is

16. Ferreira Gullar, "Teoria do Não-Objeto," Suplemento Domenical, *Jornal do Brasil*, December 19–20, 1959, in Kobena Mercer, ed., *Cosmopolitan Modernisms* (London: Institute of International Visual Arts; Cambridge, Mass.: MIT Press, 2005), pp. 170–73.

the only way to break the parochial logic of the modern art system, within which energy flows from the peripheries to the center but power to define the overall agenda always comes from the center to the peripheries. For the peripheral artist, it is never enough to do the same kind of work as well or better; you have do something that's unanticipated at the center, that makes an impact there, and, eventually even more important, makes a difference elsewhere, preferably everywhere.

MCR: Right, but with the added problem that, like every avant-garde, these people were operating in local contexts, which for the most part were not able to recognize what they were doing. In some cases, a few critics would defend them and promote them, but for the most part it took years, decades, for anyone to really pay serious attention to their work. Even many of the Constructive artists, who have had such a complete ascendancy during the last decade, were in fact completely unknown or marginal at the time. This was the significance of exhibitions like *Inverted Utopias*: to put forward this immense body of work and theoretical pronouncements—more than 350 works and ninety-two documents in total—which had been there all along but had not really been understood in terms of their true contributions, as a result of which they had not been legitimized. Some artists had received some local recognition, but internationally, almost none. Artists such as Débora Arango, for instance, from Colombia; El Techo de la Ballena from Venezuela, a quite intriguing group; Juan Carlos Distéfano and Alberto Heredia from Argentina; Carlos Raquel Rivera and Julio Tomás Martínez from Puerto Rico. Not only were all of them figurative artists, but very few curators had really dealt with their work; they were literally unknown.

CONSTELLATIONS AS EXHIBITIONARY FORM

MCR: Before *Inverted Utopias*, most exhibitions of Latin American art were based on the survey model—for example, *Art in Latin America: The Modern Era, 1820–1980*, curated by Dawn Ades at the

Hayward Gallery in 1989, after which it traveled to the Palacio de Velázquez (part of the Reina Sofía) in Madrid. It included a lot of important work—a whole section on Constructivist artists curated by Guy Brett—but it was based on an art-historically *linear* narrative. I, for one, had criticized this model in "Beyond 'the Fantastic'" and other essays, so there was no way that we could adopt it for this project. Instead, we took up the challenge of coming up with a new format that was more in tune with the theoretical debates about exhibitions that were emerging at the time. Actually, the idea of grouping artists diachronically (in order to underline the differences or affinities between them) was a dialectical model that I had already used in *Re-aligning Vision*, an exhibition about experimental drawing that I organized at the Huntington in 1997.[17] However, it was Héctor who went straight to the source—Theodor Adorno's *Negative Dialectics* [1966]—and from there developed the flexible model that we used throughout *Inverted Utopias*: the constellatory approach.

TS: In modern philosophy, a constellation is the figure, or, better, the configuration, through which we recognize the true relationships between a particular, or a set of particulars, and the generality of which it, or they, are part. This procedure differs from applying a given theory about the world to phenomena, as traditional philosophy did, or, as science does, observing the phenomena until it suggests a theory. Walter Benjamin introduced the constellation metaphor for seeing the truth in his study of tragic drama in Germany, and Adorno adopted it as the primary task of philosophy a few years later, in his inaugural lecture at the University of Frankfurt in 1931.[18] Benjamin's later idea of the dialectical image is an especially dramatic, and relevant, version of how constellations occur. In his famous

17. Mari Carmen Ramírez and Edith A. Gibson, *Re-Aligning Vision: Alternative Currents in South American Drawing* (Austin: Archer M. Huntington Gallery, University of Texas at Austin, 1997).

18. Walter Benjamin, "Epistemo-Critical Prologue," in *The Origins of German Tragic Drama* [1928] (London: Verso, 2003), and Theodor Adorno, "The Actuality of Philosophy" [1931], in Brian O'Connor, ed., *The Adorno Reader* (Oxford: Blackwell, 2000), p. 32.

metaphor, historical truth appears always as a shocking surprise.[19] So, was your goal to understand how these moments occurred to the artists and their original publics, and then to, as it were, re-create, or at least evoke, that experience for viewers as they moved through the exhibition?

MCR: Well, yes and no. When you put two objects together, you're generating a dialogue between them, which creates another type of knowledge, an innovative understanding of the works and the physical and conceptual relationship between them that does not necessarily relate to established art historical narratives. In line with Adorno's dialectical idea of negativity, Olea argued: "Given that we are oriented by constellations in this exhibition, an understanding of the history locked in each object requires a thorough knowledge of the paradoxes in whose negative light the assertiveness of Official History remains concealed and endangered."[20] As I wrote at the time: "The most significant aspect of the *constellation* model is its unapologetic assertion of the relative and arbitrary nature of curatorial authority. Rather than pretend adherence to the presumed objectivity or even neutrality of 'history,' such a model cannot but rely on the acumen and creative vision of the curator."[21]

TS: Isn't that the whole point of making an exhibition, any exhibition?

MCR: It may be, but not everyone understands it that way. Most curators use exhibitions to illustrate specific arguments or narratives through artworks. In the constellation model, the juxtaposition of objects takes on a decisive role, stressing the richness of contradiction, of discrepancy, of conflict, even inconsistency. The idea is to generate a new kind of material and

19. See Walter Benjamin, "Theses on the Philosophy of History" [1940], in *Illuminations*, ed. Hannah Arendt, trans. Harry Zohn (London: Fontana, 1973), pp. 255–56.

20. Olea, "Versions, Inversions, Subversions," p. 443.

21. Mari Carmen Ramírez, "Constellations: Towards a Radical Questioning of Dominant Curatorial Models," *Art Journal*, vol. 59, no. 1 (2000), p. 16.

conceptual dialogue by approximating similar or disparate works in the gallery space. Sometimes one work is the opposite of the other and their clash creates a new connection, or, contrarily, it shows disconnection. At other times, there are parallels and affinities or differences that resonate within a cluster of pieces or proposals. So, the whole exercise is to really bring together those similarities or antinomies into a specific array, or constellation. In Houston, all of these elements evolved through oppositions: "Cryptic and Committed" in reference to Latin American Conceptualism, "Progression and Rupture" with regards to Constructive and geometric art, and so on.

TS: In his critique of your approach, Daniel R. Quiles suggests that your choices nevertheless evoked an art historical narrative.[22]

MCR: Well, you have to bear in mind that in the case of *Inverted Utopias* we were dealing with a historical frame—the period between 1920 and 1970—and that certainly imposed certain parameters, which were underscored in the title of the Madrid version: *Heterotopías: Medio siglo sin-lugar: 1918–1968*. Obviously works made during a particular decade all originated in certain unavoidable historical conditions and exhibit a similar period sensibility. However, we mixed things up in unconventional, frequently radical ways; there were instances in each one of the constellations where we put contemporary artists in dialogue with their more historical counterparts. For instance, we placed Torres-García and Lucio Fontana from the 1930s in dialogue with the Grupo Madí of the 1940s and the Concretists and Neo-Concretists of the 1960s. We also aligned Siqueiros's radical experiments with dynamism in the 1930s with those undertaken by Jesús Rafael Soto and Cruz-Diez in Paris in the 1950s and 1960s in the context of the Kinetic art movement. In an unprecedented move, we also included Gego in dialogue with

22. Daniel R. Quiles, "Exhibition as Network, Network as Curator: Canonizing Art from 'Latin America'," *Artl@s Bulletin*, vol. 3, no. 1 (2014), article 7, pp. 65–66.

these last two artists and juxtaposed Soto's white vibrations with Armando Reverón's white landscapes done three decades earlier. Another polemical gesture was placing Oiticica's color-in-motion *Parangolés* next to Cruz-Diez's *Chromosaturation* environment. All of these juxtapositions generated unconventional, non–art historical readings of these works, and, in our view, this process was more in accordance with the way artists relate to each other and to the idea of the avant-garde itself.

TS: Quiles claims that, in the first iteration of *Inverted Utopias* at the Reina Sofía, you inaugurated the use of the network as a curatorial model, and that this has "permanently altered" the geographic conception of the region and its artistic production. He suggests that "[t]he network allows for a paradoxical rejection and reinforcement of Latin America's peripheral status… [because] 'Latin America' can be at once seen as a (provisionally) bounded periphery in which important new ideas are formed and circulated, and as a set of nodes in a global art ecology—an essential part of a system."[23] This is neat, perhaps too much so when we think of the more eruptive, and disruptive, sense of constellations that Benjamin and Adorno had in mind. Yet you have often spoken about the relationship of Latin American art to Europe and North America as one of usurpation rather than co-existence. *Inverted Utopias* certainly did map connections to Europe and, somewhat, to North America, but your overall argument, as I understand it, is that this work was avant-garde in its own contexts, and was also avant-garde in a universal sense. How consciously did you and Héctor think about the network as a model when you were putting this show together?

MCR: The network model was present through the influence that the writings of Michel Foucault had exerted on my work in particular. In my catalogue essay I cite Foucault talking about our times as "the epoch of simultaneity… epoch of juxtaposition…

23. Quiles, "Exhibition as Network," p. 63.

epoch of the near and far, of the side-by-side, of the dispersed."[24] That passage was very influential in my initial thinking about the exhibition. It struck me that he was invoking the sense—given by the Internet especially—that we are now in this profoundly interconnected world. In our view, the notion of constellations offered a more complex model capable of harboring contradiction as well as countering the reductive effects of the Internet.

TS: Quiles also suggests that your approach somehow tames Latin American art for North American consumption, especially for the markets, and makes the point that the show in Madrid was different from the Houston edition. It had a more specific title and a different design.

MCR: Our aim was to legitimize these artists within the broader narrative of the twentieth-century avant-garde. This required a huge axiological operation, in the sense of translating the cultural values they represented into an alien context. Yet "translating" and "taming" are two very different operations. Hence, I strongly disagree with the view that the exhibition "tamed" Latin American art for U.S. consumption, or even for the markets. You have to remember that in 2004, when the Houston version of the exhibition opened, more than ninety percent of the artists represented had no presence whatsoever in the U.S. Think about it: I am referring not only to the likes of Débora Arango or Carlos Raquel Rivera, who were literally "unknown," but to by now well-known figures such as Cruz-Diez, Soto, Julio Le Parc, Gego, Lygia Clark, Hélio Oiticica, León Ferrari, Armando Reverón, Antonio Berni… the list goes on.

Not only did we take a big risk in showing these artists, but some of their works were also very challenging. For example, there was a lot of tough, sacrilegious work in the exhibition,

24. Michel Foucault, "Of Other Spaces," cited in *Politics, Poetics: Documenta X, the Book*, ed. Catherine David and Jean-François Chevrier (Ostfildern: Hatje Cantz, 1997), 262. Cited in Mari Carmen Ramírez, "A Highly Topical Utopia: Some Outstanding Features of the Avant-Garde in Latin America," in Ramírez and Olea, *Inverted Utopias*, pp. 1–15.

of which Ferrari's 1966 depiction of Christ crucified on a U.S. bomber jet—*La Civilización Occidental y Cristiana* [Western Christian Civilization]—is just one example. Even geometric and Constructive abstraction was heavy stuff for an audience whose only contact with Latin American art (until then) had been Mexican art. Additionally, there is nothing "tame" about the fourteen essays that we published in the exhibition catalogue—all written by scholars from Latin America—which laid out the conceptual framework for the show. For the most part, they reached a sophisticated level of writing that atypically combined art history with politics, philosophy, literature, and anthropology. From all of these angles, *Inverted Utopias* was a tough, unconventional show for people—including the academic establishment—to absorb. I think Quiles confuses "legitimization" with "market validation"; these are not exactly the same.

The show was basically unchanged with the exception that in Madrid it had seven constellations while in Houston it only had six. This was because the owners of the works by the Uruguayan artist Rafael Barradas—featured prominently with Torres-García in the first constellation—refused to lend them. Beyond that, there were a few other works that had to be substituted or eliminated due to the fact that they were not available for travel, and a few adjustments made here or there, but this is a normal procedure for traveling exhibitions. Of course, the space made a huge difference. There is no comparison between the narrow, rigid galleries of an ancient Spanish hospital (used during the Spanish Civil War) and the gloriously minimal, wall-free, and light-infused spaces of Mies van der Rohe's 1958 galleries at the Museum of Fine Arts, Houston. Believe it or not, it is the difference between night and day!

TS: Finally, I would like to understand how you have negotiated the fact of your commitment to art in South America while being based firmly in the U.S. I know that you are always traveling there, and have an extraordinary network—here the term makes sense—of contacts throughout the continent and the Caribbean. As well as spotlighting Latin American art here in the U.S., what have you done for art and its infrastructures there?

MCR: Well, it is important to emphasize that I am working in Texas, which—because of its geographic location, its history, and its rapidly changing demographic profile (it is by now over forty percent Latino)—has provided an ideal location to carry out my work in the United States. As I implied earlier in this conversation, what I have done there would have been impossible to do here in New York or anywhere else in this country. I have enormous support—both financial and professional—but also an enormous freedom to propose and realize projects. Moreover, the presence of a large and robust Latino population endows my work with urgency and excitement, since whatever I do has an immediate impact in the community.

I would like to think that my work has also had an influence in Latin America in that it has set very high standards for the scholarship, publication, and display of works by outstanding artists from the region whose production lacked (until recently) international recognition. Beyond the specific model it embodied, *Inverted Utopias* has certainly stimulated young curators in the region to reflect upon and experiment with new exhibition formats. Héctor and I are amazed at the number of theses and essays about this exhibition that have appeared in the last few years, both here in the U.S. and in Latin America. The eighteen catalogues and books we have published at the museum and ICAA have also had an impact. Beyond that, it is difficult to assess concretely what kind of long-term effect my work may have at the infrastructural level.

One notable exception, however, is the model established through the Documents of 20th-Century Latin American and Latino Art Project, which is sponsored by the ICAA, of which I am the founding director. This multi-million dollar project involves a digital archive of over 14,000 primary sources for the study of this art that are available free of charge through the Internet, as well as in a thirteen-volume book series. To recover these sources we had twelve research teams working in sixteen Latin American and U.S. cities. Our partners included research foundations, universities, banks, and libraries. In the end, over 150 scholars, researchers, digital cataloguers, translators, and editors worked on this initiative that established the first North-South network of its kind in the Americas. The methodology that we developed for the project (editorial framework, selection criteria, training, technology, controlled vocabularies) is already being replicated by centers in Latin America and is also contributing to major databases such as the Getty Art & Architecture Thesaurus and the Union List of Artists Names [ULAN]. In that sense, the ICAA Documents Project has had a clear impact at the infrastructural level of how knowledge of this art is made accessible and digitally transmitted: "Derivative works no more," I believe was how the *Wall Street Journal* described its impact.[25]

Right now I am busy launching a related think tank, the ICAA Ideas Council, which serves as a platform for the active exchange of ideas about the field of Latin American and Latino art at the macro level. That is, issues concerning institutions, cultural policy, patronage laws, tax incentives for art, the next generation of leaders, and so on. This is an area where nothing is happening and no new knowledge is being produced. Our hope is that by bringing together collectors, philanthropists, and artists with corporations and foundations, we can stimulate a host of new public-private alliances throughout the region that will ultimately benefit artists and their production, the history of our art, and its legacy. Humbly speaking, it's a brand new idea that no one has tried out yet in our area. I am crossing my fingers that it will work...

25. Judith H. Dobrzynski, "A Cultural Conversation with Mari Carmen Ramírez: Derivative Works No More," *Wall Street Journal*, January 18, 2012.

Germano Celant

Re-Curating Attitudes, Bern 1969/Venice 2013

Germano Celant is an art historian, writer, and curator who early on became the spokesperson for Arte Povera in Italy. Since 1993 he has directed the Fondazione Prada, Milan and Venice, where he has overseen major exhibitions, including *The Small Utopia, Ars Multiplicata* in 2012, and *When Attitudes Become Form: Bern 1969/Venice 2013*, receiving the 2013 Agnes Gund Curatorial Award from Independent Curators International for the latter. He served as senior curator of contemporary art at the Guggenheim from 1989 to 2008, where he organized numerous exhibitions. Throughout his career, he has curated seminal exhibitions on Italian art, including *Identité italienne: L'art en Italie depuis 1959* (Centre Georges Pompidou, Paris, 1981), *Italian Art 1900–1945* (Palazzo Grassi, Venice, 1989; with Pontus Hultén), and *Italian Metamorphosis, 1943–1968* (Guggenheim Museum, New York, 1994). In addition, he has directed large-scale international exhibitions including the current *Arts & Foods. Rituals since 1851* at Expo Milano 2015, *Art and Architecture* for the city of Genoa as 2004 European Capital of Culture, and the 47th Venice Biennale, within the theme *Future, Present, Past*, in 1997. He is the author of over one hundred books, ranging from the seminal Arte Povera manifesto (1967) to, most recently, a monograph of Louise Nevelson (New York: Skira, 2013). A longtime contributing editor to *Artforum* and *Interview*, he received the Frank Jewett Mather Award for outstanding art criticism from the College Art Association in 1987.

We spoke at the Fondazione Prada, Venice, on August 28, 2013.

Terry Smith: We are sitting in a room in the palazzo Ca' Corner della Regina, here in Venice, where you have curated the exhibition *When Attitudes Become Form: Bern 1969/Venice 2013*. It is a remarkable evocation of the famous exhibition curated by Harald Szeemann in the Kunsthalle Bern in 1969, an almost exact re-creation of that show, yet it is inserted into this building, an eighteenth-century palazzo on the Grand Canal. How does this show differ from your memory of the original?

Germano Celant: My experience of the initial event, all those years ago, was purely existential. I organized the Italian artists' participation, and I gave the speech at the opening, but I did not think to register or to document my involvement in any way. The joy was in being part of something improvised, in being engaged directly—we were like political militants. For the generation of the 1960s, total immersion in the actual experience was absolute. No one used cameras. The photographs of *When Attitudes Become Form* were commissioned from professionals, not taken by the artists, or by Szeemann, or myself.

RELUCTANT RETROSPECTION

TS: I remember that reluctance to build distance into the experience, and the rejection of the idea that retrospect would be at all important.

GC: In those days, even as an art critic, you didn't take pictures when you visited an artist's studio—either of the artist or the place—because it was understood as private space. Later, working as an art historian, I realized the need to document works, processes, people, everything, so as to contribute to the formation of a shared memory. The drawback is that you start to visualize differently, you look at things and people as potential documents.

Now, I am trying to assemble as much objective and subjective documentation as possible for every project that I do. If I were to write about, say, Joseph Kosuth, I would start with his birth, and ask what kind of family he had, what kinds of early experiences, and so on. I am doing this with all of my "monographies," as I call them. My approach is to join my life and history with those of the artists I write about. This is what I have learned about myself over this long period. My sense of being in the art system, as a person and as an art historian, has been slowly coming together.

TS: "As a person and as an art historian"? You don't use the word "curator" to describe yourself?

GC: I don't curate. I believe that I am more of a companion to the artist, *as a person and as an art historian*. I try to be both complicit *and* detached, which is a kind of contemporaneity, as you would call it, of differences.

TS: So, you are an art historian, specifically of contemporary art, and a historian of contemporary life. Your subject is the life and work of artists such as Louise Nevelson, Mimmo Rotella, and John Wesley. I notice that they are all of a similar generation to yourself, sharing at least some of the same lifespan—your contemporaries in that obvious sense.

GC: To be engaged with the artist, to be a companion to artists, to work alongside art practices, has been very difficult for critics and historians of our generation. Starting in 1969, with the journal *Art-Language*, Conceptual artists took over writing about art—art criticism, art theory—and began doing it in another way. You will remember, you were right inside that moment. But as curators, or as critics, we were displaced. One became a *personaggio*, as we say in Italian: an actor who has to find a role for himself.

Looking back, I think that's where the adjective "independent" came from, as in "independent curator" today.

TS: Well, nowadays, not having a job makes you independent from day one, like it or not.

GC: But even then, there were few jobs on offer, and not that many university art history courses, either.

TS: And no courses in curating, anywhere, to my knowledge, apart from those devoted to conservation, which had elements of collection care built into them. We are identifying a period when everybody who was active in their local milieu took on the responsibility of performing a number of roles. Often, artists were curators, even directors of museums; they created alternative spaces, and wrote art criticism. Particularly in small-scale scenes such as Sydney or Genoa, where a few individuals in effect generated an art scene, based on an ideal: the perfect situation for artists that we imagined actually existed in Paris, or New York. At the same time, we wanted to create art worlds that, in crucial ways, would be different from those centers, which we perceived as decadent.

You're also reminding us of the moment when art history, as a profession, resolutely looked back at the art of the past.

GC: In Italy, you know, everything stopped at Impressionism. I began by studying the Baroque. There was no conception of modern, let alone contemporary, art history, which scholars felt was particularly contaminated by the market.

TS: But the Renaissance wasn't? The complicity between Bernard Berenson and Joseph Duveen must have been repressed.[1]

GC: Of much more positive effect than art historical study, especially in Italy, was Umberto Eco, with his concept of the open work.[2] Everyone could study semiotics, and anyone could practice semiology. This message was very important in suggesting that you could have a role as a thinker, a writer, and a curator, and so on, without being bound by the codes of a profession. As well, finally, after years and years of discussion, it became acceptable to be subjective. The feminist critique was very significant here, in emphasizing the personal within the political, and vice versa.

ARTE POVERA AND AFTER

GC: For me something shifted around 1970, a moment when I became a little more conscious of having a historical perspective. Since 1963, I had been living as a protagonist, sharing everything with artists, operating like an art guerrilla—we thought of it that way. But when I did the show *Conceptual Art Arte Povera Land Art* at the Galleria Civica d'Arte Moderna in Turin, in 1970, I realized that the rebellion was over, and that already, one year

1. See Colin Simpson, *Artful Partners: The Secret Association of Bernard Berenson and Jacob Duveen* (London: HarperCollins, 1988), and Rachel Cohen, "Priceless: How Art Became Commerce," *The New Yorker* (October 8, 2012).

2. Umberto Eco, *Opera aperta* (Milan: Bompiani, 1962); for an English translation, see *The Open Work*, trans. Anna Cancogni (Cambridge, Mass.: Harvard University Press, 1989).

after the exhibition in Bern, I was historicizing the moment that radicalism had ended. This exhibition was "conclusive" for me because the rupture with the past was healed, and I could begin to use historical and linguistic analysis.

At the same time, within the artist groups I had been working so closely with, differences were emerging. In 1972, I decided that the period characterized by exchange and reciprocity was now ending, and that I, at least, needed to concentrate on singular contributions, such as those made by Vito Acconci.[3] From that moment on, I said to myself, okay, I don't want to be involved in groups any longer, I will deal with artists one-on-one only. So when Ileana Sonnabend asked me to write a book in 1972, I did the first monograph on Giulio Paolini. After this book, which employed the traditional historico-scientific approach, I dedicated myself to using the method of close personal engagement with my subject, a method pioneered by Eugenio Battisti, himself inspired by Erwin Panofsky. This began the idea of monography that I mentioned earlier, which has led to many, many books.[4]

TS: What specifically triggered your move from collectives and groups to individual artists?

GC: A group is a conglomerate of identities, so you cannot pay attention, scientifically, to one language, or to a single person's language.

TS: Why not?

GC: Well, in principle, yes, you can, but at the time, in practice, it was important for me to detach myself from the previous eight years of involvement with Arte Povera.

3. Germano Celant, "The Physical Language of Vito Acconci," *Domus*, no. 509 (April 1972). http://www.domusweb.it/en/from-the-archive/2012/10/27/the-physical-language-of-vito-acconci.html.

4. These include books on Joseph Beuys (1972); Piero Manzoni (1975); Jannis Kounellis (1983); Michelangelo Pistoletto (1984); Mario Merz (1985); Claes Oldenburg and Coosje van Bruggen (1985); Giuseppe Penone (1989); Mimmo Rotella (2007); and Louise Nevelson (2013).

TS: As you know, Charles Harrison and I, both of us art historians, critics, and teachers, were absorbed into the Art & Language group. You might say, cynically, that we were recruited initially as the critics and historians of the group, and we did play that role to varying degrees, Charles especially. But we were also part of the push to override distinctions between artists and critics, those who did and those who wrote, between what we called "first- and second-order discourse." So, I, for a time, and Charles, always, maintained roles both inside and outside the group.

GC: But Art & Language was a very small group, so specific, so tight that you had the same kind of impact as one person, although magnified: stronger, more radical, tougher, like a knife, let's say, always ready to cut anyone's throat who did not, in your opinion, measure up. Lawrence Weiner, for example. The Arte Povera grouping was much looser.

Still, after a time, many artists with highly individuated personalities broke away: Michelangelo Pistoletto from Arte Povera, Joseph Kosuth from Art & Language. My shift toward individuals was reinforced when I went to Los Angeles in 1973 and discovered the Light and Space people: Maria Nordman, James Turrell, Robert Irwin, Doug Wheeler, Eric Orr, Michael Asher, and others. Writing about them was a way of discussing both individuals *and* a movement that had larger implications for art in general. I felt that I had found my territory, my environment.

However, I was regularly accused, at the time, of being much too friendly with artists.

TS: Yes, I remember that people would say, here comes Germano, the voice of the artist.

GC: Many art historians regarded this as something negative. Perhaps because they regretted the fact that they could not, obviously, participate in a discussion with Titian, and Leonardo da Vinci could not be their companion. From a contemporary perspective, it makes their profession an impossible one.

TS: Except if they project themselves into the moment of the origin of the work, and imagine its conception, creation, and immediate effect. For many of us, this is the starting point for any art history worthy of the name. It was the core idea behind what came to be called "the new art history" during the 1970s and 1980s. Recently, in a more contemporary move, we try to compare and contrast what we learn from this effort at time travel—this desire to be a contemporary of the artwork when it first became public—with what that work from the past is saying to us, its contemporaries now, in the present. Artworks contain the seeds of many temporalities, like envelopes that will be opened many times, to disclose a letter that is re-written every time it is read. Perhaps the same is being asked of exhibitions these days, now that we are treating them more like artworks or acts of creative publicity.

BERN, 1969

Which leads me to ask you a direct question. What did you say, in Bern in 1969, when you gave the speech at the opening event for *When Attitudes Become Form*?

GC: I think I read a part of the Arte Povera text, the "manifesto" essay of 1967–68.[5] It was ten, maybe fifteen minutes long. Nobody paid much attention because I spoke in English and I was addressing mostly German speakers.

5. Based on the text in *Arte Povera* (Bologna: Galleria de Foscherari, 1968), exhibition catalogue. See also Germano Celant, "Notes for a Guerrilla War," *Flash Art*, no. 5 (1968). http://www.flashartonline.com/interno.php?pagina=articolo_det&id_art=352&det=ok&title=ARTE-POVERA.

I wanted to convey the idea that a new sensibility was emerging, that artists could now use all kinds of different materials, you know, the four elements—water, air, earth, fire—and I wanted to make clear that this art was not "anti" anything, not anti-art, anti-painting, but rather more connected to the possibility of the open—in Italian, *aperto*—field. The open possibility to utilize language: that was the idea, I remember stressing that.

TS: To me a lot of that language reads as incredibly European. Which makes it totally different from what inspired the work produced by the American artists in that show. Does this distinction make sense to you?

GC: Of course. But we were Europeans, and I *am* Southern European, so sensuality, physicality, passion, are still part of my way of working. That's why I use a personal approach in art history.

TS: I have always had the sense that the works of art in *When Attitudes Become Form* "happened to" the gallery space, to this museum-like venue run by artists—an older generation of artists than those in the exhibition. Szeemann anticipated the kind of work that would be installed, but could not be entirely sure of the form that the artists' attitudes would take.

GC: Exhibitions back then were curated on the basis of sketches of possible works. Usually, there was no money to make them beforehand and to cover the costs of transporting them. That is why the exhibition had some rooms full of drawings.

TS: That's right. You would send a letter with a diagram of what you were thinking you might do. And then arrive at the venue and do something else, something better that you had thought of, or thought up when you saw what the others were doing.

GC: Yeah, always bringing with you the material, and always improvising. We have to remember that this is the moment of the Situationists. For Guy Debord, for the whole group, the word "situation" did not imply establishing a settled situation, being *in situ*, but rather adapting to wherever you found yourself. You arrived with your bag of stuff, you put it down, and you improvised. I remember Barry Flanagan arriving late, in 1969. He was always late. And I have this memory—perhaps it is a fantasy—that all the spaces were taken by other artists. So, he made his rope piece, a work that extended through three rooms.

TS: *When Attitudes* was not the first provisional exhibition, because you made the show *Arte Povera + Azioni Povere* in Amalfi in 1968, and there are many other precedents for various aspects of *When Attitudes* as a curatorial action. Yet that show has become the paradigm of the provisionality that is now the rule in exhibitions of contemporary art. It represents the originary moment when art's character came from artists interacting with materials and place, outside the history of art and museums. Therefore, the appearance of this work in a museum-like space was strange, uncanny. It is as if the works themselves had no respect for the idea of an art museum.

GC: No knowledge that museums predated them, or would claim them in the future.

TS: So, in 1969, the museum explodes, and the idea of alternative and different spaces enters it for the first time. *When Attitudes* becomes an archetype.

GC: That is the core paradox. Without it, there would be no accounting for why this show has become so important, why it has accumulated such an enormous impact.

A BRIDGE: A DIFFERENT EUROPE AND THE U.S.

GC: To me, two other arguments about this show are also important. It's the first time that there was collaboration, on the same level of exchange, between America and Europe. That was the major excitement at the time. Otherwise, it would have been just another exhibition of new European art, like the Arte Povera shows, or another new American art show. Artists were just discovering that other artists were doing similarly strange kinds of things in other places. There was a worldwide thirst for the exchange of letters, visits, meetings, et cetera, and finally, there was a *bridge*, a European curator *invited* the Americans, and, another first, Philip Morris sponsored tickets for artists from both sides of the Atlantic to travel to see each other.

I think if you read through Harald's notes, you can see how important the complexity of exchange between the artists was to the way that show came together.[6] I will never forget the moment in 1969 when I was sitting in the foyer of the Kunsthalle, near the front door, and these seven Americans came in. It was like the gunfighters arriving at the OK Corral. For us, you know, it was a myth come true.

TS: A fantastic image. In the Swiss TV documentary made at the time, the interviewer asks Keith Sonnier, I think it was, why the work by the American artists is so different, to which he replies, "I'm from New York. It's a hard city."[7]

GC: It is important to understand that there were very few people involved in the art world at that time, and that there was no market for work. In fact, that's why a lot of pieces were destroyed. Artists had to re-use materials to make new work. There was no money to fight over, no power structure to control. The only currency was the circulation of information, the interplay of ideas for works.

It's also true that artists, at the time, had no regular places to show their work, so they were busy creating their own spaces,

6. See the Harald Szeemann Archive and Library, Getty Research Institute, Los Angles, at http://www.getty.edu/research/special_collections/notable/szeemann.html.

7. Radio Télévision Suisse, *En Marge: The Attitude of the Artist*, directed by Marlène Belilos, Geneva, 1969.

their own galleries, usually temporary ones, or testing out other kinds of spaces. When I did the exhibition *Arte Povera + Azioni Povere* in Amalfi in 1968, academicians like Giulio Carlo Argan and Maurizio Calvesi said, Amalfi? Who wants to go to Amalfi? But all the artists came. As official venues were not offered to us, we used the city's Arsenale and a number of other unorthodox sites. Jan Dibbets unrolled a ten-meter-long white rope, under the water, just off the coast, for example. However, the key to this kind of work is less where it is done, but rather the idea of going somewhere to do the work, going together, and doing it together.

To go back to cultural differences, I want to underline something that I think is very important from a European perspective. People forget that during the 1960s France absolutely dominated the visual arts: the Nouveaux Réalistes, Art Informel, local action painting, Tachisme, Georges Mathieu performing his paintings...

TS: And yet there were very few French artists in the Bern show.

GC: Only two: Alain Jacquet was a friend of one of the Italian artists; he just tagged along. And Daniel Buren invited himself, and showed his stripes outside, on the streets.[8] So, you see, the second important thing underlying the choice of artists was an idea of a different coalition within Europe: the show took place in Switzerland, Belgium already had some interesting collections of new art, Holland supported experimental artists such as Jan Dibbets, as did England at the Saint Martins School and elsewhere. Germany remained a problem, due to the war and the echoes of fascism. The only German artists in the show were Joseph Beuys, of course, because he was already a key, anti-fascist figure, and, because he worked collectively, his students Reiner Ruthenbeck, Bernd Lohaus, and Michael Buthe. Franz Erhard

8. French artist Yves Klein was also featured in the 1969 catalogue for the exhibition, through a letter written by American artist Ed Kienholz about one of Klein's immaterial works.

Walther, also a Beuys student, had already moved to New York. Interestingly, two of the three women artists included were German, Hanne Darboven and Eva Hesse, the third being the American artist Jo Ann Kaplan (who was only represented in the catalogue). France was rejected. It was very political in that sense. We, in Italy, wanted to join this new alliance in Europe—Bern, Brussels, Amsterdam—and to add Turin, and then London and New York as outliers. We were desperate in a certain way; we had no power. And we didn't have a capital city. Berlin? No, for obvious reasons. Paris? No, because its culture was decadent. London had not developed its scene, so New York became our art capital.

TS: A fresh perspective on post-post-war art in Europe. I had not understood it from this angle before. I wonder what Serge Guilbaut—with his influential thesis that the American artists did not originate the breakthroughs to abstract painting with which they are usually credited, but rather stole the idea of abstraction from European, especially French, artists—would have to say about this reading?[9]

GC: I think Guilbaut's political perspective on the larger cultural Cold War context is correct for the years 1946 to 1964. Of course, everything changed in 1964: after Rauschenberg was awarded the Lion d'Or at the Venice Biennale, America dominated the art world. Remember also that Europe had been "liberated" by the Allies and Americans, and its citizens wanted to reject the nationalism of the previous generation, which had been influenced by the extreme ideologies of communism, fascism, and Nazism. Our generation sought to overcome these conflicts by seeking alignments with the United States and England. Culturally, we wished to create a "new artistic alliance," to invalidate political iconographies tied to these ideologies. So,

9. Serge Guilbaut, *How New York Stole the Idea of Modern Art. Abstract Expressionism, Freedom, and the Cold War* (Chicago: University of Chicago Press, 1985).

artworks became totally aniconic, or iconoclastic, with regard to previous imagery. Artists were in dialogue with a culture of action that was not pictorial, but "factual," by virtue of their free use of materials. They left color and canvas behind in order to engage with a wide range of materials—from those drawn from industry to those inspired by nature—all of which were at the time not the traditional territory of art. The result, in the years from 1966 to 1969, was an admixture that embraced Minimalism, Conceptualism, Land art, and Arte Povera.

PHOTOGRAPHIC FICTIONS: BERN 1969

TS: Let us turn to focus on the actual experience of being inside the exhibition. One thing that struck me, very strongly, while seeing the show here in Venice was how small the Kunsthalle Bern must have been. The photographs that we have been devouring for years make the exhibition look much bigger; the sense I mentioned before about the works exploding in the space seems to be a photographic fiction. Is this a distorted historical memory?

GC: It is distorted, because the spaces at Bern were indeed relatively small. What we discovered in researching this exhibition was that while the local photographer, in 1969, used normal lenses, and recorded details, the commissioned photographers—Shunk-Kender, Balthasar Burkhard—used wide-angle lenses, and recorded installations. Only a few people actually saw the show, so its visualization through these photographs has certainly contributed greatly to its mythos.

TS: This expanded photographic constellation has created a definitive image of the incredibly productive conjunction between open-form art and curating. In this specific sense, the photographs of *When Attitudes* have set a standard for the look of what I call the "post-avant-garde exhibition." By this I mean that the historical avant-garde had arrived at the stage where it thought that it no longer needed the museum—whether as its opposite, its foil, or its eventual destination. Something like this, anyway, was the hope shared by these artists. 1969 is a moment *before* this outcome is widely designated as "neo-avant-garde," a term I have always hated, probably because it declares that that hope was already, and perhaps always had been, a false one. It seems to me that, here in Venice, against all kinds of odds (for starters: history, this building, the structures of the contemporary art world, and so on), you have tried to re-create what that time might have felt like: to evoke, without slavish repetition—indeed, through a deliberate artificiality—the avant-garde's final moment of authenticity. That is to say, the last occasion on which artists working together could transform art into something utterly other.

GC: To me, the original power of *When Attitudes* rests, as I said, on the strong relationships that the artists, working together, established between the works.

Taken as single, discrete pieces, they are variable, but viewed as a totality they were amazing. In fact, the idea to do this show, now, here in Venice, came from the realization that few art historians or curators still take the trouble to document such specific relationships. Today, exhibitions are usually arrangements and rearrangements of individual works, or works by an individual artist, or a group, or they are displays that explore a theme. When curators make shows that recall past exhibitions, and move even just one artwork in relation to another, the language of the original is changed. That's what pushed me to revive *When Attitudes*. I wanted to show the kinds of relationships that these works created between each other.

EXHIBITIONS AS ARCHAEOLOGY

TS: This kind of approach has led some people to complain that you are just repeating, in an antiquarian way, an exhibition that everyone already regards as a classic, the paradigm of its type. They claim that you are doubling up the capture of these works by the art historical/museum machine, rendering them twice impotent, sending then back to their time of origin, and locking them inside a frozen picture of *When Attitudes*, as if we were visiting an archaeological excavation site.

GC: No. It's not an archaeological exercise. We were obliged to rope off Richard Serra's huge steel "prop" pieces and Alighiero Boetti's *Me Sunbathing in Turin, January 19, 1969*, which takes the form of a hundred crumpled clay balls in the shape of a human figure lying on the floor. But otherwise there is a minimum of territorial marking, nothing separating the spectators from the works, even though they are in a very complex and confined set of spaces. Walking through the exhibition the viewer cannot focus on each piece in the traditional way, as if it were a step in a sequence along a white wall, or an illustration on a white page that you turn by walking along.

TS: Yes, it's amazing to think that those very precarious works were once exhibited without any thought of stopping people getting close to them. At the same time, there was even an element of deliberate risk associated with some of them, such as Jacquet's electrical wiring, and Robert Morris's fire piece.

GC: People responded to that invitation in ways we cannot imagine now. The Serra lead spatter work was damaged, over and over. You can see the marks in the photographs. People pulled at the works, tested out the materials, sometimes even kicked and walked on them. That kind of immediate physical reaction is unthinkable today.

TS: Is the fact that there is no designated pathway, that you can take many pathways through the exhibition, part of that intention?

GC: I have imposed no framework on these works. The frame is whatever emerges as the totality of your experience of the exhibition. As a viewer, you are part of that frame, which I think of as being as physical as it is intellectual, or being about memory. When making the exhibition, we tried to allow for every possible relationship to the works or to their documentation. So you can feel their presence, and the absence of the original exhibition, as the same element. And you feel that everything here—the original works, the copies, the photographs, the markings on the floor—is equally present *and* absent, at the same time.

DIFFERENCE AND REPETITION

TS: Let us focus on the differences between the two exhibitions.

GC: Well, one key factor is this historic building. You know, we cannot transform the actual walls of the building; we cannot remove them, or add to them in any permanent way. We cannot even hang works on them. Yet our basic premise for this exhibition was that whatever was included in the exhibition in Bern had to be shown, and shown as it was at the Kunsthalle.

TS: So, this apparent impasse led you to the idea of reconstructing the Kunsthalle's display areas inside this palace in Venice: windows, floors, doorways, door handles, heaters, power outlets, everything. It's amazing...

GC: It is manically exact. That was part of Thomas Demand's contribution. His art centers on the reconstruction of detail, so he went immediately to that dimension. Our team of four people included also Miuccia Prada and Rem Koolhaas, who thought mostly about space. My concern was getting the historical material right. Once we had the idea of revisiting *When Attitudes*, our discussion went like this: if we do it in an empty hangar, it would be just an archaeological reconstruction, with no curatorial idea to it. But, we have an eighteenth-century building, so let's do it there—but how? First, we thought of re-creating the show at a fifty percent scale, so that visitors would always know where they were relative to the whole. Then Rem, through moving transparencies of the two ground plans over each other, saw that we could fit the entire Kunsthalle, at its actual size, into the palazzo. So, we realized that we could be very faithful to the original, if not totally, of course. Thomas worked on the detail of the reconstruction, and he thought carefully about the conjunctions between the two buildings. You will notice that the inserted walls do not quite touch those of the palazzo.

TS: In the catalogue there are intriguing photographs of the details of their conjunctions. I presume that they are Thomas's?

GC: Yes, indeed. Finally, the team got into a really heavy discussion about how to show the missing works. It was three or four weeks before the opening, and two of us were saying, let's just ignore the missing works, or reconstruct them entirely. Thomas and I said, not without permission from the artists. The others said we were being conservative. It went back and forth, like a tennis match. At a certain moment, you know, it was really tense. So, we had to find some other solution. To-scale photographs of the missing works would be construed as artworks in themselves, replacement artworks. Re-creations would be simulacra. Thomas was fantastic—he said, "Then we can label the show, 'When Attitudes Become Fakes.'" Finally, we stumbled on the idea of outlines, like those the police use at accident or murder scenes, as a similar way of marking the exact spot where something existed, and thus preserving its relationship to other works.

TS: It is rather forensic, in a strange, Warholian sort of way, but overall it works. Mainly because you keep it up throughout, and are really clear about the distinctions between re-presenting the original works, showing exhibition copies (made by other museums with the artist's permission), and these ghostly records of absent works.

To be pedantic for a moment, the Ryman wall-piece should have been in the room with the Sol LeWitt and the Fred

Sandback, which made a lot of sense back then as a dialogue between painting and drawing and a representation of what could be absented from both when trying to delineate what LeWitt called "the idea" of a work.

GC: Right, that's the only work that's shifted. It is also the only exception to the restrictions against doing anything to the palazzo walls, because the only way of securing the loan was to agree to inscribe it directly on a wall, as it was originally.

TS: In terms of the overall effect of the show, my one major sadness is that the palazzo's interior architecture would not let you reproduce the entrance hall of the Kunsthalle. Instead, we have to imagine the ground floor foyer wrapping around the well of the main staircase two floors up. In Bern, it must have been a profound experience to walk in and see those amazing tiles, to see Serra's lead spattered against the floor and lower back wall [*Splashing*, 1968], and then, above, his hanging belts and neon piece [*Belts*, 1966–67]. I saw *Belts* last month, at David Zwirner in New York, in an extraordinarily concentrated show of Serra's early work.

GC: This grouping of Serra's works lacks only the belts from the Panza Collection, now in the Guggenheim Museum. Unfortunately, as you noticed, it was already promised as a loan to Zwirner. A couple of other pieces are also missing: Eva Beuys allowed us to execute Joseph Beuys's fat piece [*Fettecke*, 1969], but not the felt one [*Wärmeplastik*, 1969]. Its owner, who is ill, uses that piece as a kind of reference to orient himself. So, there were often very personal reasons for what we could or couldn't show. The artists themselves and their estates were most cooperative. Sonnier, Saret, Jenney, De Maria, Ruppersberg, Weiner, Zorio, van Elk, and others not only reconstructed their historic pieces, but even in some cases re-created their ephemeral works for us.

TS: The clearest structural difference between this version and the original is the fact that you show the works that were displayed in the school across the street from the Kunsthalle on the top floor of the palazzo, under the roof.

GC: We found a school near here that agreed to participate, but the opening was planned for when it was still in session, so we couldn't use it after all. In 1969, the idea was less to use a school as such, and more to have an alternative, open space for works that could not fit into the Kunsthalle, or that had a different aesthetic impact from those on display there. Curators can always use some flexibility, you know. So we decided to occupy a floor of the palazzo that had never been employed as a display area. We were able to create what we believe is the same amount of exhibition space, and to show the works as close to how they were originally shown as possible. Not easy, as there are around a thousand images of the Kunsthalle, but only five photos of the school. Everything was reconstructed from memory, from interviews with people who were there. To be honest, I have no recollection of it.

Another important thing that we have done is exhibit more works than were shown in 1969. Some of the materials that artists wanted to use back then were held up in customs, as illegal imports. Works by Jannis Kounellis and Emilio Prini, for example, were thus refused entry. We included these works, and those by artists whose works were not documented in the original catalogue. Pino Pascali and Pier Paolo Calzolari were included on the basis of the testimony of Franz Meyer. We managed also to identify the one hundredth work, two colored, vertically arranged hearts, by James Lee Byars, with an inscription dedicated to Szeemann. Finally, we included works by artists who were invited but could not participate for one reason or another. Other works, those that appear only in the televised documentation of the opening, are referenced in my catalogue essay.

There was just one piece we couldn't include in any shape or form—Michael Heizer's *Bern Depression* [1969]. You can't dig a big ditch out of the Grand Canal, nor can you put a dotted line there. I went to Nevada to discuss options with him, and he proposed something involving a picture of a church and then a cut. But, we decided not to do it. So, this show is ninety-nine percent true to Szeemann's vision.

TS: Thank you for these stories. It is helpful to remember how such pragmatic factors actually shape exhibitions.

IMMERSION AND CONNECTION

TS: Going back to the general experience of the show, I must tell you that I became so absorbed working out which work was by whom, where it fitted, and if it was in the right place that I actually forgot about the palazzo itself, despite it being right there. I went around this morning for the third time, and had the same experience. As you said, the connections between the works are so interesting that everything else falls away.

GC: That was also the biggest impact at the time, along with the spirit of openness, not competition, at a time when American Pop was regarded in Europe as the invader. Also, *When Attitudes* included certain American artists whom nobody knew much about in Europe, or even in the U.S., at the time. Since then, some have faded from view. Hopefully, our show will bring some attention back to them.

TS: Yes, Keith Sonnier appears as a more interesting artist than he has subsequently seemed. As does Neil Jenney, and his two works *Curtis Mayfield Piece* and *Siegmund Biederman Piece* [both 1968].

GC: Oh yeah, a fantastic artist. I recall visiting him on Mercer Street, where he had a huge loft, and created his own gallery, selling only his own works. There was a room for his kids, and a small bed for him. Every room had the theme of a particular painting—that's how he began, as a painter. Alan Saret is another example of an artist incorrectly overlooked. Sonnier didn't have any documents for his work in *When Attitudes*, the untitled neon and cloth wall-piece [*Untitled*, 1969], so we provided him with the opportunity to re-create it. His original inspiration, he explained to me, came when he walked into a commercial lighting store on the Bowery in New York City and saw some broken neon lying on the floor. He got it for free. Today, reconstructing the work cost $50,000.

THE DANGERS OF MUSEUMIZATION

TS: There is an interesting section in the catalogue where your team asks you some very challenging questions about the motivations behind the show.[10] I've got what may be a similar one. What you have done with this restaging of *When Attitudes* strikes me as, in a particular way, very Venetian. This is a city that has been performing as a museum of itself since the fifteenth century, and especially since the early nineteenth, when it basically stopped modernizing, or, at least, did so out of sight, away from the tourist centers, in disguise, one might say. We come to Venice precisely to experience the contradiction between a museumized city and contemporary art. It is what we expect, what we are accustomed to finding: the enchanting contrast between slow time and fast happening, between entropy and the instant. In a certain sense, and in fact rather dramatically, this exhibition enacts this exact contradiction, doesn't it?

GC: Venice has always been a scenario for the contemporary. It consciously uses its past as a backdrop to the present. From the beginning, it has been the goal of the Fondazione Prada to present modern and contemporary art in, let's say, a contemporary manner, but also to present it in ways that are consciously historical, if not art historically linear.

10. "Why and How: A Conversation with Germano Celant," in Germano Celant, *When Attitudes Become Form: Bern 1969/Venice 2013* (Venice: Fondazione Prada, 2013), pp. 393–421.

TS: You have said in press releases that this exhibition treats the original one as a kind of readymade. However, to be pedantic again, unlike Duchamp in 1917, you clearly did not choose to present *When Attitudes* on the basis of your "aesthetic indifference" to it, nor to imply that it was an exhibition like any other. Perhaps it is, for you, a "repeat readymade" in the manner of Duchamp in 1964, when he authorized Arturo Schwarz to issue an edition of eight of each of his key readymades?

GC: I use that term in the sense that our decision to re-create this "already made" exhibition did not require my curatorial participation, except for the "territorial changes" required by the shift from yesterday to today, and from Bern to Venice. A "linguistic" displacement is, of course, inevitable, because, using the Ca' Corner della Regina as a pedestal, we had to reconstruct an event or object created by Szeemann that was, itself, in its time, overturned and repurposed, its meanings reassigned. The team tried to adopt an attitude of "indifference" as to how that dislocation might affect a re-reading of the exhibition, or might give it new meaning today.

The catalogue is organized to reveal the readymade aspect of the exhibition. It is divided into sections that show as much as possible about the making of both versions of the show. Like the experience of the exhibition itself, the sections are put into explicit conjunction. All the problematics that we faced as people participating in the show's organization, or working as art historians, are made clear. At the same time, we wanted to demonstrate that history could be reconstructed in a proper way, not only through documents, or as documentation, but also through reality. Jens Hoffmann recently told me that he wants to re-do the exhibition *Primary Structures* at the Jewish Museum, in the same rooms in which it was first shown in 1966, but with a new generation of artists. That's not reconstruction; it's interpretation.

People ask me, what do you want to reconstruct next? Which of the exhibitions from the 1960s, or 1970s, or 1980s, or whatever? I say, no, that's it. Another would be formulaic.

RECONSTRUCTING THE ORIGINS OF CONTEMPORARY ART

TS: *When Attitudes* has come to stand for all of the shows around that time that marked the various ways that late modern art was turning into contemporary art. In this (modern) sense, it stands for all the contemporary art to come, and it is, therefore, the most representative exhibition of its era—that is, it is *more* contemporary than the others, the *most* contemporary among them. Restaging it is a gesture that can only occur once, if you want your gesture to be *so* contemporary.

A number of historical surveys have included reconstructions of famous exhibitions, or rather bits of them. The Los Angeles County Museum of Art has done this twice, to great effect: parts of the *Degenerate Art* show [1937] were included in their 1991 *Degenerate Art and Art of This Century*, and remakes of 1960s exhibitions by Heinz Mack and Volker Bradke were featured in their *Art of Two Germanys/Cold War Culture* in 2009. In Eastern Europe recently there have been some highly evocative remakes of exhibitions from the period of the breakup of Yugoslavia, those by the group IRWIN, for example. In fact, a vision of radical repetition has inspired the program at the Moderna galerija and the Museum of Contemporary Art Metelkova in Ljubljana. In New York, there have been at least two returns to the *Pictures* exhibition of 1977: it was restaged in its original venue, Artist's Space, in 2001, and suggestions of it were folded into *The Pictures Generation* at the Metropolitan Museum of Art in 2009. And in Eindhoven, Charles Esche has been mining the archive of the Van Abbemuseum and the history of pivotal exhibitions all over the world constantly in recent years, in order to restage museum installations and definitive temporary exhibitions.

Each of these approaches is motivated differently, and each has their own specific validity. But the pace is increasing, and one fears that if more and more are made, and done with less precision as to purpose, an art historical narrative may begin to build up, and these exhibitions will become less and less remarkable. They might become reified, artifactual, like beads on a necklace. One hopes, instead, that with this exact and extraordinary restaging of *When Attitudes* the literalist re-curating of path-finding exhibitions will come to a halt. Certainly, it will be hard to match this care, thoughtfulness, setting, and outcome.

GC: Too literal repetition undermines the original exhibitions, rather than making clear how consequential they were then, and what they mean now, for present practice.

THE SZEEMANN EFFECT

TS: Before one comes here, one's deeper, non-visual memory focuses on Harald Szeemann—the masterful exhibition maker, the innovator of contemporary curating—for whom *When Attitudes* was a breakthrough achievement (although some might feel that Documenta 5 of 1972 fits that bill better, or even one of his later, more speculative shows). As I walked through this exhibition, however, another, unexpected effect slowly dawned on me: there's no trace of him.

GC: It's like going to an opera. You see the spectacle, but mostly hear the sound. You forget about the direction. It's very simple.

TS: Some have commented that in this staging, *When Attitudes* becomes your exhibition, that Germano Celant has become the curator, the not-so-invisible director of this fabled opera. You definitely had a role in curating part of the original show, specifically the participation of the Italian artists, but the Szeemann effect has been so great that the input of others (such as Piero Gilardi and yourself) has with time been occluded. What do you think about this?

GC: If you think of Szeemann as both the "director of the orchestra" and the person in charge of the funds, then his attitude as author of the entire operation is understandable. You are right to emphasize, however, that his sources were diverse. Piero Gilardi certainly encouraged the selection of many of the artists, from Richard Long to Jan Dibbets, from Marinus Boezem to Ger van Elk—artists whom I had also included in *Arte Povera + Azioni Povera*. Seth Siegelaub and Bruce Nauman were also among Szeemann's sources. While he has been identified as the sole protagonist, this dense informational network is clear if you read his correspondence, and diary, which also registers his fear of competition.

TS: In one sense, your challenge in 2013 is the opposite of that facing Szeemann in 1969. If it is true that he welcomed the provisional, open-ended, unexpected nature of whatever the artists decided to do, then his task was to contain that experimental energy within the structure, the surroundings, and the city while at the same time honoring its spirit. Your problem is how to bring excitement to the restaging of an exhibition, the elements of which are already given, fixed, and well known.

GC: Any restaging, or re-enactment, of *When Attitudes* runs the risk of annulling the energy so masterfully brought to public attention by Szeemann in 1969. We were aware that the disruptive force of the original exhibition would be lost if we presented a sterile reconstruction, elegantly integrated into the historic spaces of a Venetian palazzo. By now, the "historic" objects have—as individual works and as an ensemble—certainly lost some of the impact that they had originally. Our response to this diminution was to risk a radical gesture: to reverse the traditional logic by which curators adapt artworks to a new exhibition setting, by having the works disrupt the building itself, as the artists did in Bern, and by severing architecture with architecture—penetrating the palazzo with the Kunsthalle. This is, in fact, a gesture toward Gordon Matta-Clark's radical splitting and "voiding" of buildings. Except that both the Bern exhibition and ours are a tearing away, a splitting, a shifting in time and place that generates not a void but fullness, different kinds of equilibrium. Thus there is a contemporary resonance, however equivocal or incomplete, between artistic strategies—Michael Heizer's "cuttings," Ger van Elk's "substitutions," and Weiner's "removals"—and our curatorial and architectural intentions.

TS: Was choosing to stage your exhibition during the Venice Biennale simply to do with optimizing attention, or did you have a particular point to make—say, about this biennale or biennials in general?

GC: To be concurrent with the Venice Biennale is certainly desirable. The Fondazione Prada is increasingly interested in thematic ideas and exhibitions that present a problem, rather than only in personal anthologies and retrospectives. So we have decided to dedicate our energies to ideas that can be explored over long periods of time, or to revisiting events that played a key role in creating the history of art. The ultimate goal is to re-read history in a contemporary sense. The next exhibition, *Art or Sound*, will explore the osmosis between art and sound from the Renaissance to the present day. We are collecting artistic objects that produce sounds, and musical instruments that are at the same time aesthetically surprising.

BIG CONCEPT CURATING

TS: Let us conclude by thinking back over your career, not as a curator but, to use your own words, "as a person and as an art historian" who works with artists. When I look back at catalogue essays of yours, and to the 1997 Venice Biennale and other major shows, such as the three surveys of various decades of Italian art that you have mounted in Paris, Venice, and New York over the years, I notice that you frequently choose a very large issue, and then try to constellate everything around its historical unfolding. For example, in the exhibition *Arts and Architecture* in Genoa in 2004, you examined every possible relationship between art and architecture during the twentieth century. These were ambitious exhibitions, much larger in historical scope than the one relatively small exhibition we have been dissecting in such detail. They were ambitious in their presumption of universal validity, but the artists included were very particular about how they realized their ideas in specific materials, places, or conjunctions. They tended to be suspicious of grand series, or big concepts, and against over-arching, integrative ideas. Over time, that's what you've paid attention to, I believe.

GC: I take on a subject that is not being analyzed, one that is, as you said, too big, seemingly untouchable, and very difficult to realize. My intuition is that the subject is important to contemporary art and thinking, so I try to read it from today's perspective, but in reverse, by going back to its various origins, and tracking all the threads that actually constitute that subject now. I discovered that this method works for individual artists as well. I think about, say, Lawrence Weiner's use of words as descriptors of spatial relationships, and then I go back to Marcel Duchamp, then to Filippo Tommaso Marinetti, and so on.

Art and Architecture in Genoa was organized like this. *Art and Fashion* [1996], in Florence, was exactly the same. I was "massacred" by artists such as Jannis Kounellis, and curators such as Rudi Fuchs, for doing this show. They said, you're giving up, you're studying dresses, this is not important. But, you know, I studied the history of the avant-garde, and Balla, Tatlin, Delaunay, Dal*í*, and many others were involved in fashion. Not only that—Ellsworth Kelly, Jim Dine, Lucio Fontana, and Louise Bourgeois all showed me evidence that they experimented with dresses. In those days, everybody was somehow involved with fashion, and nobody was touchy about it.

TS: What I understand you to be saying is that a method or idea used by modern or contemporary artists strikes you as somehow essential to a key aspect of art as such. And then, instead of looking across the world as it is now for the manifestations of this idea, or looking forward to how it might manifest itself, you turn around and say, what in all the actual historical factors that have occurred before now was the seed that makes this so definitive right now? Is your approach something like that?

GC: Exactly. For *Art and Environment, From Futurism to Body Art* at the 1976 Venice Biennale, I divided the Central Pavilion exactly in two, so that one half took you from Futurism to 1966, represented by Andy Warhol's cow wallpaper. In the other half I showed the work of twelve artists, including Joseph Beuys, Bruce Nauman, Jannis Kounellis, Mario Merz, Michael Heizer, Michael Asher, Maria Nordman, Doug Wheeler, and Robert Irwin. I laid out *Art and Fashion* on the same principle, from Futurism and Constructivism until 1995, including not just artists but also fashion designers who collaborated with artists: Miuccia Prada and Damien Hirst, Helmut Lang and Jenny Holzer, Karl Lagerfeld and Tony Cragg.

For Expo Milano 2015, I am curating an exhibition on the relationship between art and food, from prehistory until 2014, that will encompass the "instruments" of food, from the kitchen to the dining room, from the bar to the restaurant, from still-lives to the Last Supper.

THE ARCHITECTURAL LANGUAGE OF EXHIBITION MAKING

TS: As you describe these exhibitions, you are drawing on pieces of paper the thematic movement within each of them as ground plans for the exhibition spaces at each of these venues.

GC: And I try to integrate the main venues into the rest of the city as much as I can—to irrigate the city with exhibitions, you might say. *Art and Architecture*, for example, was on two floors of the Palazzo Ducale—one taking you from Russian Futurism to Lucio Fontana, the other from early modern architecture to

Frank Gehry—and also in five spaces around the city, as well as on billboards in public squares, plus in constructions by Hans Hollein, Renzo Piano, and Frank Gehry.

TS: This is curatorial thinking in action. It posits a historical, aesthetic vision, and then makes an exhibition on the basis of the spatial concept inherent in it.

GC: Absolutely. All my life I have worked with the language of exhibitions because that's what I have learned through working with architects on shows over the years. I have realized that the language of space is a key element of how an exhibition actually communicates its meanings, as important as the relationships that you establish between the works on the walls or on the floor. Few people noticed at the time, but for *Art and Environment*, in 1976, made in collaboration with Gino Valle, we cleaned up the inside of the building. That was the first curatorial decision. The process begins when you start to think about the spaces you will use, before you begin to assemble the artworks, and then mount the exhibition. When I did the biennale again in 1997, and in collaboration with Gae Aulenti, I covered the interior walls of the Central Pavilion and painted everything white, which had never been done before. This kind of gesture, I think, is curatorial. That's also what working with artists teaches you. You don't need to accept the space. You interact with the space. You bring in an architect, like Pierluigi Cerri, Massimo Vignelli, Matali Crasset, Renzo Piano, Frank Gehry, Gaetano Pesce, Rem Koolhaas/OMA, or Achille Castiglioni, and automatically the space changes. It is not only the experience of working with these architects; it is also the process of sharing a mode of thinking about the spatial organization of the exhibition, so that the architecture interacts with the art.

TS: Architects and artists always understand that the space can be changed. Whereas for everyone else—

GC: —space is a given, unalterable. All these elements are, for me, part of the curatorial process. In the end, you become a small business, a *bottega*, as we say in Italian. You put together a research team. The more you bring a team into focus, the better it is for the show. Because together you create a curatorial community, which enriches what you are able to say, especially if you create a team for the show, and another for the book, as we have done here.

The complexity of these kinds of curatorial operations is really why I never worked much inside public institutions: with such amounts of public money at stake, there is no possibility of taking a major risk. I was fortunate to work at the Guggenheim during the period when Tom Krens was expanding—in fact, exploding—the idea of what a museum could do. But even in such a place, at such a time, you had to stay within budget. I find it difficult to discuss bureaucratic details and procedures. I am always thinking, like artists do, how you go against yourself? How do you not conform? By taking another risk, if at all possible. Here, at the Fondazione, the only requirement is to do whatever we decide to do in the best possible way.

With thanks to David and Ann Wilkins for assistance with translations from the Italian.

Jens Hoffmann

When Ideas Become Form Become Exhibitions

Jens Hoffmann is the author of many texts on art and exhibition making and the curator of over fifty exhibitions. Currently deputy director at the Jewish Museum, New York, Hoffmann was previously director of the CCA Wattis Institute for Contemporary Arts, San Francisco (2007–12), director of exhibitions at the Institute of Contemporary Arts, London (2003–7), curator at the Museum Kunstpalast, Düsseldorf (2001–2), and assistant curator at the Guggenheim Museum (1998–2000). Since 2012 he has been senior curator-at-large at the Museum of Contemporary Art Detroit. With the artist Harrell Fletcher, Hoffmann founded the nomadic People's Biennial in 2010. In 2009 he founded *The Exhibitionist: Journal on Exhibition Making*, and he has been editor-at-large of *Mousse* magazine since 2011. Hoffmann has contributed to a number of catalogues and authored books, including *Theater of Exhibitions* (Berlin: Sternberg Press, 2015), *Show Time: The 50 Most Influential Exhibitions of Contemporary Art* (New York: D.A.P., 2014), and *(Curating) From A to Z* (Zurich: JRP/Ringier, 2014). He has also edited a number of books, including, most recently, *Ten Fundamental Questions of Curating* (Milan: Mousse Publishing, 2013) and *The Studio* (Cambridge, Mass.: MIT Press; London: Whitechapel Art Gallery, 2012). He has co-curated a number of biennials, including the 9th Shanghai (2012), the 12th Istanbul (2011), and the 2nd San Juan Triennial (2009). Hoffmann has been a guest professor at the Nuova Accademia di Belle Arti in Milan since 2003, and was previously an assistant professor in the Graduate Program in Curatorial Practice at California College of the Arts in San Francisco (2006–12).

Our conversation began at the Wattis Institute, San Francisco, on October 23, 2012.

Terry Smith: One of the exhibitions you organized while director of exhibitions and chief curator at the Institute of Contemporary Arts [ICA], London, was *Surprise, Surprise* [2006]. You and Rob Bowman, a junior curator at the ICA, invited forty contemporary artists to, as you put it, "contribute a piece that is atypical of the work for which they had become well known." By using this strategy, what did you intend to show that seemed to you hidden about these artists' works, about contemporary art, and about the expectations that we bring to exhibitions of contemporary art?

Jens Hoffmann: It started out in a relatively banal way. I was going over my exhibition program at the ICA about eighteen months before the show opened and didn't know what to do about the empty summer slot, so I just noted the words "surprise, surprise" on the schedule. When the time came to really think about the summer show, I imagined something that could surprise us, defy expectations and ways of viewing, and take audiences down a different path. At that point Tate Modern had become incredibly successful and museums and exhibition spaces in London were coming under enormous pressures from their boards to raise audience figures. My board chair said, "Why can't we do a show with big-name artists that people interested in art will recognize?" The question then became how to make a surprising show with the least surprising group of artists. That's how the idea was born.

TS: So there was a positive sense of wanting to break habits of seeing, but some might say you were assuming that contemporary art had become so conventional that something altogether different was needed to revivify it. They might also say that showing just one unusual work per artist does nothing more than recognize that everyone is capable of doing something different, or exceptional (in an ordinary or, as you say, banal sense). It might lead to a footnote type of exhibition, a collection of minor works.

JH: Most interesting to me were the dialogues I had with artists about what work to show. Many did not see their "unusual" works as minor. I remember Andreas Gursky happily saying that he could finally show a work no other curator or gallery had wanted to exhibit before, because it was not typical. And he wasn't the only one. Some artists also chose to show something they'd made very early on in their careers, so there was nice possibility to see a development.

It was definitely a curatorial game. We didn't put labels next to the works, so people kept trying to find clues that would help them identify who made what. A London radio station started a contest: they came in with four art critics and challenged them to figure out who made certain pieces. It was quite amusing, actually.

The show was more than a gimmick, however. It was about how we look at art, how much we depend on mediation and context, how name recognition works to bring in audiences, and how audiences orient themselves without labels and other didactics. I wanted visitors to look at the works, study them, and to try to understand what they were saying in that moment.

AMERICANA

TS: When you arrived at the CCA Wattis Institute for Contemporary Arts in San Francisco, in 2007, you immediately launched into a program of exhibitions about San Francisco in particular and the United States in general. For *Pioneers* [2007] you chose local artists, from Ant Farm to Katherine Westphal, who had "achieved something pioneering, something that had never been done before in exactly that way." You also said in the catalogue that you wished the curatorial team at the Wattis to "present ourselves to audiences here as the pioneers we aim to be in our specific field—that of exhibition making." But in contrast to your ICA show, the works chosen didn't seem like surprises; to me, they were typical of the artists in question. In what way was that exhibition pioneering? Was it through the inclusion of artifacts from the Society of California Pioneers?

JH: The exhibition gave me a chance to familiarize myself with the art of San Francisco and with a big part of its historical context: the pioneer era that lasted from 1849 to 1906. I think what was pioneering about that show was the relationship I suggested between artists from the Bay Area such as Emory Douglas, Jess, Bruce Conner, Lynn Hershman Leeson, Jay DeFeo, et cetera, and the pioneers from the Gold Rush area. All of them wanted to break new ground. The exhibition installation drew on cultural history museum displays, and we situated material from the Gold Rush—maps, diaries, tools, and ship models, as well as early photographs—next to artworks. For example, a beautiful set of drawings in a pioneer diary was placed next to collages by Jess, or a map of San Francisco circa 1849 next to paintings by Robert Bechtle, or portraits of gold miners next to portraits of Black Panther members by Emory Douglas. The juxtapositions revealed something about both and brought out the artistic qualities in the artifacts.

TS: I want to ask about the exhibition *Americana*, which was presented in a wall-mounted vitrine in the shape of the U.S., just outside the Wattis offices, from September 2007 to May 2012. It was structured as a series of mini-shows, each relating to one of the fifty states of the union, and organized by students from CCA's Graduate Program in Curatorial Practice. Their brief was to focus on "the overlooked, the suppressed, the marginalized, the little known" about their assigned state. The display changed each month. Some of them retreated into stereotypes, but most did not, or if they did, they exposed the stereotypes as constructed myths. It must have been interesting to see this kind of counter-history of the U.S. unfolding. What was your overall sense of what it revealed? How did you and the students deal with the inevitable temporal fatigue?

JH: I worked with five successive cohorts of curatorial students on that project, but fatigue was not an issue, because each student worked with me on one display only. It was mostly an exercise in understanding how site and history should play a significant role in the development of curatorial ideas—how art does not sit autonomously in this world but is part of a larger cultural and social context. It was also about how much we form our own identity by looking and displaying what we feel is important to discuss publicly. Many of the projects touched on obscure events or particular historical occurrences that I, and most others in the class, had never heard of so, we all learned quite a lot. I liked the diversity of the subjects covered, from Elvis to the civil rights and workers' movements, to the abolition of slavery and the American road trip.

EXHIBITIONS AS JOURNEYS

TS: One of your big efforts at the Wattis was organizing three exhibitions, one per year from 2008 to 2010, each focused on a different classic of American literature: *The Wonderful Wizard of Oz*, *Moby-Dick*, and *Adventures of Huckleberry Finn*. Great texts, certainly, but why these and not other classics, such as *Absalom, Absalom!* or *Leaves of Grass*?

JH: At the ICA I did a show based on Jules Verne's *Around the World in Eighty Days*. It was a terrific experience to look at a city like London, and England's role in colonization and globalization, through the lens of a book. I wanted to follow that up with exhibitions about two other books set in London, *Peter Pan* and *Through the Looking-Glass*, but then I decided to move to San Francisco and I started to think about books that are quintessentially American.

The book that instantly came to my mind was *The Wonderful Wizard of Oz*. It was the first fully American fairytale, meaning that it did not draw on European traditions of storytelling at all. I also liked the fact that most people here are so familiar with it. I think it foresaw the predicament of many people in the twentieth century, and it was the element I focused most on in the exhibition: the desire for a home versus the longing to leave. I identified quite a bit with Dorothy in her longing for a place she could call home and her simultaneous desire to explore different places. Thinking of Dorothy and her trip down the yellow brick road made me think of Ishmael and his voyage across the Pacific Ocean, and then Huck's journey on the Mississippi River.

I think the best exhibitions are journeys, paths along which we have experiences and struggles, encounter new people and new ideas, and so on. Each of the three exhibitions was in a different way trying to figure out how one could translate the narrative of a book into the narrative of an exhibition. In each case I focused quite a bit on the author. I think Mark Twain ended up getting the most attention simply because he was such a character—a trickster, an illusionist.

TS: In the catalogue for the *Huckleberry Finn* exhibition, you say that "taking literature as a departure point for the making of exhibitions carries the implication of the curator as an author, who over the course of several shows presents a larger argument, or group of arguments." What is this larger argument? How would you outline it discursively? How do you think it became apparent in the exhibitions?

JH: Each exhibition was about intellectual growth and development—coming to terms with certain realities and with the understanding that the world is an utterly irrational place, and being able to deal with that. Each character has to face a challenge but is successful in the end. They reach a form of freedom that all of us should have, intellectually as much as physically.

THE CURATOR AS BOOK MAKER

TS: I was impressed by the fact that each of the catalogues approximated the original publications, especially in their design and layout. The catalogues also serve as books of record—that is, they include installation shots. This is great, because as you know, unless you were there, that's the only way you can get some hint of what I call "exhibitionary knowledge" (things you learn from actually walking around the show in real space).

JH: It's very important to me to document the staging of an exhibition, as all the details—from the lighting to the design of the wall texts, the placement of each work, the colors, and the graphics—are carefully thought out to create an almost theatrical reality. It was my goal for visitors to feel that they were stepping onto a stage and *becoming* Dorothy, Ishmael, or Huck.

TS: Are your texts within the catalogues also retrospective? They do not seem to be.

JH: No, in each case I wrote the essay before the installation was finished. All we needed to do then was to slip the installation shots into the design and send the book off to print.

TS: Overall, your exhibition catalogues look like a section of a bookstore—the product of many minds—your exhibitions, however, all seem organized along a consistent set of principles. They are all group exhibitions, not one-person shows. Each takes up a theme, or a set of ideas, or a place, and contrasts elements of its original appearance in past time with a perspective from the present—from your point of view, usually expressed in a catalogue essay, and from the viewpoints of the contemporary artists involved. So, there is always then and now, history and the present. Are you consciously trying to promote a sense of historical consciousness in the present (which is frequently inclined against such a consciousness)?

JH: This is very interesting. Many people tell me that my books have a certain look to them, which perhaps becomes more apparent when you consider the attention to detail, the paper, the binding, the colors, and so on. History is one of my main points of interest in many of my exhibitions. I am simply curious to understand how we got to this point—what events brought us here, and how they continue to inform our behavior. We always need to take one step back to go two steps forward, I think. I believe also that all intellectual and cultural output is a possible answer to the big questions we face as humans: what's the meaning of life, what's wrong and what's right, what comes after death, is there a god...

REVISITING HISTORY NOW

TS: In another of your Wattis shows, *More American Photographs* [2011], you contrasted classic Farm Security Administration

[FSA] photographs taken in the mid-1930s in the Dust Bowl, small towns, and rural communities across the U.S. with, again, commissioned photographs and installations by contemporary artists—actually twelve artists, from Walead Beshty to Hank Willis Thomas. The FSA images were hung on freestanding screens in the center of the galleries, while the contemporary works were installed on the surrounding walls. You also included documentation about Roy Stryker, the head of the bureau that commissioned the FSA photographs, who wrote outline "scripts" for the photographers, almost like plot outlines for a play (although not as detailed as stage directions). Did you see yourself as having a parallel role in relation to the contemporary artists in your show?

JH: I did not see myself as a Roy Stryker. Although I did play around with all the elements he employed—for instance, sending scripts to the artists—I was not as dogmatic about the parameters. The photo program of the FSA was one of the most impressive artistic undertakings of the twentieth century, but it is not that well known anymore, so I was happy to be able to bring it back, especially at a moment when the U.S. was facing a big recession. The photos by Dorothea Lange and Walker Evans have shaped our understanding of U.S. history so much, and their style had a massive impact on photography as a medium. That exhibition was one of my personal favorites and toured quite extensively. There was a lot of interest in the subject.

TS: You say in the catalogue, "Whereas the FSA photographs were characterized by directness and consistently carry out the documentary mandate, the contemporary artists followed much more individual interests that were not necessarily tied to education and social change." This leads you to see this exhibition less as a "sequel" to the FSA enterprise and more as a "footnote" to it. Is this a judgment about the different kind of political valence that art has today? Does it parallel the weaker role of art exhibitions today compared to the impact of those photographs in their era?

JH: Yes, there might be a judgment there, but I think maybe photography no longer holds the place it did as a medium of documentation and social critique. The representation of social hardship in photography is a big issue, with many possible arguments. I personally believe that art should be less about the representation of reality and more about the reality of representation. *More American Photographs* wasn't a sequel—it was a playful reconsideration.

CURATING AS DRAMATURGY

TS: Your background in theater informs the way you think about exhibitions as consciously framed, staged experiences that are organized like acts in a play, unfolding through time in space, with introductions, accumulative plots, peaks, downtimes, and climaxes. You have made this explicit in exhibitions such as *Painting Between the Lines*, at the Wattis in 2011. For that show you commissioned fourteen artists to make paintings that related to a novel or poem in which a painting is described in detail. For example, Laura Owens made a work in response to Sylvia Plath's *The Bell Jar*. You say that your goal was "to bring the experience of exhibition viewing as close as possible to the experience of reading," yet your staging of the show turned the texts into very large images, whereas the works by the artists were often smaller things, situated adjacent to them. The paintings were spotlit, so that the experience of viewing the show was not unlike walking through a sequence of flats on a stage. But the viewers were not performers, right? Or if they were, who was their audience?

JH: The architecture of this show was very important. The walls were built to look like open books, with facing pages for each pairing: on the left wall/page, we installed the description of the painting as it appeared in the book, a first edition of the book in question, and a summary of the book's narrative; on the right wall, the new painting. The walls were additionally numbered like pages in a book, and the numbers corresponded to the pages in the first editions in which each respective painting is portrayed.

It was about realizing paintings that never existed, or rather that only existed in the imaginations of the writers who described them and seeing how artists would interpret their words. I chose the descriptions of the paintings together with the artists, and those were very exciting conversations. I thought of the audience as walking among gigantic books in an imaginary library, like something out of a Jorge Luis Borges novel.

TS: Have you made an exhibition about a play?

JH: Not yet, but I would like to. One of my focuses when studying the history of theater and directing was absurdist theater, and especially the works of Eugène Ionesco and Samuel Beckett, whose *Waiting for Godot* is such an elemental play, with so many possible interpretations, that I am sure I will make an exhibition out of it sooner or later.

TS: For you, is being a curator closer to writing a play, or directing it? Or, perhaps, producing it? Here we might be moving into roles, such as programming a season, or managing a theater, that are closer to what a museum director, or deputy director, does.

JH: This is a very interesting question. I would say that my job entails two different types of roles: the one in which I curate exhibitions, which is definitely closer to directing, and that of the director who programs an entire exhibition schedule over several years. I am intrigued by both types of work. I think that curating is about having a larger vision for a certain argument you want to bring across in an exhibition space, and that vision (in my opinion) includes not only the selection of artworks and how they are placed, but also how one talks and writes about them, and what context one creates around them, including the architecture and the staging. When I work with architects or designers, the process is very collaborative but with a director at the helm, like in the theater.

ARTISTS AS CURATORS/ CURATORS AS ARTISTS

TS: Your 2003 project *The Next Documenta Should Be Curated by an Artist* struck me as an interesting way of provoking serious, as well as playful, thoughts about the convergences between art and curatorial practice since the 1970s. Framing the statement as a question, you invited twenty-five artists to "propose a brief concept of how they could imagine putting together an exhibition such as Documenta." The results were a fascinating mix, ranging from "why not?" (Marina Abramović) to jokey refusals (John Baldessari), neat parodies (Elmgreen & Dragset), and lengthy speculations, such as that of Daniel Buren, who reprised his 1972 letter attacking Harald Szeemann for imposing his perspective on the artists invited to Documenta that year, and argued in detail that this dynamic has proliferated over the years. Alfredo Jaar said that the world situation was so serious that only a "great mind" should do it, irrespective of discipline. Most respondents proposed ideas involving collaborative teams, including artists and curators working together, which of course happened that year at the Venice Biennale, in the *Utopia Station* section.

It seems to me that you proposed your own possible answer in the concept that you and Adriano Pedrosa put into practice at the 12th Istanbul Biennial in 2011. You created five group exhibitions and fifty solo shows. The group exhibitions all departed from a particular work by Felix Gonzalez-Torres, and the solo shows took up themes from the group presentations. Did you think of this as, in a way, an artist "curating" the exhibition in absentia, or in spirit, given that Gonzalez-Torres died in 1996? And were you and Pedrosa acting as mediums?

JH: I never thought about Felix curating the exhibition and Adriano and me being his mediums. That's a possibility. However, more likely is the fact that Adriano and I both feel a responsibility to the formal and the political, and so we wanted an artist who had, in our opinion, carefully combined those concerns. We looked at Gonzalez-Torres's works and reflected on Istanbul and its history, ultimately selecting five of the artist's works that we felt spoke to war and violence, identity and geography, history, the personal and the political, and abstraction in a way relevant to the context. We organized the five group shows and the solo exhibitions around these concepts.

TS: Some reviewers faulted you for overemphasizing formal resonances, especially compared to the previous two editions that were curated by Hou Hanru and the collective WHW, respectively. They felt that your structure somehow constrained the political connotations of the works, giving the displays a quality more like temporary exhibitions in a museum than a biennial.[1] But Gonzalez-Torres was, as you said in your curatorial statement, an artist "deeply attuned to both the personal and the political, and also rigorously attentive to the formal aspects of artistic production, integrating high modernist, minimal, and conceptual references with themes from everyday life." The ghosts of certain artists—Duchamp, Warhol, Judd, it's a long list—certainly hover over some exhibitions. And if we are to be haunted, it seems to me that Gonzalez-Torres's ghost is one of those we might prefer to have around. What is your response to the criticisms?

JH: I do not think that each edition of a biennial has to look the same and engage with its location in the same way. I think ours was distinguished by the attention to detail, the rigor in terms of focusing on the themes, the installation, the juxtapositions, the hanging, the level of finish, et cetera. It was less chaotic and confused than most biennials, with their rather loose and imprecise plotlines, and more on a par with museum standards. We were fed up with lazy, pretentious, sloppy curating. We wanted to put an exhibition together that emphasized works

1. Reviews of the 12th Istanbul Biennial: *Frieze*, http://www.art-agenda.com/reviews/untitled-12th-istanbul-biennial/; *Artnet*, http://www.artnet.com/magazineus/features/watts/2011-istanbul-biennial.asp.

on paper, photography, and printed matter—all mediums used by Gonzalez-Torres—and avoided large video projections, installations, or sculptures. We also wanted to create a biennial that was, despite its size, very intimate and personal. The political was one aspect of a larger investigation into the relationship between politics, representation, and art that we were trying to reveal.[2]

RE-CURATING

TS: Recently you have turned to what I call "re-curating," meaning revisiting a historical exhibition that has had the kind of impact on art making, and on subsequent curatorial practice, that novels such as *Moby-Dick* and *Adventures of Huckleberry Finn* have had on the American social consciousness (and, hopefully, conscience). You haven't remade exhibitions of the work of individual artists, but you have revisited single exhibitions, or the creative acts of an individual curator. In *When Attitudes Became Form Become Attitudes* (at the Wattis in 2012), you evoked Harald Szeemann's iconic 1969 exhibition at the Kunsthalle Bern. The show wasn't a re-creation, but rather an exploration of the legacy, and the mythology, of *When Attitudes*. I think your biggest curatorial decision was to invite viewers to make the leap from 1969 to 2012. A curator with heavily art historical instincts would have done a thorough tracking through art and exhibition history from 1969 up to the present, showing us each step and all the currents of that amazing journey. Can you tell us why you left all that out?

JH: Let me cite one of your injunctions to curators: "Re-invent the exhibition format." One of the impulses that led me to curating in the first place was my interest in how art is displayed. I remember vividly several visits to the Museum of Modern Art

2. Jens Hoffmann and Adriano Pedrosa, curatorial statement, *Untitled (12th Istanbul Biennial)*, 2011, http://12b.iksv.org/en/giris.asp?c=3&id=38.

in Frankfurt when Jean-Christophe Ammann was running it. I was fascinated by the fact that the building was designed around the museum's collection. There is a space especially for Christian Boltanski, one each for Katharina Fritsch, Andreas Slominski, and Gerhard Richter, and a long gallery especially for Stephan Balkenhol. I thought it was fabulous—I had never seen anything other than uniform white boxes before.

I think my whole desire to challenge exhibition formats really has its roots in that experience. You have to find the right context, one that is the most appropriate for what the art is trying to say. So in each of the exhibitions that I've done over the years, I've always tried to find another format, one that suits the art exactly.

SEQUELS IN SEQUENCE

JH: What does it mean to organize an exhibition as a sequel to another? The first room in *When Attitudes Became Form Become Attitudes* briefly summarized Szeemann's exhibition, by centering on a specially commissioned scale model of the original exhibition to give you an idea of how it looked in Bern. Also included nearby were a copy of the catalogue—now a much sought after item—and a video of a film made for Dutch television that tracked the installation of the works in 1969 and the opening, and includes a very entertaining interview with Lawrence Weiner. On another wall were lots of photographs of the artists installing their works, the exhibition spaces, and of course the opening.

Then you stepped through a large, life-size photograph of the doors of the Kunsthalle Bern and what you saw was not, of course, the 1969 exhibition, but the sequel, or today's episode, featuring artists of a more recent generation, all aged between twenty-five and forty-five. Most of the artists that I have worked with most closely, many of whom were in that show—Claire Fontaine, Ryan Gander, Mario Garcia Torres, Tim Lee, Tino Sehgal, Luisa Lambri, Nina Beier—have at some point mentioned to me that the period that really informs their way of thinking about art is the late 1960s and early 1970s. My question was always, why that particular period? Why don't they think about the 1980s, or the late 1970s, or the early 1990s? Their answer was always that this was the last truly radical moment in art. They admire artists who were really interested in challenging the concepts, frameworks, and institutions of art, whether through Conceptualism, Minimalism, or Arte Povera.

TS: Yes, we have to reach back, but what does it mean to be a historian, a curator, or an artist now, realizing that you have to go back to the late 1960s to actually find inspiring art, incendiary art, challenging art, art that is relevant to the present? I am old enough to be able to tell you that they weren't wholly magical times and shouldn't be overly mystified.

It is extraordinary that a middle-size exhibition in a marginal venue should have had such an impact, and that its resonance seems to grow rather than diminish in time. After all, in 1969 the Kunsthalle Bern was about as prominent on the map of European art institutions as the Wattis is in the U.S. today—perhaps less so, relatively speaking.

My sense is that, in Bern, the art erupted in a building that was absolutely not designed for it. Serra's *Scatter Piece*, all that molten lead thrown at the wall-floor juncture of a highly graphic, black-and-white mosaic floor! I think the art actually transformed the spaces into a kind of suspended state. I agree that the experience also transformed Szeemann's outlook.

JH: As the images show, the installation was so dense, the situation so intense.

TS: Yes, absolutely. So, thinking about your exhibition as a whole, as movement through a sequence of rooms, it is clear that some odd disjunctions can happen when one juxtaposes things of the same kind but coming from distinct temporalities, as we constantly do in making exhibitions. Strange effects can occur when you put a scaled-down version of something up against an actual-size instance of the same kind of thing. Or when you place an idealized rendering of something against an actual item of the same kind. In your show, the miniaturization embodied in the scale model of the exhibition made the original exhibition come alive to me as a gargantuan project, but the fifty works in the surrounding galleries—however much they echoed, or played off at tangents, the concerns of the earlier artists—somehow became smaller as I walked through the rooms. Not necessarily physically, but, in a funny way, conceptually.

I am thinking, for example, of Hank Willis Thomas's riff on the long, heavy rope that Barry Flanagan trailed through the galleries in 1969. Willis Thomas tics a noose at one end, but few, if any, of the artists in *When Attitudes* would have done something like that. Perhaps Beuys. Yet, for a black American artist today this makes absolute sense, even if, visually, it is a kind of narrowing. Which does not make it a lesser work, because current contexts—where instantaneous reading is required—demand such trade-offs.

Some works in your show understand that this legacy is a more complex one. Marcelo Cidade's *Addition by Subtraction* [2012], for example, which delineates the frame of a large wall-mounted work using broken glass shards, echoed works by Lawrence Weiner, Keith Sonnier, and Allen Ruppersberg, among others, that dealt with removals, voiding, edging, and so on. The piece relating to real estate in San Francisco by the Palestinian artist Taysir Batniji also used Conceptualist protocols to make a sharp political point, one that you got by unpeeling its layers.

These examples highlight, by contrast, the almost absolute absence in the works shown in *When Attitudes* of any specific reference to the events of May 1968, the political conditions of the time.

JH: Many contemporary artists are trying to find a connection to something that exists outside the world of art galleries and auction houses. To do that, if you think historically or look for precedents, you have to go back to the late 1960s. In regards to the work by Hank Willis Thomas, while the noose of course invokes the history of lynching in America, it is also about being suffocated by a certain history and style, that of Conceptual art in this case.

San Francisco in 1969 was a center in terms of political movements, the anti-war movement, the free speech movement, the feminist movement, and the radical art practices that developed out of these movements. I asked myself, how can we introduce this work, this way of thinking about art and exhibitions, to a new generation not only of curators, but also of artists, especially those who are studying here at California College of the Arts, the art school of which the Wattis is part? How do we respond to our location in the city but also on campus?

TS: Why didn't you re-curate, or do a sequel to, a San Francisco show from that time?

JH: There was no equivalent show.

TS: To revisit a past exhibition, and do so in a way that transforms our understanding of the exhibition and then looks for resonance in the present—that's what I think you did in the show. Do you want to comment on this broad tendency, or on other re-curated exhibitions?

JH: I deal with the history of exhibitions in the most direct way: by making another exhibition. As a curator, I think it makes sense for me to do this, rather than writing a book or teaching a seminar. Well, I have done that, too, but making an exhibition is most satisfying for me.

TS: If we take literally your idea of a sequel, we might wonder if you saw your show less as a re-curation of *When Attitudes* and more as a survey exhibition of current conceptual/political art? This would make the reference to *When Attitudes* more an homage, a gesture of acknowledgment, as opposed to the main focus. Do you think that the works in the main rooms at the Wattis added up to a survey of conceptual/political art in its current manifestations?

JH: You are absolutely right. It was a survey exhibition of art made today that has been influenced by the artworks made in 1969 and the artists who made them, and it was definitely in homage to that earlier show.

OTHER PRIMARY STRUCTURES

TS: Kynaston McShine certainly is one of the curators who shook up curating in the later 1960s and early 1970s by responding quickly, and sharply, to changes in contemporary art. While his show *Information* at MoMA in 1970 was pivotal, his *Primary Structures* at the Jewish Museum, New York, in 1966, was just as important in marking the first stages of the shift away from traditional mediums. It brought together the breakthroughs that were occurring in sculpture in England and those being made by "Minimal" artists in North America.

In your *Other Primary Structures* exhibition at the Jewish Museum in 2014, you contextualized *Primary Structures* with some generosity in your catalogue essay, but clearly your triggering insight was that the 1966 show was entirely about the work of forty or so U.S. and British artists, and that everybody concerned had no hesitation in claiming universal relevance for them as radical transformers of Art, as such. There was no regard for the fact that, in many other parts of the world, artists were subjecting sculpture to similarly radical transformations. So, in your first major New York show, you seemed to want to set an agenda, part of which entailed revisiting past acts of definition to

redefine them more completely, in a world context. To me, this is curating as a kind of radical art historical supplementarity.
JH: *Other Primary Structures* was the result of a number of histories, or precedents. One was the history of exhibitions and what *Primary Structures* did to the narrative of art history. The other element was an examination of the history of the Jewish Museum itself, and the idea that I could review its most important exhibition by bringing it into the present and by presenting a global perspective on the subject McShine investigated. The show was also a reaction to the fact that the Jewish Museum has to date been incredibly Euro-centric and our goal is to radically change and challenge that fact.

TS: The two-volume catalogue repeats the design of the 1966 publication, and includes a reprint of that publication together with a volume reflecting your show, uniting the two in a very 1960s-style plastic sleeve. Your exhibition presented works made around the time of the original show, the mid-1960s, by artists active in South America, Asia, and Eastern Europe, plus a few, such as Rasheed Araeen and David Medalla, who had migrated to London from Pakistan and the Philippines, respectively.

Why did you decide to include the actual works shown in *Primary Structures* as life-size, wall-mounted photographs of the original exhibition? This meant that although the works in your exhibition were affirmed in the present, they were surrounded by image-ghosts of great works past, which took on, in their actual absence, almost mythic stature. It is hard to compete against such things. Even when your implication is that you are focusing on the absent half of the exhibition that could have, or maybe should have, been mounted in 1966.

JH: I was definitely thinking about ghost images, and a past that the museum, also, has to overcome. The fact that the original show took place in the very same spaces gave the whole undertaking a somewhat uncanny undertone, at least for me. I was less interested in making a direct comparison between the

Western works and works from other areas of the world than in thinking about placing the new works *inside* the old exhibition. A mirage-like merging of past and present. You might have noticed that the large blow-ups were tilted, implying that history is unstable.

TS: Works from the original *Primary Structures* also appeared, I think compellingly, in the final room of the exhibition, as miniatures inside a scale model of the building. It was a very dramatic culmination to a rather theatrical sequencing of the rooms. Some commented that this arrangement cut against the character of the artwork itself, and fed into the misleading reading of Minimalism—famously mounted by Michael Fried in his essay "Art and Objecthood" [1967]—that it was an overly literal, theatrical turn, and therefore anti-modernist. I can't recall whether Fried mentioned *Primary Structures* in his article, but I can imagine the exhibition shocking him—and Clement Greenberg, for that matter—to their foundations.

JH: It took me a long time to decide whether I should put the model at the start of the show or at the end. I decided on the latter, believing that it would lead to fewer comparisons between the two shows. I was not interested in comparing the works as much as showing what other work was being made at the same time elsewhere. The model was about us being voyeurs of the past and the present simultaneously.

TS: Work from this period by Lygia Clark, Hélio Oiticica, Gego, Lee Ufan, David Medalla, and some of the other artists you selected has received a lot of attention recently. Curators are searching for the origins of what I call the "transnational transition" in contemporary art, and historians are researching what they call the "multiple modernities" that were actually being pursued in localities all over the world during the past two centuries or so, but have been downplayed or ignored by mainstream modernism.

Obviously, your project was part of this tendency, as was made very clear by the North-South comparative timeline that we saw as we entered the exhibition. Yet in most recent exhibitions and histories, the radical artistic innovations of these artists are valued as manifestations of forces and dynamics at play in their locations, with connotations and meanings that are specific to their places of origin. They are also usually read as having national or regional significance, as well as more "universal" (actually, international) relevance. These qualities are often highlighted in publications and in the exhibition spaces. Taking in *Other Primary Structures* room by room, however, we experienced a very different framing, almost as if the predominantly formal aesthetic of *Primary Structures* refused to disappear back into history but, instead, had revived itself to now incorporate these artists. As an overall historical and curatorial strategy, does this not leave the West-versus-the-Rest binary intact? What would be a more suggestive strategy?

JH: I think I am actually interested in this dichotomy. I do not advocate assimilation or absorption: Asian art, or Latin American art, does not need to be part of the Western or Northern canon of art. Canonization is such a Western/Northern concept anyway, a leftover of modernism, and I think it has been done and is finished ideologically speaking. The dialogues that interest me more are the ones between the South and the South, between the East and the South, the East and the East, consciously excluding the West and the North for once. I did not do *Other Primary Structures* to say that the West *has* to look at these artists; I did it because the South and the East are just as much part of my region as the North or the West. I think it's about a form of delocalization, undermining the structural principles of Western society, which are very much about domination and demarcation.

TS: For pragmatic reasons related to limited space, you divided the show into two "halves": works from 1960 to around 1967 were on view for the first few months, works from then until around 1970 in the second part. (I have to say I find it dismaying that the museum did not give you sufficient space to do the whole show together.) You did not change the overall style of presentation in *Other Primary Structures: Others 2*. What is your sense of how different the work was between the two moments? Or was it mainly a matter of continuities?

JH: The idea was also that the works in *Others 1* were made before the Jewish Museum mounted *Primary Structures*, and the works in *Others 2* subsequently. Several of the works in *Others 2* were actually direct reactions to *Primary Structures*, and I wanted to present how that show influenced particularly the Latin American artists. I would have loved to do it as a single large-scale exhibition, but the museum did not have enough space and the schedule was already set for the lower galleries. Also, because it was a relatively radical show for the Jewish Museum to do, I think we all decided that it made sense to only use the second floor, and keep the ground floor for something with more general appeal—as it happened, an Art Spiegelman retrospective. This is simply the reality of how museums have to operate these days.

Zoe Butt

Infrastructural Activism: Alternative Spaces And Curatorial Networks

Zoe Butt is executive director and curator of Sàn Art, Ho Chi Minh City. From 2007 to 2009 she was director of international programs at the Long March Project (now known as Long March Space) in Beijing, China. Between 2001 and 2007 she was assistant curator of contemporary Asian art at the Queensland Gallery of Modern Art, in Brisbane, Australia, where she assisted in the development of the Asia Pacific Triennial of Contemporary Art (APT) and in key acquisitions for the contemporary Asian art collection. Her curatorial range is pan-Asian, and she works with private collectors and researchers, independent curators, and major museums globally.

Our conversation was triggered by our membership of a panel entitled "Infrastructural activism: building alternative spaces and critical curatorial networks," which introduced the conference *Knowing Through Showing*, convened by Lizzie Muller at the National Institute for Experimental Arts, College of Art and Design, University of New South Wales, Sydney, on September 9, 2014. Blair French, director of curatorial and digital at the Museum of Contemporary Art, Sydney, chaired the panel, and participates in the conversation.

Terry Smith: I want to focus our discussion on your work at Sàn Art, Ho Chi Minh City, which the New Museum describes as "the most active independent, artist-initiated contemporary art space and reading room in Vietnam." But let me begin by asking about your experiences in Brisbane during the early 2000s, when you worked at what was then the Queensland Art Gallery, now called the Queensland Gallery of Modern Art [QGOMA]. It is, of course, best known for the Asia Pacific Triennial of Contemporary Art, the first of the mega-exhibitions that are now so common in the region, which it inaugurated in 1993. I presume that something about working on those exhibitions drew you to Asia as a place where you felt you might make a difference?

Zoe Butt: Absolutely. While training as a museum curator for nearly eight years, I worked closely with a number of artistic communities across the Asia-Pacific region, often on projects where artists chose to risk cultural controversy, or place themselves in dangerous positions in terms of local politics. I made some site visits, but most of the time I worked remotely, in Brisbane. There were all sorts of logistical obstacles resulting from the discrepancy between what our museum required and took for granted and the almost total absence of parallel infrastructure at the other end. There were financial hurdles in trying to match the quality of local artistic materials and levels of skill to our presentational standards, which, we would grumble, were not universal. Above all, there were constant reminders of how different values, cultures, and terminologies determined the limits of artistic possibility. Meanwhile, inside the curatorial department in Brisbane, an old-fashioned kind of theoretical soccer match was constantly being played out between the "conceptual studies" team and the "cultural studies" team—back and forth between reading value and meaning as residing in each art object itself, or seeing the work as a nexus of multiple social roles and influences on the artist. Lots of learning went on in both directions.

It was, and still is, easy to lament the absence of a museum network in Southeast Asia and the Pacific, the lack of critical art expertise, and the relatively small and confused local collector base. Intriguing to me in this context was how essential the triennial's commissioning funds and acquisitions program became to furthering the ambition and local projects of artists in the region, and especially in communities that had had little prior opportunity for experimentation. For instance, for APT5 [2006–7], QGOMA funded six new commissions with the Long March Project. Zhou Xiaohu produced his largest installation up to that time, titled *Utopian Theater*, a series of ten fired ceramic tableaux depicting various world tragedies as perceived via popular televised media. This work was subsequently purchased by QGOMA, bringing much-needed funds to the Long March Project's ongoing enterprise. And Vietnamese artist Dinh Q. Lê made *The Farmers and The Helicopters*, a video installation, which was eventually acquired by MoMA, New York, boosting recognition of his work in Vietnam, as well as in the U.S., and bringing more donor support to Sàn Art.

I often think back to the glass icebox of an office I occupied at the Queensland Art Gallery, to how I struggled to write reports about artworks for collection acquisition, or for curatorial consideration in the APT, with limited textual resources, usually snippets of email conversations or notes from hasty visits to artists' studios. I now feel incredibly privileged to have had the opportunity to experience the interpretative process inherent in curatorial labor through living, witnessing, and contributing to the shape, growth, and meaning of that artwork's production. Ultimately, I think that the APTs were important in the creation of what was a fluid platform for more equitable exchanges between artists, critics, curators, and audiences in the region. By the way, *sàn* means "platform" in Vietnamese.

A PLATFORM IN SAIGON

TS: What led to the founding of Sàn Art?

ZB: Four artists created it as a platform for contemporary art in 2007: Dinh Q. Lê, Tuan Andrew Nguyen, Phunam Thuc Ha, and Tiffany Chung. Dinh is one of Vietnam's most renowned artists, and Tiffany Chung is probably the best-known female artist in the country. Tuan and Phunam constitute the Propeller Group, a collective founded in 2006 known for their sculptural video installations parodying the mixture of neoliberal values and ideological thinking disseminated via popular channels of online and off-line social media. (A third member, Matt Lucero, joined in 2009.) Social science methodologies underlie all their practices, which are based on investigative journalism and a lot of documentary fieldwork. Their artistic approach has heavily influenced the mission and purpose of Sàn Art, yet they early on decided that their individual practices should remain separate from the institution. At the same time, Sàn Art benefits from sharing the strategies that inform their artistic practices, which are widely respected abroad and, increasingly, in Vietnam. Artist-entrepreneurs such as Dinh Q. Lê (and Lu Jie of Long March Project), in particular, are social figures of high, if controversial, standing in their respective communities. These artist-curators are infrastructural activists of the kind you celebrate in your book. Their significant international reputations provide leverage in securing overseas funds to maintain their organizations and are especially valuable in contexts plagued by local misunderstandings and different understandings about contemporary art. Despite occasional friction, both the Long March Space and Sàn Art have contributed significantly to cultural production in their locales.

It strikes me that the Western impulse to categorize the labor and products of creative collaboration as either "artistic" *or* "curatorial" is in a curious state of flux. Especially so in Asia, where the distinction does not translate, particularly when you look at where a lot of the creative energy is now focused. There are numerous artist/curator/intellectual collectives like Ruangrupa in Indonesia, Sa Sa Art Projects in Cambodia, Green Papaya in the Philippines, Raqs Media Collective in India, Total Art Studio in China, Alternative Space LOOP in Korea, AIT in Japan, and Sàn Art in Vietnam, to name but a few. These are potent examples of artists with a range of interdisciplinary motivations collaborating to make their work and engage their communities. In these contexts, the practice of collaboration is itself considered a medium. The role of interpretation, typically the purview of the curator, is here a mechanism powering an artwork's *production* as opposed to an after-the-fact necessity.

TS: Is this why the Sàn Art artists felt the need to bring a professional curator on board?

ZB: When I expressed concern to the founders of Sàn Art that I was not Vietnamese and could not speak their language—a worry I had voiced when Lu Jie wanted to hire me to work with him in China—they responded in the same way: we have translators already. What we really need is someone to write and talk about contemporary art; to provide historical analysis and make comparisons; to help train arts administrators in the handling and care of art objects; to facilitate and introduce an international network to the local art scene; to be a sounding board for local artists seeking critical feedback on their ideas; to be a cataloguer of the historical artifacts we collect, including the masses of fakes and items of doubtful authenticity that we love; to assist in the documentation of little-known interdisciplinary histories; to help deliver critical discourse; and to brainstorm strategies for dealing with government restrictions. Basically, they said, we need you to come and work with us to create our own systems of making culture and talking about it, here and everywhere else.

THE SILENCE OF MOLD

TS: I have not been fortunate enough to visit Vietnam—what kind of visual art world exists there?

ZB: I recently wrote a few scenarios that might evoke a picture. Here is one based on a visit to the official Fine Arts Museum of Ho Chi Minh City:

> *A large, yellow, peeling, Vietnamese-French Art Deco colonial villa compound belonging to the Communist State (previously owned by a wealthy Chinese merchant).*
> *The second floor stands still and silent beneath the whir of lazy fan blades as an army of mold spores marches across the surfaces of a meager collection of oil paintings, lacquers, and silks.*
> *War and its consequences are a common theme and influence.*
> *Aesthetic technique is granted small pride of place in gold identification plaques; authors appear in name only (no place or date).*
> *These rooms, full of what are most likely copies, are prefaced by a ground floor dedicated to a rotating menagerie of works authored by whoever can pay the rental fee.*
> *I ask reception for more information on the oil-and-wood assemblages that cover the lower walls and am given the price list.*

TS: This is certainly a picture of a society without curators, or at least lacking curators of the visual arts, of their histories, and their present possibilities, except as they might be marketable. How developed is the idea that curating is a profession, as distinct from an activity that anyone can undertake?

ZB: The word for curator in Vietnamese, *giám tuyển*, translates as "to control/to select." It's a hotly contested term that has not yet entered the broader Vietnamese lexicon as attached to a particular profession. Another story:

> *A steamy and sweat-filled opening at Sàn Art.*
> *A journalist asks me, "What do you do?" to which I reply,* "Toi la giám tuyển" *(I am a curator).*
> *Her eyebrows furrow in evident confusion, and then a flashbulb of a grin, "Aha! You are the stylist!"*
> *I consider it an appropriate quip; we both laugh.*

I remember the incredulity of my old boss, Lu Jie, when I announced in 2009 that I was resigning to take on the position of executive director and curator of Sàn Art in Ho Chi Minh City. "This is curatorial suicide!" he exclaimed, impressing upon me his opinion that the lack of cultural infrastructure and support in Vietnam was worse than in China in the mid-1990s. He feared that such a context would consume me whole. Looking back at that conversation I always laugh, because I believed even then that my work in Vietnam would critically shape and inform my curatorial practice in a way that the system of international art commerce then burgeoning in China could not.

EXHIBITIONS BY INFERENCE

TS: One of the ideas I explored in *Thinking Contemporary Curating* was that curatorial thought about art was distinctive in being centrally focused on the exhibition value of artworks, things, ideas, attitudes, feelings, everything. Instinctively the first question is always: is *this* exhibitable? How can I exhibit it with *other* works? How can I work with an artist to create an exhibitionary situation, environment, scene, display, something that may be shown to this or that audience? Yet you are working in situations of precarious cultural fragility, with almost no infrastructure, and the hovering suggestion of censorship. You are a curator who, for these reasons, has had great difficulty producing exhibitions, yet nonetheless something has to be visible at Sàn Art nearly all the time. What do you actually do in such a situation?

ZB: You have no idea how many fantastic exhibition proposals we get, but we have no money, we have almost no space, and we have no political agency. So, what do we actually do? Let me begin with another of my vignettes:

> *A fine arts student wishes to take part in a group exhibition at Sàn Art.*
> *The Vietnamese Ministry of Culture, Sports and Tourism requires an exhibition license.*
> *He submits a sketch of his artwork, an artist's statement, and a CV.*
> *He is proposing a ziggurat of upside-down televisions on red steel shelves, in front of a camouflage-patterned wall.*
> *The top row of televisions represents Hanoi and displays segments of state-sponsored news.*
> *The second row represents Saigon as seen in popular dramas from Korea.*
> *The third shows static.*
> *The ministry refuses him firstly in his desire to place the televisions upside down and to show state TV.*
> *A second missive is issued saying he cannot use the color red.*
> *A third missive says he must paint the background a solid green.*
> *No explanations are provided.*
> *The Vietnamese Ministry of Culture, Sports and Tourism has seemingly become a collaborative artist.*

Welcome to Vietnam, where museum directors struggle to provide even the most minimal of facelifts to their sad, dying collections from nearly forgotten pasts; where journalists are the promoters of culture; where artists must negotiate their aesthetic choices with government clerks; where fortune tellers determine the auspicious day of an art opening; where *feng shui* masters bless the communal kitchens of artists-in-residence; where artists have to console each other's shattered egos after a foreign curator visits their studios and leaves with a rude dismissal. In this environment, in the absence of social structures that are in the West default settings, the local curator becomes the backup system.

Working in the Vietnamese context over the last five years has really challenged my understanding of the role of curators and what constitutes the shape, purpose, and content of our work. Broadly speaking, a strong track record of exhibition making is the criterion by which a curator's labor is typically measured and evaluated, just as an artist's exhibition history is used to determine his or her historic and market value. However, when working in places such as Vietnam, where public and private space for art, and its online equivalents, are heavily monitored by the state, it becomes very difficult to pursue "normal" curatorial practice. It is even more debilitating for artists whose understanding of their role in society is limited to the staging of exhibitions that are sanctioned by a communist government with no comprehensive cultural policy. These experiences emphasize how important the context of place can be to the curator's commitment to "knowing through showing," to creating interpretive spaces. Our compass points have to be socially and politically sensitive, and the form, shape, and content of our labor has to keep shifting in order to survive. For the infrastructure to gain relevancy, we have to keep producing. To answer your question of what do we actually do in such a context: well, we organize a vast array of educational activities.

SUSTAINING AN INFRASTRUCTURE

TS: Let's come back to that after spending a moment longer on the issue of sustainability, which is a challenge for alternative art spaces all over the world. Those that have been around for a long time, in some cases for decades, face problems of maintaining their innovatory edge. The Long March Project has become quite a successful commercial enterprise in the form of Long March Space, which showcases art that is usually more interesting than anything else in the 798 Art District. You and the artists have managed to get Sàn Art up; what are you doing to keep it running?

ZB: Within such a landscape, the sustainability of an independent contemporary arts organization is fragile to say the least. Because, like in China, non-profit status does not legally exist, Sàn Art is registered as a small family business and events company. When dealing off-shore, we are a separate entity, being registered as a charity in the U.S. At home, we act and speak officially as if we were a business: our programs create "products," our exhibitions are "product showcases," our artists are "producers," and our artist-in-residency programs are our "factories." Seen from abroad we look like an alternative space, but this term sits awkwardly, because there is no museum world, or even a substantial commercial scene, to which we stand opposed. We are, though, a space of interpretation that operates as an "alternative" to the official voice of local political culture.

Sàn Art's sustainability is crucially dependent upon people, and their networks, across all sectors of society, both locally and abroad. It is essentially structured like a family unit, based on trust and commitment, and dependent upon a large group of individuals who are passionate and believe in the mission of the organization. This friendship network is the collaborative backbone of a community infrastructure that takes the concept of collegiality beyond the requirements of professionalism to a wholly different level of social conscience, one where ethical and moral responsibilities act as barometers. In Vietnam, the expression is *co qua co lai*. It means, "only through give and take can we satisfy each other."

Within this system of elders and successful entrepreneurs, the young cannot ask seniors beyond their friendship circles for tutelage; stigma and tension between locals and Viet Kieu, overseas Vietnamese, is rampant; and the staging of effective program partnerships to deter government attention can be tricky. Success often relies, as in my case, on a foreign curator with no local cultural baggage to step in and play politician. I have learnt that the greater the number of interdisciplinary players—from politics to business, from social science to bio-science, from fashion to film, from architecture to welfare—and inter-generational players invested in an organization in Vietnam, the greater the need for the organization to be seen as being utilized by sectors of the community that defy easy categorization. Vietnamese society, you have to understand, is governed by official departments that do not communicate with each other. As per my sketch, every proposed exhibition must be submitted to the Vietnamese Ministry of Culture, Sports and Tourism. But if the idea requires additional input from the Department of Medical Sciences and the Department of Foreign Affairs, forget it. Directing an arts organization here means playing a game of political chess with lazy kings and queens.

TS: A tiny organization usually needs to partner with other larger, stronger, more resourced operations if it is to survive. What kind of support structure does Sàn Art have? Is this where you map onto educational institutions?

ZB: Sàn Art currently runs three continuous programs that focus on discussion, critique, and collaboration as inherent tools in the definition, production, and presentation of art. Each program possesses its own international and local advisory board to assist in the strategic direction, content, and promotion of its activities in Vietnam and abroad. These boards of highly qualified individuals (artists, curators, historians, teachers, and businessmen) are the curator's critical support network; they offer a lifeline of knowledge, experience, and caution regarding the running of programs that seek to inform two totally different audiences, at home and away.

When a strong project really can't be realized for either practical or political reasons, I turn to education. I build a validation of the artist's idea discursively, by bringing in external speakers and interdisciplinary participants to work on the concept, to share it, imaginatively. This has the effect of creating a larger community of people, and it emboldens them to say, well, we should be able to help this person realize that work. Right now, this is coming to fruition with a program we call *Conscious Realities*. This is an endeavor that is supported by an advisory board of experts from Colombia, Thailand, Senegal, Moscow, Colombo, New York, and Hong Kong. It is a three-year program funded by a Network Partnership with the Prince Claus Fund, which is based in the Netherlands. It focuses on the complex, interwoven histories and geographies of the Global South—namely Southeast Asia, South Asia, Latin America, and Africa—inviting critical creative thinkers with interdisciplinary backgrounds to give lectures, run workshops, or be creators-in-residence, working in tandem with the local community of producers and supporters. Sàn Art has partnered with the Tri Viet Center for Social and Educational Research, Vietnam National University, Hoa Sen University, and the Royal Melbourne Institute of Technology to carry out this endeavor. The individual programs often require us to collaborate additionally with local music, film, literary, or scientific community organizations. All of these activities rely on the operating licenses of our program partners, which are mandated to provide educational opportunities to their constituencies. Under such arrangements, Sàn Art is "hired" to provide expert services. It is a tricky landscape at the best of times, and often Sàn Art cannot openly promote its activities. Nevertheless, people are slowly starting to say, well, yeah, maybe we should give this discourse more social space...

Strategic leadership, a commitment to training, readiness to speak publicly, and the ability to listen—these are the crucial skills of a curator at the helm of an organization in this context. There is no way that any of our programs would gain support, visibility, or credibility were I not willing to play the daily game of cat and mouse with the political and social powers. Nor would Sàn Art be able to contemplate the next generation of "Sàn Artians" if I was not prepared to train our willing team. Belonging to a "family" of artists whose vision seeks to stay one step ahead of the game, not only with Sàn Art, but also with their individual art projects, I am emboldened by their imaginative innovation, the criticality of their art, and their determination to outwit officialdom.

A FAMILY OF ARTISTS

TS: The artists who you work with seem to be inspirational, not only because of the kinds of work they do, but also because of how they go about their work. There is the aesthetic dimension, but also an ethical one.

ZB: As a curator, what is of particular interest to me in my current role at Sàn Art is how heavily involved I am with the journey of an artwork's production. I am an interlocutor from the concept stage, through to material experimentation, securing funding, display, promotion, and commercial distribution. Throughout this journey I am asked to provide interpretations of what is happening from a myriad of different angles. This becomes a kind of rehearsal for the various political and marketing obstacles that cause a local artist's nerves to wobble and twitch. The insight I am afforded into processes of research, the considerations of intent and purpose, the desire for social visibility, and, most excitingly, the revelation of little-known cultural or social histories—these are the gems of curating in this context.

As well, migrating from an institutionalized museum to an artist-run initiative has impressed upon me the critical role that artists play in building supportive networks for artistic production in localities that suffer political restriction, and consequently despotic cultural infrastructure. In Vietnam, government funds for art favor the commercially viable (read decorative); commercial galleries cater to the tourist market; museums lack curatorial and conservational expertise; and critics of contemporary art and culture are silent (in large part due to government crackdowns). The biggest gap is that the education system provides very little comparative historical analysis of cultural or artistic ideas beyond 1954, the year the French left Vietnam.

TS: My sense is that, despite these obstacles, you are building a kind of network of creative potential between groups of people—young people who you're training as curators, and artists whose work you are helping to realize—but you are also, in a way, curating social relations on a broader scale. I mean, you're assisting in the coming-into-being of cultural relationships, of anti-bureaucratic protocols, of connections between friends, thus spreading the model of the artist-friends who set up Sàn Art. Do you see yourself as having a role beyond simply supporting that network, by helping to move it forward through generations, for example? These are all infrastructural elements to be activated—indeed, curated—aren't they?

ZB: Yes, absolutely. Actually, last year the Vietnamese Ministry of Culture, Sports and Tourism asked me to attend a government panel with the Asia-Europe Foundation, the British Council, and the Vietnam Institute of Culture and Art Studies. It was the first time that I have been invited to such an event. Questions concerning how a nation's cultural strategies could contribute to its economic growth were central: what is required in a local cultural infrastructure to increase international tourism? What kinds of programs are successful? What kind of expertise is required for their sustainability? Curiously, the labor of a curator was not mentioned at all, and museum members were not present in the audience. At this event, however, I met a number of key influential people who are trying to educate the Vietnamese Ministry of Culture about why the facilitation of culture is so important. They were very happy to hear that I had museum curatorial experience and that I am committed to Vietnam.

So, I am now beginning to participate in much bigger conversations about these relationships because they can see that I'm working between disciplines through culture. And they can see that our audiences are expanding.

When we first opened in 2007, our audience was almost entirely foreign. Now, it's mainly local, which is fantastic. We've got businessmen. We have anthropology students. We have translators. We have designers, architects, and a lot of students. More and more kids. Don't get me wrong; we're tiny. Our space is so small. But every year the interest is increasing. As well, partners in the region are slowly recognizing the value of our inter-generational, interdisciplinary focus. It means that we stand, I'm hoping, a reasonable chance of eventually being able to have a solid financial base. That will help with exhibition making.

FROM THE SOUTH TO THE WEST

Blair French: Within this idea of the curator being right at the heart of the artistic process and bringing a very specific, potentially multi-faceted set of skills to that situation, we often encounter a concern that in so doing the curator might be stepping in front of artistic practice, somehow leading it rather that facilitating it, however fully. What you've described, however, is a very different process, one that is quite complex and quite integral. Looking back to the self you remembered when working at what is now QGOMA, and comparing it to the situation you're in now, how do you think what you're experiencing would alter your approach to being a curator within a Western institution?

ZB: Actually, this is a conversation I'm currently having with the Guggenheim. I really believe that museums need to change, fundamentally. I think that the global network of museum practice has reached incredible heights. We have the ability to do things that we couldn't decades ago. We have access to artists working on the ground within war zones and can organize exhibitions of their work simultaneously online; we have ever increasingly mobilized art production, so that a work concerning Britain is highly likely to have been fabricated in China. How the contexts and backgrounds of a work's creation become a communicable part of its experience is something I have learnt a great deal about over the last eight years. Living the experience means my interpretation of the work is so much deeper. How can museums better provide opportunities for such in-depth articulations of an artwork? How can their resources be better attuned to experience rather than deadlines? I believe that museums with great resources should be globally responsible for the narratives of their collections. Of course, all museums should be responsible in this way, whatever their capacity or their location.

From a Western perspective, the starting point should be the expertise of locals who think about art production and interpretation from very different perspectives than those of the metropolitan centers. The first step must be to insert these perspectives into the curatorial departments of Western institutions. Then, the process of acquisition requires an enormous amount of rethinking. QGOMA was amazing in this respect, and still is, especially through the APTs, even though recent funding cutbacks in Australia are threatening that kind of support. It's very sad because the curatorial expertise behind acquisitions has thus largely left the institution, not to mention that the time afforded for research has been greatly reduced, leaving behind collections with few mediators who can really speak to the objects they comprise and to the relations between them.

Other museums are beginning to take up research into contemporary Asian art. The Guggenheim, through its UBS project, appoints a curator for a two-year period to produce an exhibition of freshly acquired work, representing the regions of, firstly, South and Southeast Asia, followed by Latin America, and then North Africa. The South and Southeast Asia platform was curated by Chinese curator June Yap, whose exhibition traveled to the Asia Society in Hong Kong, and the Centre for Contemporary Art Singapore. However, there were many problems with this project concerning unrealistic timelines stemming from funder demands. I think it is also interesting that Tate Modern has finally set up a South Asia Acquisitions Committee, equipping staff with the time and funds to travel while also being open enough to the idea of an adjunct curator who is based between his/her own respective locale and London. It's a slow, step-by-step process of change in the methods and experiences afforded an institutional curator that give me hope that things are improving.

TS: Well, tackling these questions from the West looking toward the rest of the world makes one kind of sense, because it at least acknowledges where the main power used to be and how what remains is trying to reinforce itself. We can try to reassure ourselves that the age of imperialism is over, and that colonialism is a thing of the past, but the centuries of exploitation cannot be glossed over, because they drained local resources while at the same time holding out models of culture that are possible only when based in vast, deep, and sustained resources. This is the provincialist bind, a dichotomy that remains such a palpable part of on-the-ground actuality in many parts of the world, as you have been evoking for us so eloquently. It resonates in the West, too, because established institutions, such as the great metropolitan art museums, must work harder to maintain their relevance during a period of relative decline—not collapse, or implosion, but decline from dominance. "Masters" and "slaves" are obliged to take on new roles because we need each other in different ways nowadays. Those who can switch between these roles, and do so with a degree of global mobility, are in high demand, but face acute ethical dilemmas.

You are active in situations that could scarcely be at a greater distance from the Guggenheim headquarters in New York, and from its global effort to franchise itself at selected would-be centers in various locations around the world. Yet the Guggenheim will not succeed in its plans unless it adopts—or at least appears, convincingly, to share—the values, and the politics, of the localities.

Most everyone involved, at each stage of this food chain, is well aware of these complexities. Many continue to seek critical pathways within the jarring contradictions and inevitable compromises. This includes the curators driving the Guggenheim's Asian, Middle Eastern, and South American programs, and those doing parallel work at the New Museum, MoMA, and elsewhere. Yet as far as the New York presence is concerned, at end of the day the Guggenheim wants to put on a spectacular exhibition of art from the region in question, usually a show of recently collected work, with the added dimension that this exhibition could then travel to Guggenheim venues around the world, tying them together as if the network were a dispersed cultural knitting machine. It could market itself as the globalizer of the experience of art. To me, however, these are inevitable but lesser outcomes of what should be the real quid pro quo here: the input into local arts infrastructure, into supporting local artists to make work, which you highlight as the best effect of the APT project during its heyday in the 1990s and early 2000s. Brisbane was so prescient, and QGOMA so far ahead of art galleries elsewhere, at that time.

ZB: The really positive side of international exchange is that I can work to the best of my ability to enable a Vietnamese artist to make a work by finding international support and getting that project realized abroad. The result is that we do many exhibitions overseas, such as Dinh Q. Lê's installation *Erasure* at the Sherman Contemporary Art Foundation, Sydney, in 2011.

TS: That show was of particular importance to me, as an Australian with some political conscience. A number of artists have tackled the fraught subject of "boat people," the political and economic refugees, usually fleeing from war zones in which

Australia has had some role, who have no chance of being included in the small intake of legal immigrants and so risk their lives to travel illegally to our shores. Mostly, they drown at sea, or are taken by the Australian navy to off-shore detention centers on various Pacific islands where they can remain in legal limbo for months, years… this includes entire families.

There is a backstory here in that the first great wave of "boat people" to Australia were refugees from Vietnam and Cambodia, fleeing the U.S. war against those countries during the 1960s and 1970s. Dinh Q. Lê was born at that time, on the border between those two countries. His installation in Sydney included a projected image of a boat from the eighteenth century (the period of Australia's settlement) beached on a shore and slowly being consumed by flames, together with actual wreckage from a more recent refugee boat, and thousands of photographs, passports photos, pictures from family albums belonging to refugees and asylum seekers. These were strewn around as if they had spilled from suitcases and been dumped on the shore. They were all over the floor, I recall, and visitors were invited to pick them up, and reflect on the possible histories of the people pictured. Dinh's installation thus drew parallels between Australia's settler past and our asylum-seeker ancestors (mine were Anglo-Irish), by personalizing stories that we more normally find out about through the media.

NETWORKING THE REGION

BF: You have listed a range of organizations, collectives, or entities throughout the Asian region that have come out of the practice of artists working in various platforms, including the curatorial in its broader sense. I'm interested in the extent to which they form a peer group, as I sense an underlying feeling of isolation in the way you talk about Sàn Art, as if it were engaged in a single, solitary struggle against the odds in Vietnam. What peer relationships exist regionally that you're able to draw from and work with?

ZB: Well, I recall a recent meeting in Bangkok of dozens of people from Asian alternative spaces. We had been brought together by the Guggenheim to give advice on its UBS program, the one that supports its acquisition of art from countries beyond the U.S. and Europe. At one point the Guggenheim staff left the room for a mini-meeting outside, so I looked around the table and said, "Well, this is embarrassing." They said, "Why? Why is this embarrassing?" I said, "It took the Guggenheim to get us together."

The biggest complaint from all of us is that we're operating with bare bones resources, and simply don't have the time and energy to think about doing something on a broader network scale. Whenever we do meet, we think up great ideas, but then it all gets lost in the mechanisms of local shortages, censorship, or exhaustion. We haven't managed to find a solution to this problem.

TS: Assuming that Sàn Art keeps growing and gets to a point where you could curate exhibitions that reflect your perceptions and experiences of working in Vietnam, exhibitions that might travel, what kinds of ideas would you tackle?

ZB: I am still astonished at the casual attitude of Vietnamese artists to a decaying or mold-covered painting, say. "No problem, I will paint another one." People working in museums and galleries instinctively feel that a fake version of a work is not as valuable and interesting as the original. We might be appalled at the thought of something slowly rotting, dying, or being readily substituted, but we should also acknowledge that the central pillar of Buddhism is impermanence. So, how do we start to encapsulate that spirit into our collections and displays? I love the idea of the copy, to be honest. I've done one show, in Vietnam, where we played with that a little. But in Vietnam they don't really understand how pioneering it is to do this. They think, oh, this is just our reality.

Maria Lind

Stirring the Smooth Surfaces of The World: The Curatorial and The Translocal

Director of the Tensta Konsthall, Stockholm, since 2011, Maria Lind is a curator, writer, and educator. She was curator at Moderna Museet in Stockholm from 1997–2001, and, in 1998, co-curator of the second edition of Manifesta, Europe's nomadic biennial of contemporary art. From 2002–4, she directed the Munich Kunstverein, and then, from 2005–7, IASPIS in Stockholm. She was subsequently director of the graduate program at the Center for Curatorial Studies, Bard College, from 2008–10. In 2009 she received the Walter Hopps Award for Curatorial Achievement, conferred by the Menil Foundation, Houston, Texas. In 2010, Sternberg Press published a compendium of her essays, *Selected Maria Lind Writing*, and, in 2012, her edited book *Performing the Curatorial: Within and Beyond Art*.

We spoke on April 1, 2013, at Independent Curators International, New York.

Maria Lind: To me, perhaps the most important message of *Thinking Contemporary Curating* is that the curator, or curating, is setting the agenda of contemporary art to a degree that the critic, or art criticism, did previously. Our generation has no Hal Foster among us because curating, and not art critical reflection, produces new ideas nowadays.

Terry Smith: There is an interesting echo to what you say in a recent remark Daniel Birnbaum made during a discussion with curators about these issues. He said that no one in his generation has come up with an idea equivalent to Hal Foster's "the return of the real." You remember that Foster proposed this idea against the grain of the time, during the postmodern period, at a moment in which the real was said (by Jean Baudrillard, for example) to have vanished forever.[1] In so doing, he made a decisive contribution, one that recognized and reinforced an important critical tendency in art practice, a "postmodernism of resistance." As for today, I don't buy the notion that we are in a "post-critical" age, if taken as a totalizing idea. Yet it is true that, given the rule of the contemporaneity of differences, it is unlikely that a single art critic or historian, curator or theorist, could plausibly describe where art is at, and where it is going. A layered approach to the multiplicity of our contemporaneous differences is what is needed. By no coincidence, knowledge is increasingly being spawned collectively, or through processes that usually involve more than one specialist. Indeed, it is in this spirit that I drew attention to the interactions between artists and curators in the book. If you look at the changes within the whole exhibitionary complex from the 1960s onward, it's obvious that artists have had a huge impact. And, since the 1990s, it is equally obvious that curating has had a definitive effect on the ways artists think about their practices, and make and present work.

ML: Yes, exactly.

TS: We are additionally starting to see that curators were almost as important as artists in precipitating and shaping the aesthetic revolution that erupted in the 1960s and 1970s. To be sure, the new values suffered major setbacks during the 1980s, and again during the 2000s, but younger people now seem to be rejecting neoconservative closures, and are instead picking up the promise of the 1960s, puzzling over it, and doing different things with it. Meanwhile, some of the artists from that 1960s/1970s moment have gone on to elaborate their visions, sometimes on gargantuan scales. For younger artists, however, it is the exploratory, provisional nature of the early work that really resonates.

1. Birnbaum's remark can be found in Daniel Birnbaum et al., *Defining Contemporary Art* (London: Phaidon, 2011), p. 458. See also Hal Foster, *The Return of the Real: Art and Theory at the End of the Century* (Cambridge, Mass.: MIT Press, 1996).

Perhaps, in the bigger picture of what counts in contemporary art, we're looking at a convergence of these temporal currents, and, at the same time, their dialectical interaction against each other.

WHAT IS THE CURATORIAL?

ML: It may help us if we think less about positions, less about the artist, the critic, the curator, and more about processes: art making, writing, and curating. The notion of the curatorial, at its best, involves all these aspects.

Contemporary art is adept at addressing existence today, at imagining our contemporaneity, like a seismograph sensing what is to come before other spheres of society. It is privileged because it is able to suck everything in as it is happening and, at the same time, it has traditions, centuries long, of reshuffling, articulating, and criticizing. Compared to all other forms of expression in society, it is a very advanced form of analysis and knowledge production.

Working curatorially is beyond methodology, it's the next step almost, a kind of meta-methodology. Like contemporary art itself, it is very inclusive. I use "working curatorially" rather than "curating," because for me there is a qualitative difference between the two. "Curating" encompasses the technical side of things, and can take different shapes and forms: making an exhibition, commissioning an individual artwork, organizing a screening or seminar series, a workshop, et cetera. But "working curatorially" implies doing these things with a sensibility and urgency as to why they are being done *precisely* this way, *precisely* right now in relation to *this* art and the questions that it raises or proposes. And it is based on an ambition to go beyond the status quo.

TS: In your article "The Curatorial," in *Artforum*, you say something like, "the curatorial should be beyond the expanded field, a multidimensional role that includes critique, editing, education, and fundraising."[2] But putting it in terms of a list led many people to think, well, everything anyone does in a museum, every role anyone takes, could therefore be considered "curatorial." But that's exactly what you did *not* mean, right?

ML: Right.

TS: In *Thinking Contemporary Curating* I quote an exchange between you and Jens Hoffmann on the subject, which I find really interesting.[3] Jens counters with the term "paracuratorial," that is, like curating but not it exactly, on analogy, I suppose, to a paramedic or a parateacher. You respond by saying that "rather than being the product of the curator's labor per se, curating is the result of a network of agents' labor." You go on to say something quite fascinating: "The outcome should have the disturbing quality of smooth surfaces being stirred, a specific multi-layered means of answering back in the given context, so, rather than representing, the curatorial involves presenting, it performs something in the here and now, instead of merely mapping it from there and then." Clearly, this draws a distinction between the core act of curating and that of art historical research and writing. It claims that the curatorial act exhibits something beyond that which is already known, as distinct from the obvious, apparent contemporaneousness of certain relationships. Yet you can imagine an institutional curator reading your words and saying, all right, I'm going to apply *the curatorial* to how I install the permanent collection. Or an independent curatorial collective saying, we are going to do whatever, and whenever things become chaotic or disordered, we will know *the curatorial* has appeared. We can see both of these things happening in museums and in alternative spaces today. For you, however, the curatorial is

2. Maria Lind, "The Curatorial," *Artforum*, vol. 68, no. 2 (October 2009), p. 103.

3. Jens Hoffmann and Maria Lind, "To Show or Not to Show," *Mousse*, no. 31 (November 2011). http://moussemagazine.it/articolo.mm?id=759.

anything but a formula. Can you say more about what it actually is?

ML: It's something that you can typically identify only post-factum, after what you've done is out there and operating. It's about seeing what the project does once all the elements are choreographed together. It came home to me after working at the Center for Curatorial Studies at Bard College, and spending a lot of time with smart, committed students, yet being worried about their interest in having a career rather than in engaging with art or thinking about what their own practice does in the world. Are we just going to be apparatchiks in the machine, or are we going to try to push for change? Given the way the world is now, we need to think about things that are not flowing with the mainstream.

So, the idea of thinking about what something *does*, rather than what it *is*, becomes essential. This leads to questions of evaluation and assessment: how do you actually detect the relevant qualities of a project? And how do you then evaluate them? I don't have an answer, but I think it's only possible when it is done, when it has happened. If you declare beforehand that something is going to be critical, it's probably not going to be. If you say that you're working curatorially, that probably won't be the result.

TS: To me, it sounds as if you're describing what used to be called an "open experimental process." To work curatorially, then, is to establish an experimental situation, one that, if it works, will generate not just an outcome, but also its own value. In other words, the conditions of its valuing will be established in the process specific to it, as opposed to it having to satisfy pre-existent expectations or prior specified conditions.

THE CENTRALITY OF ART

ML: In that sense, the curatorial is radically situational. Yet certain constants, or principles, should remain. Art, for example, should be absolutely central, although over the past decade it seems to me that it is being increasingly pushed into the background by exhibition making.

I do believe that art is this amazing form of understanding in itself, that it helps us to problematize and make sense of our situation. It is a fantastic resource. That's where my allegiance is. So, how can we work curatorially and still respect art? How can we use the potential of art? How can we let it flourish? I feel that we mostly only scratch the surface.

TS: There are young curators, and even young artists, now, who would hear this and speculate that you are a figure in transition. (I know they say that about me.) A residual figment from an earlier generation when the artist was the absolute priority, and the artwork was the definitive field of exchange, while everyone else—spectators, audience, curators, critics, or whoever—came up for the count later, as lesser, and at a distance. Today, however, many curators understand their activity as *participation* in a transformative process alongside artists, writers, publicists, whomever … everyone is open to creative opportunities, waiting to seize them as they come up.

"Stirring the smooth surfaces of the world"… I wonder how many surfaces, or how much smoothness, there is in the contemporary concept of the world? There is the immediate sense of hyperactivity, and infinite opportunity, but this, as we know, exists as an effect of power sources—finance capital, advertising companies, governmental agencies, international crime, war machines—so distant that they are taken for granted until, of course, they run amok, as finance capital did in 2008. David Joselit has identified this situation in his book *After Art*, in which he identifies art practice as having become aggregative, replicative, iterative, and embedded in the flow of information that's out there on the Internet and in the rest of the world. From this perspective, art can be understood as a practice of creating events or shifts within the information flow.[4]

PIROUETTES AND OVER-COLLABORATIONS

ML: I'm thinking about tendencies in curating among, let's say, emerging curators today. While there are of course exceptions, I see two main trends—firstly, what I call "curatorial pirouettes," which occur where the theme or structural conceit is the strongest part of the project. In these cases, the whole project becomes, if not navel-gazing, self-referential, often extremely so. I think a lot of Jens's work is on the verge of curatorial pirouettes, but most of the time he ends up on what I would say is the right side.

The second tendency uses a rhetoric, which on the surface appears completely different. I call these "over-collaborations," where the curator wants to collaborate, often under the guise of questioning authorship and finding a more democratic way of working. Instead, however, such symbiosis between the artist and the curator occurs that nobody else can enter the project. Instead of having an author with one head, you have an artist, or a curator, with two heads.

In both cases there is little interest in the outside world, in a public beyond the already converted, or a particular peer group. This is an issue because the question of art's cultural legitimacy is absolutely urgent. It is really clear in Europe right now, with all the funding cuts, and so on. The post-war agreement between citizens and their governments that culture is essential to society and should therefore be publicly funded has been broken. So, how do we legitimate what we do?

4. David Joselit, *After Art* (Princeton, N. J.: Princeton University Press, 2012)

MUSEUMS AND THE CURATORIAL

TS: Are there museums that have committed themselves to the curatorial in their organization and their programming?

ML: This is a blind spot in a lot of discussions today: assessing programming over time in one institution. That the Van Abbemuseum in Eindhoven, for example, works very curatorially is evident in many of its institutional activities, including its exhibitions and commissions; the use of the library and the archive in relation to its shows; the renovations and changes made to the space; the staff structure; and external and internal communications. Through addressing all these aspects and giving them equal weight, they create slightly different conditions for understanding both the work and the actuality of curating. It's similar to the examples that I used in my 2009 essay on "The Curatorial." Like the Bienal de São Paulo in 2008, where Ivo Mesquita and Ana Paula Cohen revisited the role of the biennial itself through opening up most of the site as discussion and performance spaces, and selecting only artworks that critically engaged collecting and archival art practices. I would also mention the Welkulturen Museum in Frankfurt under the leadership of Clémentine Deliss, and Casco in Utrecht led by Binna Choi.

This leads me to say that I don't agree with the notion of "the exhibitionary complex." I would say, rather, that it is the curatorial complex that is important, because the exhibition is only one mode among many others.

TS: Oh, I should explain that I use the term in the way that Tony Bennett does, namely as making objects and ideas public in any form whatsoever, the "complex" having woven itself over the past two centuries through such massive vehicles as international expositions, department stores, and museums.[5] But you're quite

5. Tony Bennett, "The Exhibitionary Complex," in *The Birth of the Museum: History, Theory, Politics* (London: Routledge, 1995).

right to make that distinction within the terms of our discussion of curating. From my point of view, the Van Abbemuseum is also one of the few institutions—although the number is steadily increasing, especially in what used to be Eastern Europe—that exhibits contemporaneity. Charles Esche, Annie Fletcher, and the team there show us that the present is full of different kinds of pasts that have to be revisited, interrogated, re-imagined. But as many people ask: how long can you keep doing that? Can a museum keep being so reflexive and so focused on multi-layered temporalities?

ML: Well, I think that it can go on for quite a long time, but I also imagine that at one point it will be interesting to create a contrast. In order to keep stirring the smooth surfaces, you have to keep shifting your methods.

TS: You have to, as it were, revoke what become the standard structures.

ML: Exactly! The norms, the gestures.

TS: Does this imply that standard structures and formats as they've evolved during the modern period are themselves the bigger frame, which the curatorial questions? Or does it imply that the curatorial will transform the entire frame to such a degree that, over time, the structures will fundamentally change?

ML: Obviously, my elaborations on the curatorial come from hands-on experience. I have not thought through all the implications of applying the theory to the whole of the twentieth century. My sense is that the curatorial is an agent. It's almost viral in that it becomes part of something, but it also mutates its host. However, I'm very happy if other people want to try to show that there are very clear limits to what the curatorial can achieve.

TS: I keep trying to think historically, to track through twenty-, thirty-, forty-year sweeps, so that's why I am asking these questions.

ML: Which is interesting, because I think for contemporary art today simultaneity, or the synchronic, is often stronger and more present than diachronicity. It's the difference between time and space. So, which does one privilege? I'm interested in the balance, the proportions, the relations between the two. A big dilemma today is that when we talk about time, we seem unable to speak about the future without speaking about the past, or even being *stuck* in the past. It is what social commentator Boris Buden identifies as "retrotopia." So, one of my interests right now is just this: how do we think about the future? Which is why, in 2005, I worked on the report *European Cultural Policies 2015*, which explored various future scenarios, and in 2012 the report *Contemporary Art and Its Commercial Markets: A Report on Current Conditions and Future Scenarios*.[6] Art is, after all, projective.

TS: What is the value set that's operating for you when you name "art" in this way?

ML: The basic starting point is the institutional definition of art; it is what gets produced within the system in some form and manner. But that being said, there are also other things that operate as art, just as somebody can work curatorially without really knowing that they're working curatorially.

TS: But surely you are not taking any art that's generated by the system as art that you—

ML: That I appreciate, no!

TS: Or that you want to interact with curatorially.

ML: Often it's to do with how a specific approach is articulated. It's the relationship between materials, whether disembodied or specific, like wood and stone and human bodies, et cetera.

6. Maria Lind and Raimund Minichbauer, eds., *European Cultural Policies 2015: A Report with Scenarios on the Future of Public Funding for Contemporary Art in Europe* (London, Stockholm, Vienna: eipcp/IASPIS, 2005).

TS: The articulation of an idea, or actualization of a material, or one within the other?

ML: Any kind of articulation: a work can articulate a question, or a proposal, or just be. Sometimes it's the practice that is even more relevant. Sometimes it's an individual work, when the other works made by the same person are not so interesting.

TS: Are these surprising?

ML: No, not always. I think recognition can also be extremely appealing and challenging.

TS: Particularly if you know the work of an artist, and she or he has done something in a way you would have expected, but there's still another sense to it.

ML: My special interest is to take up things that seem incompatible and find interesting relations between them, to show how they can speak to each other in challenging ways, even argue. Maybe this has to do with being schooled by postmodernism in thinking about difference, and doing so without necessarily creating hierarchies. It's almost always more interesting to look at things co-existing simultaneously rather than going back into history, I find.

TS: Given that the curatorial has to be disjunctive, do you think it's a postmodern thing? Do you think it's a value that you arrived at during the postmodern moment of the 1980s?

ML: Yes, but there was also always some sort of emancipatory desire that things should be different.

TS: It's not very postmodern to require that the curatorial should have a large-scale, transformatory effect in the world.

ML: No, but *micro*-effects are possible.

RELATIVE PERIPHERIES

TS: You are predominantly working in Northern Europe, which is geopolitically a region both within Europe and the wider world. But of course there are all kinds of worlds that intersect and diverge from each other within the world in its largest sense. I believe that one of the purposes of any kind of creative activity is to make visible the connections that exist, or might exist, between parts or layers of the world and ways of being in the world. Do you see certain sorts of practices today that are particularly useful for making these kinds of connection visible? Is this an aspect of working curatorially?

ML: When I wrote about "relative peripheries" the first time, I had just completed a couple of years of intensive traveling in Europe and in the U.S.—that's also when I did the Whitney Independent Study program.[7] It was fantastic for me to discover that great art was being made outside the traditional centers of New York, London, and Cologne—which was the main center in Europe at the time—in places like Glasgow, Vancouver, Mexico City, Copenhagen, and Vilnius, for instance. It was important for me to address the power of this work, and the fact that those of us involved in it often felt more connected to each other than to the traditional centers.

At the time, there was a small network of people circulating between these "peripheral" places, sharing ideas, actively curating. So much has changed since then in the overall infrastructure of the art world, but there are still considerable differences in terms of influence, let's say, between things happening in London, New York, Berlin, and a few other places, and the rest of the world. At the same time, there has been a forking of paths between what I think of as the "minor" and

7. Maria Lind, "Notes on Contemporary Art in a Relative Periphery" [2001], in Brian Kuan Wood, ed., *Selected Maria Lind Writing* (Berlin: Sternberg Press, 2010).

the "major," or mainstream, in the art world, in Deleuze and Guattari's sense of "minor literature." Now, there's less and less contact between these two in either the relative peripheries *or* the traditional centers. So, in London, for example, you have mega-institutions like Tate Modern that operate more like global TV stations in a global network. There is not much similarity between what they do and how they do it and what happens in smaller venues like the Showroom, or Chisenhale, even though these also deal with contemporary art and are in the same global city. Instead, Tate Modern has formal connections to the Centre Pompidou in Paris, for example.

In parallel, but also in contrast, we smaller venues are starting our own networks in order to gather strength. One of these is called "Cluster." I initiated it when I started at the Tensta Konsthall. It is a consortium of art centers based in residential suburban areas. I realized that it was not so easy to talk to colleagues running institutions in more classical contexts, in major city centers, so I got in touch with people sharing our *particular* situation. Cluster consists of the Showroom in London; Casco in Utrecht; Centro de Arte Dos de Mayo in Móstoles, outside Madrid; Les Laboratoires d'Aubervilliers in Paris; CAC Brétigny, just outside Paris; the Israeli Center for Digital Art in Holon, an industrial area near Tel Aviv; and the P.A.R.A.S.I.T.E. Museum in Ljubljana.

TS: It's a dispersed, lateral network of satellite spaces?

ML: Precisely. I would say that today, we are still considered as the slightly embarrassing cousins from the countryside. We're not as exotic as centers in many parts of Asia and Africa and Latin America, but we're different enough not to be included in the classical centers. Do you see what I mean?

TS: I do, absolutely. Following a North American analogy of major and minor league baseball, what's needed is an intermediary league of second-tier museums, such as the

Carnegie Museum of Art, in Pittsburgh, that share shows with similar-scale museums around the country. Contemporary art spaces have their networks, as well, but they are not usually as explicit as Cluster. It is an effect of globalization to connect city nodes and fly over, as it were, everything in between. Such nodes tend to clear the regions around them by absorbing markets and talents.

ML: Yet most of the new ideas and ways of working come from the minors and are picked up by the majors, both in the public sector of the museum world and in the commercial sector, ten to fifteen years down the line, which raises the issue of deferred value, as Sarah Thelwall dicusses in the report *Size Matters*.[8]

The bigger picture is that the major museums offer programming that tends toward populist, mass entertainment. We all know this very well. Meanwhile, on the other hand, the very specialized, slightly inward-looking minors tend to speak too much to themselves, so I am actually quite interested in how these leagues might communicate with each other. How could we use the big museums as amplifiers to broadcast the fascinating new ideas that the minors develop? I connect this to the very legitimacy of art and culture in contemporary societies. If we don't start to address this soon, we will be in real trouble.

TS: This makes me think of New Jerseyy, the small gallery in Basel, which is run by a collective that includes the co-curator of this year's Carnegie International, Daniel Baumann. It shows work of all kinds as it is being made. It is relevant to our discussion of the co-existence of different art world spheres,

8. Sarah Thelwall, *Size Matters: Notes towards a Better Understanding of the Value, Operation and Potential of Small Visual Arts Organisations* (London: Common Practice, 2011). See also Rebecca Gordon-Nesbitt, *Value, Measure, Sustainability: Ideas towards the future of the small-scale visual arts sector* (London: Common Practice, 2013). Downloads at http://commonpractice.org.uk/position-paper.

because apparently it receives very few visits except during Art Basel, when thousands of people turn up because it is the only alternative space in the city. As a result, it has 25,000 people on its mailing list. So, it has this large presence when, in effect, it's just a little space, with occasional programming.

ML: The space in Basel also speaks to the fact that you can operate at the relative periphery and still be seen by the art world media. Nevertheless, being adjacent to Art Basel creates a big difference—hardly anyone writing for big magazines, et cetera visits Centro de Arte Dos de Mayo, even when they are in Madrid.

TS: So it makes sense to develop a layer of connectivity between places that are experimental even within their own cities or regions.

ML: Places that want to be locally embedded and are at the same time required by their funders (city councils, local donors, community groups) to work locally.

TS: Right. Yes, this is really very important, because it values locality at a kind of median, small-scale, and sees global connectivity occurring at what many identify as the "transnational" sphere—rather than according to the size of one's international profile. In so many places, like China, South America, these registers—the local, the regional, the transnational, or the global—mean such different things. Clearly, you value art practices that have something to say about this situation, or that simply come out of these circumstances. Do you value curating that makes at least some of these connections, or the nature of locality, manifest?

ML: Yes, but not exclusively so. I value enormously the work of somebody like Claire Barclay: she makes discrete objects with a very specific sensibility in relation to the combinations and qualities of different materials, objects which have nothing to do with these issues. That's perhaps why it's so interesting to work with somebody like her in an embedded situation, as it were. This is where my idea of always setting up interesting contrasts applies. From our perspective and preferences at Tensta we might wish to highlight social practice works. We can do that every now and then, but absolutely not only that. That would be uninteresting.

TS: Everyone would know what to expect every time they visited and after a while they would stop going.

ML: It would be formulaic.

TS: And not curatorial.

ML: No!

THE QUESTION OF EUROPE

TS: The European question is of interest to many people both inside and outside the European Union. British artists Neil Cummings and Marysia Lewandowska's video *Museum Futures: Distributed* [2008] is a wonderful parody of an art institution that has *totally* absorbed institutional critique, anticipating its own "radical" future to the point where everyone involved is precisely politically correct, absolutely charming, and utterly vacuous. This highlights a danger with the whole European project, which is managed by universalizing bureaucracies in Brussels. Although the disasters of the twentieth century haunt this project, constructive content that transcends national interests seems elusive, leaving the field open for reactionary nationalists. A number of artists pay attention to the way Europe is being thought about, and seek to intervene in specific instances, as well as in the general debate about its scope and remit: Thomas Hirschhorn, Harun Farocki, and collectives such as NSK, or Henry VIII's Wives, come to mind. I am aware of the history of connections between Glasgow, for example, and the more radical and socialist parts of Europe, such as Bremen, or Gdansk, via maritime workers and others. What are your thoughts on the curatorial in relation to the content and structure of the debates around Europe, whether localized or general?

ML: Europe is no more, no less, interesting today than it was twenty years ago, but it has taken on different urgencies. I don't think that there are many projects that I'm aware of that talk about Europe overall; the more interesting ones look at specific geopolitical situations. My prime example would be the work of Deimantas Narkevicius, an artist based in Vilnius, who connects his personal history with the larger history of world politics in fantastically poetic, suggestive, and discomforting ways. I also think of Dan and Lia Perjovschi and their drawings, which map these sorts of connections often from the perspective of Romania.

Another way of relating to these issues is simply to speak about normality. It's the border regimes of Europe and their problems that people are interested in, but the rest of the world is already inside Europe, so its population is *transnational.* The streets of Tensta, for instance, look more like Istanbul than Stockholm city center, which is fantastic. Europe is present, it's urgent, but not as an identity. Nevertheless, we are completely dependent on Europe when it comes to funding. Most of us would not survive without EU money.

TS: Is that because the state, the Swedish state, for example, is cutting down on support for the arts?

ML: So far, public support in Sweden has not been cut, although it doesn't keep up with inflation. If you need to expand your budget in order to operate properly, like we do in Tensta, you can't rely on getting more national funding. But the funding that colleagues at the Showroom in London get from the Arts Council, for example, only covers their salaries. They have to fundraise for *everything* else. This model is becoming more and more common. I now have to fundraise at least a third of my budget, which is radically different from ten, and especially fifteen, years ago. We did at least get some European funding for Cluster, so that we're able to visit and learn about each other's operations. EU money can fund intra-European connections, but not projects within single nations

TS: Right, but your cluster reaches beyond Europe.

ML: Yes, we have one member beyond Europe, which is acceptable within the European scheme. More significantly, I think that the commercial boom in the art world has adversely affected funding schemes, and that's what our most recent report is about.[9] The art market has grown in terms of volume, but also has spread into other areas, so it is more visible as a model of viability in what were previously considered public art sectors. Government policy makers now look at the commercial boom and unfortunately see the two sectors as linked.

TRANSLOCAL IN TENSTA

TS: Let's talk about Tensta, and about the role that the konsthall has found for itself within that suburb. To me, it seems an interesting instance of the infrastructural activism that is so urgent in current circumstances almost everywhere.

ML: Tensta Konsthall is a private foundation that grew out of a grassroots initiative in the mid-1990s. Since it was founded in 1998, its main funder has been the city of Stockholm, with a little help from the nation. Tensta suburb itself was built in the late 1960s as part of the Million Programme scheme, under which one million housing units were constructed across Sweden between 1965 and 1975. It was a huge endeavor intended to improve the country's housing options for poorer people, with mixed success. Everybody knows the name "Tensta" and almost everybody has an opinion about it—it's considered a ghetto. Twenty thousand people live there today, and ninety percent of them have a translocal background. The unemployment level is higher than elsewhere, the average income is lower, and people of color dominate these categories. Stockholm is considered one of Europe's most segregated cities, if you compare the center and

9. Maria Lind and Olav Velthuis, eds., *Contemporary Art and Its Commercial Markets: A Report on Current Conditions and Future Scenarios* (Berlin: Sternberg Press, 2012).

the suburbs. To simplify, the city center is white and the suburbs are colored. To work at Tensta is quite specific. I think of it often as a window on the future.

Maybe you've heard of the Lost Highway Expedition, a project in the former Yugoslavia in 2006? It was a swarming research action of sorts: artists, architects, activists, and others traveled independently along an unfinished highway of "brotherhood and unity" to visit the capital cities and look at their current conditions of urban development as part of a process of thinking about the Balkans as a window to the future, rather than as a primitive cave of the past. I think of Tensta in the same way.

The konsthall is located in a former storage area underneath the shopping mall, next to the subway station. We have a space of 7,500 square feet and we show exhibitions, commission new work, and organize other projects like screenings and seminar series. Despite the fact that we are a small team, five people including myself, and totally underfunded, we have a program that is part of an international discussion about what contemporary art is and how you can work with it. But we try to mediate the conversation in ways that are meaningful locally.

TS: How do you do that?

ML: It's a question of tailoring. We constantly think of contacts, surfaces, and shared concerns (which does not exclude conflictual ones) in relation to each project that we do—we are always identifying individuals, or groups of people, who can relate to a particular art project or an exhibition. But we also run separate, ongoing "mediation" projects. The most important one is the café, which is run by a local person. This might sound super basic, but it fulfills a need, as there was previously no café in the area, as such. A number of people just come for the café. And that's totally fine.

TS: It is a very good one, as I discovered when visiting.

ML: When I started, the team went out and spoke to almost all associations, organizations, and work places in the immediate area. We actually relocated a number of our staff meetings to their premises, asking them to tell us about what they were doing, telling them a bit about what we were doing, and then ending by asking, so how can we be interesting, meaningful, and even useful for you? Some responded and others absolutely did not. One of those that did was the Women's Centre, which is probably the only transethnic association in Tensta. It's an organization that works very much like an everyday, social environment for middle-aged and older women.

TS: Is it like a women's refuge?

ML: Yes, but self-organized and *really* grassroots. They wanted to use our café, and so every other month, for the past years, they have organized tea and coffee salons there.

TS: Will you draw an exhibition out of that relationship?

ML: No! The way I think of it is rather that we are as context-sensitive as any program I would make anywhere else. In a way, my nightmare would be imagining myself living in a place and having a local cultural institution constantly holding up a mirror to me, saying, look at yourself, look at yourself, look at yourself. There is an assumption when it comes to cultural institutions in residential areas of this kind that visitors exclusively want local identification as a primary model, which is not true. This is where context-sensitivity, I think, has to be balanced.

TS: But what about holding up a two-way mirror to the neighborhood, to the people? Because of course your konsthall is not only locally embedded, it's actually connected to transnational spaces of a similar kind, and has some registration within the global art world. You might want to distribute some of the values from these worlds, many of which are quite positive, into the neighborhood. And, of course, vice versa. It's not as if the neighborhood is the sole repository of value, but, clearly, it is as complex and contradictory as any human situation, including the global art world.

ML: Yes. Interestingly enough, there are six or seven konsthalls, such as Marabouparken and Konsthall C, for example, in various suburbs of Stockholm. It's a Stockholm phenomenon. Four of us interconnect, forming the network Sibling Art Centers, and during the past year, we have come together in the wake of Cluster, actually, and the report talking about funding and the working conditions of small visual art centers. We organized three hearings in Stockholm around funding. We had to start from scratch almost, because we found that people in general, including ourselves, did not know much about this subject. We invited politicians, policy makers, and other people with influence to attend. The first hearing was about broadening the funding sources that we are, in most cases, required to find. The second was about creative industries, and the third about gentrification. Out of that a national network has emerged, which is called *klister*, which is a pun on "cluster," meaning "glue." We're now meeting, and organizing discussions locally, about the conditions of working with our kinds of organizations. Everybody contributes around 500 euros, so that we can commission a report from a researcher on the kind of values that we produce. We are inspired by the Common Practice group in London, who published the report *Size Matters* two years ago.

TS: In Australia, the National Association for the Visual Arts [NAVA] does similar work. It is an artists' and craftsworkers' advocacy group led by Tamara Winikoff that has had a considerable impact on thinking about the context in which art is made there, and gaining political and funding support for artists and arts infrastructure. I was part of a team from the University of Sydney that undertook a research project to develop guidelines for the "visual arts industry," as we had to call it to get funding.

Reports from that project and subsequent research keep coming out: they include an economic model for the industry, best practices for artists and publicly funded galleries, income subsidy models for artists, occupational health and safety, professional accreditation, freedom of expression, copyright and moral rights for artists, resale and gifts of works of art, and ideas for policy and legislation. The key ideas are gathered in *The Code of Practice for the Professional Australian Visual Arts, Crafts and Design Sector*, some elements of which are supported by federal and local governments, although this of course varies hugely, depending on their politics. Despite this, the guidelines have been widely adopted on a voluntary basis within the Australian art world.[10]

NAVA also operates a website that works as a portal to all the organizations in Australia that are very similar to the ones that you have spoken about, and that have come into being during the last thirty or so years. They are mainly artist-run initiatives, and there are about forty of them in the country, with their own network. There is a constant effort to build infrastructure, to sustain it while trying to keep it "alternative." Would you say that this is curatorial activity?

ML: Yes.

TS: Is it "the curatorial" as well? Or not exactly?

ML: That's hard to say. The way I try to conceive of the overall functioning of the konsthall is curatorial somehow, but I will only be able to tell later if it works that way. One of my big aims is to try to make the konsthall into more of an institution than it has been, because it's virtually been run as a project. The whole neighborhood has suffered so much from projectification—things that have a beginning and an end—so the goal is to be agile and find ways of surviving. For a place such as Tensta, continuity is essential.

10. See https://visualarts.net.au/code-of-practice/.

In your book, you identify infrastructural activism as the next big thing, which I think is correct, but I would phrase it a little differently. I would think about it as working on conditions of production and on protocols. "Infrastructure" implies something rather set, a framework, or skeleton, which is important, but even more important is how you can operate things, or the software. This is what colleagues talk about all the time: we are all suffering from a paradigm shift, in which we have to spend so much time fundraising and defending what we do, and this affects how we operate in radical ways.

TS: That's the impact of neoliberalism and globalization, coming as it were "from above and around" art making and all of the processes that you identify as curatorial. Yet the priorities of art practice itself have changed in recent decades from object production and the provision of beauty and pleasure toward dispersed mediums, challenging content, and socially embedded practices. The perception of what art should be, or what it should do socially, that is conveyed by neoliberalism and globalization is often an older paradigm—art ameliorates the harshness of life, makes people happier, and thus better disposed toward its supporters: politicians reap votes, corporations raise their reputations, donors are lionized.

ML: One of our challenges is to make sense of what we do, of the value of art, and of working with art in society, but beyond the instrumental expectations of funders. At the moment, the briefs from our funders say that we have to work with participatory culture.

TS: For many of them, however, that's a multiculturalist formula. They see art institutions as elements in the machinery for smoothing over the rough and potentially violent edges of cultural difference. There is a real relevance to this, but it can become a problem when the expectation is that the differences will ultimately be resolved into a pattern of ongoing harmony. Especially when such an expectation is accompanied by underfunding.

ML: Yes. Absolute artistic freedom is an illusion, and a particularly time- and space-specific illusion in the post-war period in the West that is no longer credible. In the fight for space, maneuvering the conditions and protocols of production becomes essential.

TS: So, in this sense, the idea of the curatorial becomes a kind of ethics of working curatorially, as you put it. When I say "ethics," I don't mean a morality, or a moral system. Ethics is something you find in a process of seeking the right way to act in the circumstances.

ML: I would think of it rather in terms of making qualitative differences.

TS: As distinct from quantitative ones, or just better ones?

ML: Yes, and it's also in line with what I said before: we need to make distinctions. We don't need more art, we need more *good* art. We don't need more curating, we need more *good* curating. By "good" I mean a quality, something that is not universal but always renegotiated. As curators we need to share and debate in public our individual notions of quality, and hence our criteria for how we work. We started out by talking about the importance of *micro*-situations. With all due respect, that remains super important, but now we also need to think about connectivity and about raising voices collectively. I think we will see much more of that.

TS: And we need to think of generating values that are not universal imperatives that are expected to apply to everybody.

ML: Yes, but universal in the sense of being *unifying* to some degree. So, I think we are seeing attempts at formulating a new type of universalism, which includes notions of collaboration, comment, and propriety. This is not so far from the curatorial.

AUTHOR BIOGRAPHY

Terry Smith, FAHA, CIHA, is Andrew W. Mellon Professor of Contemporary Art History and Theory in the Department of the History of Art and Architecture at the University of Pittsburgh, and Distinguished Visiting Professor, National Institute for Experimental Arts, College of Fine Arts, University of New South Wales. He was the 2010 winner of the Mather Award for art criticism conferred by the College Art Association (USA) and the 2010 Australia Council Visual Arts Laureate. During 2001–2 he was a Getty Scholar at the Getty Research Institute, Los Angeles, and in 2007–8 the GlaxoSmithKlein Senior Fellow at the National Humanities Research Centre, Raleigh-Durham. From 1994–2001 he was Power Professor of Contemporary Art and Director of the Power Institute, Foundation for Art and Visual Culture, University of Sydney. He was a member of the Art & Language group (New York) and a founder of Union Media Services (Sydney). He is the author of a number of books, notably *Making the Modern: Industry, Art and Design in America* (University of Chicago Press, 1993; inaugural Georgia O'Keeffe Museum Book Prize 2009); *Transformations in Australian Art*, volume 1, *The Nineteenth Century*: *Landscape, Colony and Nation*, volume 2, *The Twentieth Century: Modernism and Aboriginality* (Craftsman House, Sydney, 2002); *The Architecture of Aftermath* (University of Chicago Press, 2006); *What is Contemporary Art?* (University of Chicago Press, 2009); and *Contemporary Art: World Currents* (Laurence King and Pearson/Prentice-Hall, 2011). He is editor of many others including *In Visible Touch: Modernism*

ICI BOARD OF TRUSTEES